BRIGHT WITH SILVER

Also by KATHRENE PINKERTON

Wilderness Wife
Three's a Crew
Two Ends to Our Shoestring

For Young People

Adventure North
Fox Island
Farther North
Windigo
The Silver Strain

Bright
WITH
Silver

Kathrene Pinkerton

WILLIAM SLOANE
ASSOCIATES, INC.
Publishers -- New York

Copyright, 1947, by

Kathrene Pinkerton

First Printing

A PATHFINDER BOOK REPRINT EDITION
Complete and Unabridged

Printed in the United States of America

ISBN: 979-8-8691-0683-4

BRIGHT WITH SILVER

I AM INDEBTED TO SO MANY FOR HELP IN THE PREPARA-
tion of this book it is impossible to name them all.
Generous with time and effort were the Fromm brothers,
Edward, Henry, John, and Walter; John A. Fromm,
Arthur's son; Dr. Robert G. Green of the University of
Minnesota; Harry J. LaDue, editor of *American Fur
Breeder;* and Dr. W. A. Young, pathologist of the Fromm
farm clinic. Also, men and women on the Fromm farms,
fur breeders, buyers, manufacturers, and other people
in the industry have given me valuable information.

K. G. P.

Chapter One

HENRY FROMM HAD ALWAYS LIKED FOXES. THE HARD-
wood land of north central Wisconsin was famous for
them, and before Henry knew A from B he could read
the story of their footprints in the snow. The forest
pressed close around the few cleared acres of his pioneer
farm home, and its creatures were as familiar to Henry
and his brothers as were their father's horses, cows, and
pigs. They were even more important, for only by trapping could they obtain the things all boys want.

Henry, youngest of four brothers who grew up together, couldn't remember when he had not heard talk
of fur, and before he was able to set his first weasel trap
he roamed the woods with John, two years older. They
were a strange pair, Henry intense and eager, and even
at six a husky chunk of a lad; John shy and remote, and
as niggardly with words as an Indian. John loved the
forest. He knew it better than the others, and sometimes
disappeared in it for two or three days. His traps earned
as much as those of his two older brothers.

The four depended for their income on skunk and

weasel but caught an occasional raccoon and mink, and there was always the possibility of a red fox. Even grown men got only three or four in a winter, but John and Henry talked more of foxes than other animals. John, a born trapper, was challenged by their craftiness, Henry fascinated by the creatures themselves. Since he was old enough to hold a pencil he had drawn pictures of them, and imagined how wonderful it would be to have a fox of his own. Then he could be near it and watch it, really know it. He never followed a fox track without thinking of this, and although he knew that he and John could never overtake one, he always hoped to catch a glimpse of a red coat.

"Maybe we could find young ones and keep them," he said.

John walked a hundred yards before he spoke.

"You couldn't put collars on 'em, like on a dog," he said.

"We could keep them in a box with chicken wire," Henry said. "You and I'd shoot birds and snare rabbits for them. And I'd take care of them."

John considered the suggestion. "Maybe it would work," he agreed at last.

Henry was thinking only of a fox, any fox, a creature of sagacity and of pride too, with eyes of intelligence and ears alert for the faintest warning. Having such an animal would be exciting, but later he became aware that there were even more glorious foxes than the reds which lived in their forests. He learned this when, with weasel pelts of his own to sell and fur prices of vital interest, he listened as the older boys read fur buyers' price lists. Always at the top was the incredible sum of fifteen hundred dollars offered for the rare black silver fox. This never failed to arouse the wonder of the Fromm boys. It was exciting even to think that so fabulous a creature existed.

They always read the placards of itinerant fur buyers tacked on trees, and whenever they could afford it they bought a copy of *Hunter-Trader-Trapper*, a monthly magazine that was the trappers' Bible. Walter, oldest of the four, always looked first at market reports. He worked hard at trapping because he wanted things, and in summer he added to his income by hoeing corn and potatoes for neighbors at fifty cents a day. He was no more industrious than the others, but he had learned what money could accomplish, and he always knew which fur buyers offered the best prices.

Weasel was usually quoted at fifty cents, and to Henry four skins from a winter's work meant that he could buy more traps for next year. The other three were concerned with bigger sales. A double-striped skunk might be quoted as low as a dollar but a single-stripe brought more, and a short-stripe was worth three times as much. Raccoons did not bring much, mink varied, and a red fox might go as high as five dollars, although a trapper was prepared to take less. Buyers and trappers always differed on grading pelts. After the boys compared fur prices, guessed at the quality of their skins, and estimated the winter's income, their eyes always went to the offer for a black silver fox. None of the boys believed a trapper would get that much, Edward least of all. He was the next oldest, but surer in his oinions than the others. He knew that the fur was precious and that only a few were caught each year, but buyers who haggled over the size and quality of a skunk were not merchant princes.

"Those fellows would never pay fifteen hundred dollars for one skin," he said. "If I caught a black silver I'd take it right to St. Louis where you could find out what it was worth. What do you suppose it would really be?"

The boys spent hours talking about how a man would feel and what he'd do if he caught a silver fox. A discussion of the most dramatic event possible in any trapper's life held a vicarious thrill for the older three. Henry listened, and wondered what a black silver would look like.

In 1901, when Henry was seven, he became sure that the silver fox must be the most beautiful creature in the world. *Hunter-Trader-Trapper* printed a picture and story of the pelt that had topped the London auction at twelve hundred dollars. Edward read it aloud after the chores were done that evening. Another skin had brought the record figure, eighteen hundred, the previous year.

"Don't you wish you'd got that one!" Walter said. "We're lucky if we get four dollars for a red."

John, now nine, had already caught a red fox, and Walter, thirteen, had two to his credit. Edward trapped as industriously as the others, but he was not an instinctive hunter. Already he was strongly set apart from his brothers. His features were finer, he was not so shy, and he looked ahead of the moment. His eyes, of the same intense blue, kindled as did Henry's to an idea. In many ways these two were alike, and yet strangely different.

When Edward finished reading, Henry reached for the picture of the famous pelt. More than the record price, it proved how wonderful such a creature must be.

Walter wished he knew where the fox was caught. "Probably 'way up north in Canada," he said. "No one around here ever got one, and that's funny when **we** have so many foxes."

"But there could be one," Edward said.

The boys knew what he meant and now, with the picture before them, they thrilled to this possibility. Only recently they had read that it was definitely established that silver foxes could be born of red parents. Trappers still spoke of them as "freaks," and Charles Darwin had pronounced them a separate species, but at the turn of the century evidence had piled up that the two were of the same family. It had been nature's whim to make the lowly commoner, the red fox, capable of producing the aristocrat of fur land, while the cross fox, with its curious markings of red, black, and silver, was merely a red fox showing silver blood.

Much proof of this had been uncovered. A Nescape Indian in Labrador found a litter of one silver, one red, and two cross pups. Similar accounts came from trappers who wrote of their experiences to local newspapers and to *Hunter-Trader-Trapper*. Men saw reds running with silver mates, found mixed litters, and even trailed what appeared to be a silver and a fortune to dig out pups that were cross, or common red. Despite this simple explanation of its origin, the silver continued to be rare. In 1901, when the Hudson's Bay Company sold 5,446 red and 1,534 cross fox pelts, it offered only 325 silvers, and these were of all grades. Some brought as little as five dollars. The rarity of a perfect black silver was one reason for its being so precious. A pelt could be marred by many factors — fur not prime, damage to a skin in capture, a red tinge in what should be lustrous black, a pepper-and-salt coat instead of veiled and gleaming silver or a long hard winter's wear by the original owner.

But to the Fromm boys the article in *Hunter-Trader-Trapper* proved that eighteen hundred dollars actually had been paid for a single pelt. They could talk of nothing else that evening until their father said boys who had work to do in the morning should get some sleep. Their mother had long since gone to bed with their baby sisters. The little girls slept in their parents' room, and through eighteen years of marriage the small cot beside the bed of Frederick and Alwina Fromm had always had an occupant. The boys went upstairs to the unfinished half-story where the cold usually ended any desire to talk, but tonight the news of the silver fox kept them excited.

Such a price seemed fantastic. In their pioneering farm life they had known only frugality, self-denial, and the need to work. A large family and a partially cleared homestead could mean nothing else. The farm had good land, but it was a farm in the making. Alwina's father, Joachim Nieman, had given her the quarter-section in Hamburg township when she married. A forester in Germany and a Social Democrat, he came to America in the political exodus of 1848, and recognized the fine soil of the hardwood country of northern Wisconsin. Alwina's wedding gift was an untouched wilderness. Frederick built a small log cabin and began to chop a farm out of the forest. It was hard and slow work but eventually he achieved tilled fields, a barn, and a farmhouse of logs hewed foursquare and sheathed with siding. The acres were claimed so slowly that when Frederick's father gave him rich cleared Iowa land he wanted to move his family to it, but Alwina, with an obstinacy rare in her, had clung to her farm, her forests, the people she had always known, and the Lutheran church she loved. Frederick, usually a man of stubbornness, did not persist, and now the land he had won was as dear to him as to Alwina.

The homestead was built by ceaseless and driving toil. Ease and comfort were unknown. Each year another field was added, and another child must be cared for. Not an hour, not a penny, could be wasted. Wool from the sheep was carded, spun, and woven, to be made into clothing for the boys. Produce was traded for groceries. Trees felled in clearing were cut into cordwood, hauled twenty-two miles by oxen, and sold to pay the yearly taxes. Barley grown for a brewery was the cash crop. As on all pioneer farms, the table depended largely on the forest. Rabbits were snared, small streams yielded fish, and roadsides and clearings were filled with wild berries. In autumn butternut trees were laden, and in spring maple sap was boiled to make syrup for the year.

Always the four younger boys turned to the forest for the money they needed, and carrying on this serious business of making a living welded a close-knit group. As early as they began to roam the woods, they called themselves "The Wolves" because they ran in a pack and believed they were invincible. There had always been an age-cleavage between them and their older brothers, Arthur and Herbert, and it had widened when these two went away to study for teachers' certificates. Frederick Fromm had encouraged this ambition. A few pioneer acres could not support so many boys, and he would never be able to leave each of his sons a piece of land, as his father and Alwina's had done before them. Teaching offered a thrifty way to education and independence, for with savings from a country school position a boy could go to normal school and equip himself to escape the drudgery of farming. Frederick was already looking forward to the time when Walter and Edward would follow their older brothers.

"I want you boys to get your feet out of the mud," he said.

If at times Frederick seemed inexorable about farm tasks — and he expected every boy to earn his keep — it was understandable to The Wolves. They had known the necessity of work and a serious purpose since they could remember, but they were aware that their father was capable of strange contradictions. To his people music was a part of living, and as a young man he had played the violin for square dances as well as on Sundays when neighbors gathered. He gave violins to the older boys and taught them to play, and when six sons made family concerts possible he bought a cottage piano, horns, and flutes, and on trips to town he took the boys along for music lessons. The instruments and occasional instruction made inroads on a scanty cash crop, but Frederick gave them to his sons at a time when a new pair of shoes would have been a major purchase. The little orchestra practiced winter evenings, and Alwina spun or knitted as she listened, surrounded by her sons. She did not worry about their future. That was for men to think of. To be sure, life was hard when so little must be spread so far, but this was only to be expected when people married and had children. She was a happy woman, for she knew no mother had finer sons.

As music was an expression of the family's self-sufficiency, so the activities of the four younger Fromm boys set them apart from their fellows. To be one of The Wolves entailed achievement. They bought corduroy to replace the homespun clothing made by their mother. They bought traps, ammunition, guns, a tent for camping trips, and at last bicycles to ride when others walked, an undeniable mark of success. Fur supplied their wants, and when their wants increased they thought more and more of what the forest offered.

Trapping pelts which brought only a few dollars had limitations, but they had never accepted these. Trapping was also a gamble. A clever set took a poor pelt as surely as a valuable one, and a trap baited for a red fox might catch a silver. It could happen, and they talked of it as they did their chores, roamed the woods, and hoed in the field. A Fromm boy catching the greatest prize in fur land! He might even dig out a litter in the spring and find a black silver among the reds. They talked of this, too.

"We'd keep it until it was grown and the fur was prime," Walter said. "If other trappers can, there's no reason why we couldn't."

Several instances had been related in *Hunter-Trader-Trapper* of men carrying over a young or late-spring-caught silver to pelting time.

"But if we had a silver why couldn't we raise some more?" Henry asked. "What if we were lucky and got two pups?"

"We'd be dumb if we didn't try to raise a litter," Edward said.

They talked of this more and more, and the dazzling idea received new impetus each time *Hunter-Trader-*

Trapper carried news of silver foxes, or a price list quoted fifteen hundred dollars. At last the boys no longer spoke of a pair of foxes, but of dozens of pairs. They had never heard of anyone who had attempted to raise them; but doing so would have the thrill of an untried venture and seemed as practical, they thought, as expecting an increase from any pair of farm animals. The greatest difficulty was that a silver had never been caught in their district.

"Maybe we could start with a red and a cross fox," Walter said. "Then we'd keep on breeding until we got pure silvers."

They talked of this, too, and how it might happen. It was nature's method.

"And we'd have to study how to raise foxes," Henry said.

He had thought more about foxes than the others; for him foxes never would be creatures to be cared for like horses, cows, and sheep. He was sure they must be fed the same food they ate in the wilds, and live as nearly as possible as in the forest.

They discussed all these matters endlessly, and finally what had been at first only a wish became so real that in their minds they no longer doubted but that some day they would raise silver foxes. Although they didn't have even a common red fox or money to build a pen in which to keep it, never did the idea seem preposterous. It grew year after year as its scope and daring caught them. Always they had been seeking ways to lift themselves above the neighborhood level, and now the dream of silver foxes became a plan, as the four boys schemed and argued until fantasy was hammered into a fixed purpose. If silver foxes could be raised and bred, they would be the owners of a herd of the most precious fur in the world.

Having determined on this they ceased to refer to themselves as The Wolves. They needed something significant to mark a solidarity the dream had brought, and since they bought traps from one company, sold fur to another, and read advertisements of many companies, they began to ship fur and buy traps as a company. "The Company" had more than a fine sound in the ears of teen-age boys. To them it meant maturity and permanence, and an impersonal power behind which they could move onward against any obstacles. "The Company" it became.

In 1904 they recognized how tremendous these obstacles were. Walter was sixteen, Edward fourteen, John twelve, and Henry ten. They knew they could not depend on so frail a hope as finding a litter with silver foxes.

"There's only one other way," Edward said. "We've got to get money to buy a pair, and we'll never make enough by trapping."

"How much would we need?" Walter asked.

They didn't know. They had no way of knowing. For a time the boys did not talk so much of silver foxes. The forest had closed in upon them. It had been their friend when they needed little, but it could not give what they needed now. This was in their minds one Sunday afternoon when they took a stroll with their father to estimate the fall butternut crop. The first tree at the edge of the woods was usually heavily laden, and Frederick looked at the upper branches.

"We'll have plenty of nuts if the neighbors don't get them first," he said and started on, only to stop and poke at a plant with his toe and chuckle. "Here's the thing Reinhold Dietsch is going to get rich on."

Edward bent over the plant. It had broad, bright green leaves and a stalk of red berries.

"How can he make money out of this?" he asked.

"I don't know," his father said, "but to hear Dietsch talk he's already got the money in the bank. He's even built a house of laths to grow it in."

Walter examined the plant. "We've seen this all through the woods," he said. "What is it?"

"Ginseng, Dietsch calls it. He claims Chinamen pay so much for it that he can make twenty thousand dollars an acre."

Frederick had his sons' entire attention. They had read price quotations for ginseng root on every fur list.

"Does Dietsch say he can grow this in a garden?" Walter asked. "Did he get seeds from the berries?"

"He dug up plants. Went all around these woods to find them. He says it will be five years or longer before he can dig the crop."

"What kind of soil did he use?" Walter asked.

"How would I know?" his father said. "I didn't ask him. I've got something better to do than listen to such crazy ideas."

He was through with the subject, and they walked on to another tree. Butternuts at least supplied good food for a family, and when the crop had been inspected Frederick returned to the farmhouse. The Company did not go with him. The four boys went back to the plants with the broad leaves and red berries.

Chapter Two

As they stared at the bright green foliage and the stalk of handsome berries, they marveled that so conspicuous a plant had not caught their attention long before. Walter brought some dry branches and propped them carefully above a plant.

"We've got to cover every one," he said. "The cows might get them."

The plants had survived all summer despite cows, but no one spoke of that, for now they had become company treasure. As they carried brush and built barricades against browsing cattle, John suggested they dig the ginseng at once to insure possession.

"We can't move them until we have a place to put them," Walter said. The oldest, and with a natural aptitude for growing things, he had taken charge. "Besides, we should wait until the seeds are ripe."

They had no idea when that would be, and they were dismayed at how little they knew about ginseng. The plants they'd found grew in deep shade, and Reinhold Dietsch had built an arbor. Walter sifted a handful of black porous earth through his fingers.

"We can scrape all the loam we'll need from under trees," he said. "Tomorrow we'll bring grain sacks."

"We'd better hunt more plants first," Edward said. "We can spot them easy while the berries are red, unless Dietsch got them all."

Already Mr. Dietsch was a competitor. As they walked home they planned the arbor. They would need lumber, and wondered how much the sawing would cost. Nails were no problem. For years the burned ruins of a sawmill had supplied the boys with odd bits of hardware.

"Think Pa will let us have the timber?" Henry asked.

They knew he wouldn't. Good building timber must be saved for the stable Frederick Fromm intended to have some day, and trees cut in the work of clearing as they pushed the farm farther into the forest were sold as cordwood to pay the yearly taxes.

"He can't say anything if we take dead balsam and hemlock," Walter said.

Resources were at hand but their greatest need, information, would be more difficult. It was unfortunate they had not seen Dietsch's garden, but a visit now would arouse suspicion, since he would know rival growers were searching for the plant. Nor could he be expected to reveal the secrets of ginseng culture to competitors. He might even lead them astray.

"I wonder how he found out you could grow it," Edward said. "I never knew he was that smart. And what if he isn't right about its growing in a garden?"

It always bothered Edward to be outthought by others. They'd read the prices of ginseng root in fur lists and knew medicinal plants provided summer pin money for trappers, but it had never occurred to the Company that ginseng could be cultivated. Now, if

Reinhold Dietsch were right, the possibilities were dazzling. How dazzling, they discovered at home when they looked up the market reports in *Hunter-Trader-Trapper*. Dried ginseng root from the north central states, the most valuable of all, was listed at six dollars a pound. While the boys had been searching desperately for a way to own a herd of silver foxes, a neighbor had gathered a fortune from their own forest. Edward quoted the price at the supper table.

"It'd have to be worth a lot more than that before I'd fuss with a crop that takes five years to grow," his father said. "By the time Dietsch gets his harvest, probably the Chinese won't want it."

The Company did not argue this, and it was no time to tell him that ginseng was about to invade his farm. Nor did they know how long the sale of the root had existed, nor why the Chinese desired it. It was only much later, and little by little, that they learned that for centuries the people of China had venerated the plant and that the mystical value they ascribed to it, and the astounding prices they were willing to pay, had placed it among the conspicuous flora of the world. It was a strange and exotic plant for four farm boys to seize upon as a way to earn a herd of silver foxes, but silvers were almost as exotic.

The Company's attack was intensely practical. The boys searched the woods for miles around and carefully observed the habits of the plant. Success would depend on the fidelity with which they reproduced natural conditions, and the forest could be their only guide in making the bed and arbor.

They were nagged by the need of money and time. Soon Walter, graduated from the little log schoolhouse down the road, must go to Wausaw, twenty-two miles away, to prepare to become a teacher. This had been talked of for so many years that now it was not even questioned. Arthur and Herbert had already proved how practical was this thrifty way to an education, and were attending normal school with money saved by teaching country school. Frederick realized that the initial two years in training school necessary for a teacher's certificate meant a cash outlay, and he would pay Walter's room rent and bring food from the farm for his bachelor housekeeping. Books, clothing, and incidentals must be earned by odd jobs.

Now Walter was eager to complete the garden before departure, and he dared not cut too deeply into his savings. His father would not be willing to replace funds wasted on such folly as ginseng.

The boys hauled hemlock lath bolts and windfalls to the neighboring mill for sawing. The price for this was more than they had expected, and they held a consultation and counted their money.

"Let's have it sawed into wide boards," Edward said. "Then we can rip them to what we need."

John had a truly inspired idea when they built the arbor. He suggested that the lath walls and roof be made in sections, so that if the first bed proved a failure the structure could be dismantled and moved without wasting precious lumber. This idea, although no one realized it at the time, was one of the soundest notions a boy ever had.

The first ginseng bed, five by sixteen feet, was shaded by the woodshed, and because all the plants had been found in dry places the bed was raised. It held 150 plants; not as many as they had hoped to find, for

Dietsch's earlier search had made their own the harder. The creamy spindle-shaped roots had an odor that reminded the boys of licorice, and deep encircling wrinkles gave the appearance of great age. When they counted stalk scars on the neck of the root, they found that the years varied. Those with a bud which were sufficiently young to promise greater size were used as nursery stock. Ancient roots that had ceased growing — and they found some of thirty and fifty years, and even a grandfather root of seventy-five — were put aside for sale. These were washed and dried on strings hung above the kitchen stove, and lost two-thirds of their weight in the drying process. When the prongs and fibers had been removed the Company had one pound to send to market. Shang hunting was less profitable than trapping, but ginseng culture, which Dietsch had said would produce twenty thousand dollars an acre, would be vastly different.

To get even a small part of an acre they must learn to raise plants from seed. In a second bed, each of the three hundred small flat seeds extracted from berry pulp was dropped into a separate hole made with a stick. This was Walter's last task before departure. But he considered ginseng his responsibility, and as he and Frederick were ready to start to town in the wagon with Walter's boxes behind them, he called a last direction on the winter protection of the garden when leaves fell in the forest.

"Be sure you rake leaves from under the same kind of trees where we found the plants," he said. "Maybe those leaves are the only kind we should use."

Later, when this was done and the roof of the arbor removed to prevent damage from weight of snow, ginseng work was finished. Henry and John, anxious to get out their traps, found Walter's absence made a difference. There was one less pair of hands to help with farm chores. Next year Edward would be gone. But Henry at ten was as strong as, and even bigger than, John and a hard worker.

"I chose the two huskiest of the lot to be farmers," Frederick often said. A powerful man himself, he admired strength.

The three members of the Company still at home went on their annual October camping trip, and carried tent, quilts, food, and dishes to a spot they had discovered years before and called their own. It was almost a day's tramp away, and they remained two nights, which was as long as Frederick was willing to do their chores. But they had two days of exploring and hunting in distant woods, and of talking around a camp fire. Edward was the cook and made potato pancakes which, with plenty of maple syrup, tasted even better over a camp fire than when made at home. It was the boys' favorite food. This year they talked often of the herd of silvers, for even finding a possible means to earn them had brought them nearer.

"We could begin with two pairs, or even one," Edward said. "We'd have twice that number in a year."

"Do you suppose all the young ones would be silvers?" John asked.

"Why not?" Edward said. "If you breed purebred horses and cattle, you get purebred colts and calves. Of course we'd have to wait until we could buy some pure silvers. And we'd have to build pens to keep them in. All that would cost money."

"We could hunt enough game to feed them," Henry said.

"And for a year or so we couldn't sell any fur," Edward said. "We'd have to keep the young to get a big herd started."

When they talked thus the herd of silvers sounded real, and because a distant goal never seemed impossible to Edward, he could make it sound very real to others. But many times that winter Henry stopped on his way home from school to stare at the small bed of ginseng and wonder if the plant could ever earn silver foxes. He doubted it, yet when anyone wanted anything as passionately as Henry wanted silver foxes, any means was worth trying.

In the spring, when green shoots appeared, they knew they had brought the transplanted ginseng through the winter. But the seeded bed had not sprouted. They weeded it as zealously as they did the young shoots of ginseng. No sprouts had appeared when Walter returned from school.

"Maybe I planted them a little deep," he said. "Let's give them a chance. Seeds take longer than roots."

His tone was less cheerful as weeks, then months, went by, and the seed bed remained a blank. Still they weeded, always hoping. Every free hour was spent searching for more wild ginseng, but the plants had to be left in the forest until the seeds had ripened, for these were even more important than the plants. Other farmers were now starting ginseng gardens and were rival hunters, and finders were keepers. It was desirable, however, that no one should discover that anyone had so valuable a plant on his land, and the Company reconnoitered, studied neighbors' habits, and learned what each might be doing at any hour of the day. A few apples, a melon, or handful of berries have always been a farm boy's loot, and a wild ginseng plant was not different.

But the Company was horrified on learning that a farmer's ginseng bed had been raided and a whole planting stolen. Thieves might plunder the Fromm garden, for the bed, though close to the house, was vulnerable at night, so they contrived a burglar alarm. The burned mill supplied wire which they stretched around the lath house and hooked to a battery and electric cell. They felt safe until John demonstrated its inadequacy by stepping over it.

"Any thief would expect a wire," he said.

A second and higher wire was installed, so that if jarred or broken it would not only ring a bell but flash a light. Walter backed up the alarm system by sleeping in the woodshed with a shotgun at his side, but they overlooked night-flying birds. When a night hawk or owl struck the wire a bell rang, a light flashed, Walter rushed out with a gun, and three boys dashed from the house. Frederick and Alwina wistfully recalled the old days when they had raised only such commonplace crops as turnips, barley, and potatoes.

At the end of the summer hundreds of plants waited in the forest. Blazed trees, broken branches, heaps of brush, and maps, were guides to the treasure. A new arbor would draw heavily on company capital, but land was the greater problem. In the first transplanting, roots had rotted in soggy soil; higher land, or any land, must be obtained from their father.

The boys laid their case before him. Ginseng culture

had become a nuisance to Frederick Fromm. It threatened to encroach on a farm of orderly fields and traditional crops, and whenever a boy was needed he was off trailing ginseng or weeding the useless plant.

"Cleared land is valuable," he said.

"So is ginseng," said Walter, who had become spokesman for its rights.

Frederick scowled. "Yes, to hear you boys talk you'd think — "

"But Pa!" Alwina said, "the boys work hard to grow it." Almost never did she interfere between them, and no one knew better how hard Frederick had worked to clear those fields. Now she finished mildly, "Besides, their small gardens take so little land."

Her husband didn't answer for a moment. He knew his refusal would hurt Alwina, for her faith in her sons was unbounded, but if he gave land freely he would be retreating from his position.

"A boy who wants good cleared land should be glad to earn it," he said. "You can have the ground under the pile of rocks behind the barnyard, but I want those rocks carried to the woods."

The rocks had been there since he had dragged them off the field on a stoneboat, and the woods were a quarter of a mile away. His proposal was infuriating. Land for oats, barley, or any other farm crop would have been given gladly, but this was a contrived slur on ginseng. The boys knew their father was no man to argue with and, angry though they were, they carried away the rocks. Being angry they worked the harder, and as they saw the good land they uncovered — rich, cleared, free from weeds and as virgin as the forest — they laughed. This was better than they had expected. In the struggle between farm crops and ginseng, the strange wild root had won.

The new bed held four hundred plants. This forest booty was brought home in an oilcloth-covered box so that if, by some misjudgment, they encountered the real owner, he would not see what they carried. From the berries they extracted three hundred seeds, although not one of the previous planting had sprouted. The day for Walter's and Edward's departure for school in Wausaw was drawing close and time was precious. Also there was much to do, and they had wasted a summer's weeding on an empty bed.

"Anyhow, it's ready for seeds now," Henry said.

He was beginning to be annoyed by the eccentric demands of ginseng. Such a plant was a frail hope for silver foxes. The Company considered this suggested economy in effort.

"But we've waited only a year," Edward said.

"And we still aren't sure those seeds won't come up," Walter added.

The next spring even Henry began to believe ginseng might bring silver foxes. After eighteen long months seeds in the first bed sprouted; it didn't seem possible they could take so long to germinate. Ginseng must indeed be a plant of leisurely habits. Some seeds had died from lying too long in the soil. This undoubtedly happened in the forest too, but nature could be more wasteful than boys who had extracted three hundred small seeds, washed, dried, and planted them one at a time in holes. They wondered if there were facts about ginseng culture the forest could not teach them.

"Maybe I'd better join the ginseng association," Walter said.

"It wouldn't cost much," Edward said, "and might be worth while for the Company."

Local growers had formed an organization for mutual aid and were affiliated with the National Cultivated Wild Ginseng Growers' Association. They knew the county might become an important center, and plans to interest eastern capital were already under way. Although Walter feared men might resent an eighteen-year-old, he found himself welcomed.

The Association offered a reward for the apprehension of ginseng thieves, but this service did not impress Walter. Now, to supplement the burglar alarm and shotgun, all four boys slept on the arbors. A sheepskin coat and a folded quilt made a comfortable bed on the springy lath roof. High enough to be above mosquitoes, it was a pleasant place to spend the night, and under a starlit sky a boy could contemplate his treasures. The Company would never have to call on the Association to catch a thief. The boys laughed when Walter reported the reward.

But at the first meeting Walter learned the answer to seed trouble. Eastern growers had discovered that seeds should be stratified in layers of moist sand for a year before the outer shells were ready to open, and that during this period they must have the same protection and ventilation as in porous forest loam. This was accomplished in boxes sunk in the ground. Other information was funneled through the local organization from experienced eastern growers. Young nursery stock required little space, and could be transplanted to a permanent bed after two years. This was an economy in land and arbors, and the Company adopted the idea with enthusiasm.

More astonishing was the practice of spraying to protect wild plants from the hazards of domestication. Herded together, they were vulnerable. Blight spores from the foliage traveled down the stems, might cause root rot the next season, and most certainly would infect new stock. To prevent this, all new growth must be covered with a spray of slaked lime and blue vitriol. Blight, Walter's fellow members said, was the greatest hazard and, if unchecked, would wipe out a garden.

Walter had never heard of the evil, but he wrote down the formula and directions for testing the strength of the spray by dropping a bit of the mixture into corrosive sublimate. The Company listened to this report with reservations, and inspected its garden. The plants were beautiful. Growing sturdily, the mass of bright green foliage, bathed in the subdued sunlight of a lath house, imparted a sense of tranquillity. The plants, lovelier and more exotic than any they had ever seen, spoke of far lands and ancient peoples. It seemed dreadful to mar such perfection.

"Maybe our plants are healthier than theirs," John said.

"We can wait till the blight comes," Edward added, "but it's a good thing we heard about it."

Walter learned much about blight. Because the disease left spores in the soil, ginseng could not be grown twice on the same land, and eastern growers were experimenting with chemicals and live steam as disinfectants. China, faced with the same problem centuries earlier, had turned to other lands. Further mysteries were cleared up as Walter attended meetings. He was taking a place in the community as a young ginseng grower.

Any doubts the Company might have had concerning

the permanence of the Chinese ginseng market were completely set at rest as they learned the history of the plant. Ginseng had been exported from America since 1713. The earliest Chinese literature had testified to the virtues of the root. The Chinese used it not only in sickness, but in health to retain vigor, and it was considered an effective specific against all nervous diseases and the debilities of age. In some measure this was due to the great age the plant attained — specimens ninety years old had been found in the forests of North America — but the original reason for its unique position was the root's strange resemblance to the form of man. This parsnip-like root was often split and had curious prongs and fibers, and those specimens that most faithfully resembled the human figure were so highly prized as talismans against the inevitable weaknesses of age that they brought incredible prices. This resemblance had given the plant its name. Ginseng, like the fountain of youth, promised to banish the universal dread of age.

The first description of ginseng reached Europe in letters from China written by one of the French Jesuit priests. Another Jesuit, Père Lafitau, working among the Iroquois of North America, read them, and recognized the plant as one the Indians called *Garent-oguen*, signifying the representation of a man's thighs and legs. They, too, believed that the plant insured the user a vigorous old age. Ginseng was plentiful in America while China's supply was diminishing, because it cannot be grown more than once on the same land. Samples of the North American root were sent to China, and a Canadian company was formed to export it. Iroquois were hired to dig the root, and for a time the commerce threatened to rival that of the fur trade.

Later ginseng was discovered in the Himalayas of Nepal, and hunters climbed ten thousand feet in search of the fabled root. In the United States it was found in many districts, and "cheng," "chang," or "shang" hunters — the vernacular differed with the locality — made a precarious living. Superstitions grew up among these hunters, for a plant capable of living undetected for almost a century was awesome, and they believed it would refuse to work for man if he tried to tame it. In the south shang hunters bestowed almost human attributes on the plant, maintaining that, although it was of a wild and wayward nature, it would indicate the existence of other roots to those of sympathy and understanding; but only people of deep wisdom could read the direction indicated by one cluster of broad palmated leaves.

Intensive search almost brought about extinction, and as early as 1877 a farmer in Wisconsin spent hundreds of dollars in a futile attempt to grow the plant from seed. In the late eighties George Stanton, a ginseng hunter in New York State and an instinctive horticulturist, succeeded in transplanting the wild root to his garden. He became the founder of the cultivated wild ginseng industry, which later spread to the Middle West.

The Company eagerly awaited reports of visits to other gardens, and the evening was filled with shoptalk. Men the other boys had never seen were now familiars and associates, for at each meeting a different member talked on ginseng.

"All of them complain about the cost of arbors," Walter said. "It's expensive to build a lath house for only one crop."

"Did you tell them we can take ours apart without losing lumber?" Edward asked.

"No, and I didn't tell them our roofs are flat. They build theirs peaked, like a house."

This gave the Company a chuckle. Older minds, set in the traditional pattern of fixed structures, had contrived roofs to carry off rain and snow. It had never occurred to them to duplicate forest shade and an equal distribution of both rain and sunlight. The Company was pleased to learn it had evolved an original and superior model.

"Won't you have to tell them when it's your turn to talk?" John asked. "And what will you do when they want to come here to see how we grow ginseng?"

This was a threat they had not considered. Their methods, learned by hard work and by years of watching wild things in the forest, were company secrets.

"My turn is coming soon," Walter said.

"Then you'd better quit now," Edward said. "Let them find things out for themselves the way we did."

The Association lost its youngest member and the four resumed their isolated existence, finding ginseng plants where they could and spending hot summer days weeding. When the weeds were checked they carried loam from the woods to make ready for the fall garden.

This year they would not lose Walter entirely. With his new certificate he had found a position that permitted a compromise between his ideas and those of his father. His salary was forty dollars a month, he could board at home, ride a bicycle to his school, and have Saturdays in the ginseng garden. Edward would be in Oshkosh Normal. A job as janitor, thrifty bachelor meals, and a little help from his father had made this possible, and if he had to teach to make a living until ginseng could lead to silver foxes, he intended to earn a better salary in a high school. The way of John and Henry was easy. Frederick's selection of them as the farmers of the family made trapping a possible means to a living until the Company was on its feet.

Ginseng was a summer job, but even then it could not have all the Company's time. Although the older brothers, Arthur and Herbert, were at home to help in vacations, there was still need for all of Frederick's sons. The farm was operated largely by man power. The forest still left its mark on the small clearing. Stumps of trees with deep roots which defied grubbing had been left to rot in tilled fields and made it impossible to use mowing-machine, binder, or tedder. Hay was cut with scythes and turned over with pitchforks; oats, wheat, rye, and barley were cut with cradles and bound by hand; peas for hog feed were hand-harvested and hand-threshed.

And always the forest must be pushed back. Every season more land was to be cleared, and two acres was the best a farmer could hope to gain in a year. Trees must be felled and cut for cordwood and the brush burned; the acrid smoke of smoldering fires hung in the air. Frederick was justified in his belief that cleared land was precious, and with misgiving he watched preparations for a larger ginseng arbor.

These unsightly structures were becoming an eyesore, and four boys who could be useful on a farm were wasting time and energy. But the Company was untouched by parental disapproval and, as they searched for new plants, weeded, collected loam and timber from the forest, the boys talked of silver foxes. Such talk was a prod to tired bodies and an escape for flagging spirits. Weeds were less depressing as they considered how glamorous would be their foxes.

"We could improve them like farm stock," John said. "A trapper has to take what he can catch."

"If we fed them game and the kind of food they're used to, they ought to get along all right," Henry said.

"Foxes aren't any wilder than ginseng," Walter said. "We're growing that. We'll have to build pens for foxes, though, and that will mean money. All we have to spend on arbors is the cost of sawing lumber."

"One fox is worth more than all the ginseng we can grow in five years," said Henry. He had never given his allegiance to the strange root. For him it was only a back breaking means to an end, and he wanted to make sure no one would mistake the route for the destination. But he was generous and he added, "I suppose we'll be glad we found ginseng when the Company raises the finest silver foxes in the world."

"If we make them fine enough, everyone will know a Fromm fox when he sees one," Edward said, for he had a natural awareness of horizons. "Ever think we might be the only company in the world that raises them?"

These hours when they talked of silver foxes held for John and Henry all the splendor of shining dreams. They had no second route to achievement or did they wish one, for silver foxes had taken early possession of their thoughts and their desires. To them life without silver foxes would be only failure.

Chapter Three

Henry was fourteen, and the company seemed as far from its goal as ever. Now, in 1908, he was appalled to realize that while they had talked of silver foxes and of how they must learn to raise them by experimenting with common reds, others had actually started silver fox farms. He read this in an article in *Hunter-Trader-Trapper* written by an official in the U.S. Department of Agriculture.

"Of some twenty parties known to have engaged in breeding them," Henry read, "one began fifteen years ago, another eight, while the others have undertaken the business within the past five years. Those who have persevered in spite of early failures have attained some success. Some have become discouraged while others are just beginning, and their experience is too slight to be of much value in determining the practicability of the business."

The Company had let years slip by, and if it didn't get foxes soon the boys would be old men before they even began the real business of the firm. With such articles giving not only directions for building pens and feeding, but assuring readers that the rare silver was a color phase of the red, any number of fox farms would be started.

Henry showed the article to John, who was equally disturbed.

"We should have begun with reds five years ago," John said. "But you can't keep foxes without pens."

Henry did not let that deter him, and answered a classified advertisement in the magazine in which a trapper offered four live red foxes. The signature bothered him. The company name, "Fromm Brothers," would be more impressive but might inflate the price, and he signed the letter, "Henry Fromm." The trapper replied asking five dollars for each pup, money in advance, and expressage to be paid by purchaser. The terms ended negotiations.

The Company was still financing itself precariously. Walter, after one year of teaching, had decided forty dollars less board money did not permit white-collar splendor, and he abandoned the profession for a business course at Wittenberg Academy. At least a business training would have some value to the Company, and he answered his father's protests by paying his own expenses with savings from his teacher's salary and earnings as a photographer. Modest prices — fifty cents for a mounted five-by-seven print — brought work with country school classes, new babies, and family reunions. Rumors of a neighborhood festivity sent him pedaling on his bicycle. Edward was in normal school and would not have a high school teacher's certificate until the following June. John and Henry were depending on traps. Skunk and weasel provided a small but steady income, and an occasional mink or fox was a windfall. Fur bought clothes, ammunition, and hunting gear, but the trap lines had to be fitted in with school and farm chores, which was not always easy. Henry occasionally played hooky to visit his sets, and once swaggered past the schoolhouse with a red fox slung over his shoulder.

Ginseng had not brought the returns the Company expected. Each fall the crop was larger. In the past four years it had outgrown the string method of drying, and was taken care of on a rack set above the stove. But the product still barely supported the new enterprise. The Company had learned not to expect the top price because ginseng, like fur, was graded. Through the centuries the Chinese had become discriminating buyers, and roots must be round, of good body structure, deeply furrowed, with the appearance of a vigorous old age. Dried, they must not be soft and never bonelike. Few roots in the company's harvest met all these requirements, and expenses also were increasing. Each fall lumber must be sawed for a new arbor; the supply of nails in the burned mill was exhausted; always a necessary purchase swept away resources. An orchard sprayer was imperative when blight at last came to the Company's gardens. Vigorous plants suddenly drooped, and must be sprayed zealously to avert disaster.

A company with all these problems could not afford to buy red foxes or build pens. Henry regretfully laid aside the trapper's offer, but he somewhat assuaged his disappointment by reflecting that five dollars was too much to pay for a red fox. When the Company could afford wire netting he and John would catch their own. They had often talked of how they could do this. In midwinter during breeding season they must watch for the finer tracks of the female, study her habits and the district in which she chose her den. Tracking must be cautious, and after whelping season neither parent fox must know that the retreat had been discovered. The young could be dug from the den before they were old enough to go forth into the world.

"It'll take a lot of time," John said, "but I bet you and I could get a few litters."

These would be useless without pens, but hopes ran high the next fall when the ginseng crop was the largest they had yet dug, roots of those first forest plants brought to their garden. Even more exciting, the Company planted a half acre from two-year-old nursery stock grown from seeds they had stratified. They estimated this would bring ten thousand dollars. The dazzling sum was reckoned on maximum production, and no one spoke of the five years of weeding, mulching, raking forest leaves, and constant battle against blight which lay between them and harvest.

It was triumph enough to plant a half acre. They had scraped the forest floor of the Fromm quarter section for loam, and looked with envy on the loam of neighbors. Even nursery stock had cost weeks of toil. Almost seven pounds of ginseng seeds, which ran eight thousand to the pound, had first been planted in seedbeds. The boys had progressed from the hole-and-stick method and now worked in pairs. One raked the soil from a trench, the other knelt on a board and dropped seeds in one by one, while the raker used displaced earth to cover the trench behind. They were beginning to think in assembly-line methods. They had to. Speed and effectiveness could be the only answer to what four boys must accomplish.

Soon after planting, Edward went to his first teaching

job on a high school faculty of three, salary sixty-five dollars a month. This marked for Frederick the final launching of another son, but his satisfaction was short-lived. A few weeks later Walter returned from the academy to announce he intended to grow ginseng, and with this news ginseng fell into complete disrepute. Not only did it take good land and timber and mar an orderly farmstead with untidy arbors, but now the root had dragged a son back to the soil. If Walter had never heard of ginseng he would have been a teacher like Edward. And if it wasn't ginseng it was foxes! All John and Henry thought of was how men were raising the filthy creatures.

"Crazy dreams!" Frederick said. "Ginseng and foxes! What kind of a farm is that?"

Almost at once his two foes struck again. Edward came home and said he was through with teaching. The school principal drew a larger salary, but left his work to assistants. At the end of the first month Edward protested, at the end of the second he acted. His abrupt departure shut off the possibility of teaching in that school or any other, but Edward felt completely justified. He was a member of a company with property to be looked after. It was time to give his whole attention to that.

Now the Company was together again in the fall of 1909, and doing exactly what it always had intended to do. John and Henry set out trap lines and the others prepared to advance ginseng culture. The new half-acre garden would need an arbor in the spring, and since it would be unwise at this time to ask their father for more timber, Walter and Edward found a job clearing land. In payment they received hemlock bolts for laths, balsam for support posts, and a few tamarack logs for sideboards for the beds. This arrangement opened a new avenue to a supply of lumber, which was well, for the less said to their father about ginseng the better.

In December the Company heard of a litter of live red foxes in a nearby township. John Wittkop, a farmer, had bought six males and one female from an Indian for fourteen dollars, and asked twenty-five dollars. The Company had sold its ginseng and Walter, as treasurer, said it had sufficient funds to buy the litter and a roll of netting. Edward urged the purchase.

"After we've raised reds we'll be sure we can take care of silvers," he said.

"But Wittkop's making nine dollars on the deal," Walter said. "Next spring we can dig out our own litter."

"But by next spring these foxes would have young," Henry said. "We'd be a year ahead. And if we don't find a litter next spring we'd be two years ahead. What are we weeding ginseng for if it isn't to buy foxes?"

Impatience was apt to make Henry reckless but now John, who was never swung from caution, pointed out that foxes in their own neighborhood could be inspected before buying.

"They're almost nine months old," he said. "We can be sure we'd raise them."

The Company decided on the investment and the next day, when their father made his regular trip to town, was a desirable time for the purchase, as awkward arguments with him could thus be avoided.

Henry wakened early that morning. Sometimes he had doubted if the day would ever come when they would start their fox farm. Even after his brothers had gone downstairs he lay for a time contemplating the dazzling possibilities. These foxes were red, to be sure, yet reds had been known to throw cross foxes and even silvers. Anything might happen. But, red, cross, or silver, he wanted these foxes more than anything he had ever wanted in his life.

Town days were always rushed, and the boys hurried to harness the team and load barley for the brewery. If Frederick was startled when no boy appeared in his best clothes he made no comment, and the Company managed to conceal its excitement. The wagon was scarcely out of sight before the boys had a horse hitched to the buggy. Walter had the money, and he took precautions to have small bills in case they were able to strike a better bargain. They had grain sacks in which to carry the foxes, and when they reached Wittkop's farm these may have revealed their determination. Although the haggling was lengthy, the Company won some sort of victory when it bought the litter for twenty-four dollars. A dollar was important.

The foxes did not have the predominance of black markings that might indicate the possibility of cross or silver offspring. They were the rich fulvous hue typical of the district, in good winter fur, and had full brushes with white tips. But even red foxes were a beginning, and the return home was a journey of pure enchantment.

The litter was housed in a large box covered with wire netting, and Alwina came out to admire it. She knew how much it meant to her sons, and she and the Company were standing before the box when Frederick Fromm drove through the gate. He stared, but until he climbed down from the wagon and looked through the netting he did not believe the box contained seven foxes.

He had thought fur farm talk was merely the chatter of sheep-headed boys, and it had never occurred to him that foxes might become as great a nuisance as unsightly ginseng arbors. And when he learned that they actually paid money for the animals, he knew the time had come to stop such nonsense.

"You'll not keep those miserable creatures on my land," he said.

The boys knew he meant it. Ginseng may have won after five long years of struggle, but foxes did not have a chance.

No one thought of Alwina. In the years of ginseng quarrels over land and timber she had remained apart. Those were problems for men to settle. Her world was the home and the care of her family. But now she stepped forward.

"Put them on my land, boys," she said.

It was the first reference she had ever made to the actual ownership of the quarter section.

Chapter Four

THE PENS WERE BUILT CLOSE TO THE HOUSE AS A precaution against theft. It was December, the ground was frozen, and for days the Company worked with pickaxes to set poles and wire netting in the earth. Hollow logs were used for houses, since foxes chose them in the forest.

From the first Henry was the official "fox man." The article in *Hunter-Trader-Trapper* had emphasized the importance of a regular keeper, and the Company knew from watching wild creatures that foxes, nervous and distrustful, must not be disturbed. Custody of the Company's herd was a big responsibility for a fifteen-year-old, but Henry liked foxes, liked hunting small game and snaring rabbits for them, and became adroit in getting extra tidbits from the kitchen. The job of keeper, however, changed Henry's life. No matter how exciting a forest expedition, the foxes' supper hour was a must.

He spent hours watching them from his special lookout on the roof. He watched in daytime and in moonlight, and because foxes behave naturally only when they think they are not observed, he learned many things about them. Some were only interesting bits of nature lore, such as the fact they never ran alongside the netting but always described a figure eight. Yet everything he saw was of interest to Henry, for a good keeper must be able to think as foxes think.

His first effort in fox thinking brought tragedy. The animals fought the netting, and he believed they had too much leisure in which to resent captivity. Finding busy work for penned foxes was difficult, and Henry's scheme to hang meat on wires, so that they must jump to get it, seemed inspired. He was confident that he would have tired and contented foxes, but next morning he found one hanging from a wire, strangled. It had caught its head in a loop holding the meat.

The Company lost more than one fox. The victim was the only female, and unless another could be had before breeding season there would be no increase. The four boys had been searching for wild foxes, and now John worked hard with his snares. To everyone's astonishment he brought in a live female a short time later. He refused to reveal his technique, calling it a trade secret and claiming that skill enabled him to catch a fox by both forelegs and neck to avoid strangling. He proved this by catching a second female a week later. The Company had begun to believe John really had a secret method when Walter saw a fox lying in the woods, apparently asleep. He decided he, too, would be a hero, the only man who had sneaked up on a fox and captured it with his bare hands. He crept forward by inches, only to find the fox was dead. One of John's snares was around its neck.

The females John caught gave the Company a chance

for two spring litters, or so they thought until Henry saw one was growing thinner. They knew nothing of fox diseases and the mystery was not solved until a few days later, when she died of abdominal strangulation. A snare wire had caught around her body and had gone unnoticed in the thick fur. John's technique had imperfections, and again they had six males and a female.

Henry began to understand why fox farmers failed, and still all the usual hazards — sickness, escape, lost litters and infertility — were ahead. This job required more than forest thinking and he needed help. Since the article on fur farming had been written by a member of the Department of Agriculture Henry wondered if the government had not issued bulletins for fur farmers as it had done for others. He wrote and received one.

It became his Bible. He found directions for feeding, warnings against excitement in breeding and whelping seasons, and diagrams of pens and houses. The bulletin stressed the need of proper nesting boxes and large pens, thirty by forty feet. Many fox farms had failed through ignoring a fox's need for space.

Netting for such pens would cost more than the Company's treasury held. The next ginseng harvest could not be sold before fall, and in any event the hastily-built winter pens must be replaced and construction finished while the ground was soft. Even now the posts had begun to lean at drunken angles, and the only reason the foxes were still inside was that they found it as difficult to dig in the frozen soil as had the boys. The situation appeared hopeless until one of the boys saw an advertisement in *Hunter-Trader-Trapper*. Funsten Brothers, St. Louis fur buyers, offered fifty dollars for the best picture and story of the successful use of their "Trail Scent and Animal Bait." Henry had a bottle of the bait, and the directions read:

"Foxes are the most cunning of all wild animals to trap. The traps should be boiled in hemlock water, or sprinkled with blood to which has been added a few drops of Funsten Trail Scent. In setting the traps, be sure to sprinkle a half-dozen drops of Funsten's Animal Bait. The powerful odor, which is irresistible, will draw the animals from long distances right to your traps and into them. Every trapper knows that animals continually sniff and smell in their prowling, and once they smell an odor or strike a trail that appeals to their passions they will follow it to the end."

A bait for which the manufacturer made such claims demanded a spectacular picture, and it was reasonable that Fromm foxes should earn their own housing. Not one fox lured to death, but seven! If they were tied in traps and a bottle of animal bait were set in the foreground, a picture of the scene must certainly win the fifty dollars. An outer fence of netting (not showing in the photograph) would prevent escape.

Next morning the seven foxes, in grain sacks, lay outside the door while the boys gathered equipment. John looked up to see a sack was empty. Walter picked up a rifle and ran out as a fox went down the road. After two miles he decided a pelt was better than no fox, and a pelt was all he brought back. The Company lost interest in posing the herd for pictures.

But the dead fox gave the boys a new idea. By freezing it and others they might trap, they would have enough dead models; but this, too, was abandoned. Pelts might be damaged through delay in skinning. The eventual scheme was depressingly unexciting. The skins of a winter's hunt were draped over Walter's shoulders. His look of maturity might add weight to the claim that all the foxes had been caught in a single morning as a result of using the Animal Bait. Henry signed the picture, as he was the only member who'd had financial dealings with Funsten Brothers, and that too might be considered in the award. The picture and a fulsome account of the miraculous properties of Animal Bait were mailed. For a month the Company waited, and then gave up hope.

In April the question of greatest moment was what might be happening in the nesting log of the only pair of foxes. The Company had no way of knowing. The bulletin warned that if fox mothers were upset or frightened they might destroy the pups in an ill-advised attempt to save them. Henry, attuned to fox thinking, could not follow this fox reasoning, but he took care not to vary his feeding routine by an incautious step. From his outlook post he saw the pair carry meat to the hollow log, which must mean young were being fed; but that could not be confirmed until the pups should come out, when they were about four weeks old. The Company must endure the suspense as best it could.

Waiting was hard because of the electrifying news of the winter sale in London. For the first time rumors and conjectures as to the possibilities of fox raising were settled. The Dalton fox farm on Prince Edward Island in Canada had sent twenty-five ranch-bred black silver pelts to the London auction, a dramatic proof that the rare creature could be bred and reared in confinement. With these foxes, which were unusually fine, man had carried an experiment of nature to new standards. Buyers paid $34,000 for the twenty-five skins, and one brought $2,600, a record price for a silver fox. The pelts were well furred, the guard hairs were long and glossy, the color was good, the black had no tinge of rust, and the silver was well veiled. The farm had successfully competed with the forest.

The last was the most exciting news of all. Until 1910 the fox farms of Prince Edward Island had been operated in secrecy. A few pelts were sent to London and sold by C. M. Lampson and Company under a pledge not to reveal their source. Charles Dalton had been experimenting since the late eighties, and in the middle nineties was joined by Robert Oulton. To these two men is given the credit for pioneering fox farming on a commercial basis. Others had made contributions to the domestication of the fox, and eventually six Canadian firms combined in what was virtually a monopoly. They owned all the breeding stock and refused to reveal their methods. Finally a member broke the agreement not to sell and, the secret out, Charles Dalton sent twenty-five pelts to London.

This meant many things. Not only was the silver fox, once wholly a creature of luck and accident, now an established strain, but the future of a fur threatened with extinction was assured. The animal had been growing rarer until in the previous decade the supply had fallen off 45 per cent. Similar decreases had been recorded in other fur bearers. The world's traffic in raw pelts, which had grown into ninety-five million dollars annually, was threatened by the inevitable dwindling of supply due to greater areas of settlement, more skillful tools for hunting, aggressive trapping, and clearing of forests.

The hunter-trapper era in North America had passed its peak, but man's ingenuity had rescued the fur trade. Until now good pelts had come only from the wilderness, and it was still believed that if animals were confined the quality of fur must suffer, be of poor color and, more important, lack luster. Thus the sale of twenty-five ranched silver fox pelts, acknowledged to be as beautiful as those taken in the wilds, was of far greater significance than the mere fact a few men had discovered a way to fortune. It was a signpost to the great fur trade itself. A new and profitable industry had been founded, and already it was being called the "Industry of the Golden Pelt."

To the Fromms in Wisconsin this was confirmation of the soundness of a boyish dream. Men had succeeded in raising silver foxes by the same methods the boys had planned, but this priority did not affect the Fromms' purpose. Their goal was still ahead, still as tempting, and now could be even more audacious. If selective breeding could produce pelts that as a whole were better than those from the wilds where nature often fumbled, then the Company could by the same process produce an even finer strain of silvers, and become owners of the most beautiful silver foxes the world had ever known.

News of the Dalton sale quickened the Company's eagerness to know what was happening in the hollow nesting log, but all Henry could report was that both parents had been carrying in food. At last, when whelping season was long past and pups should be taking the air of a morning, Henry investigated.

There were no pups. There never had been. A heap of gnawed bones filled the den. What Henry had presumed to be parental solicitude was merely a desire for mealtime seclusion, and the Company's first breeding season was a blank. It was little comfort to know this was an old story in fox farming. With one female, a hollow log, and pens so near the house, the boys should not have expected an increase, but they determined to have proper equipment and more females before another breeding season. Additional stock was the immediate problem. They had searched in vain for dens, and their only hope lay in purchase from a luckier trapper.

"We might get an answer from my advertisement in *Hunter-Trader-Trapper*," John said.

This was the first the others had heard of it. Caution had made John less sanguine about the explanation of the secret meals, and he had not wanted to risk missing a spring litter. It would be June before he could expect replies to his ad, but Edward began to figure on the probable cost of pups and measures to raise the money.

"We may not have to buy a litter," Walter said. "We've still got a chance if it snows in May."

A May snowstorm was capricious. It might be only a light powder, gone by noon and of no value to a tracker, or it might lie on the ground a day or two and give the Company one last chance to hunt a den. Again, it might not snow at all.

But a promise of snow was in the air one day when Walter entered the forest, and an hour later lazy flakes floated down. Before dark he not only found a den, but had seen the tracks of pups in fresh snow at the entrance.

Next morning the wagon delivered Walter to a place from which he could pack his gear to the nest. One hunter could be more quiet than two or more, and it might take three days to capture a litter. The pups, he learned, had not emerged since the previous day, and after he had made camp he prepared his traps, padding the jaws with cloth so they would not break the pups' legs. Before dark he set them at the entrance and through the night he waited in the tent. In the morning the traps were as he had left them, and there were no fresh tracks. The foxes had smelled man at their front door. All day he watched and not a fox appeared. The second night he dozed and was wakened by a shrill scream. He had caught a pup.

It was not injured by the padded trap, but Walter had not realized how trying the lamentations of his tent mate would be. Through that night and all the next day the pup whimpered. It refused to eat or be consoled, and its constant cries began to break down Walter's resolution. More than anything else he wanted to restore the pup to its mother and go away, leaving her family unmolested. He knew he would not have minded the usual method of getting pups — chopping a litter from a hollow log. The zest of discovery and the need for speed would carry a hunter through. But now he could only wait, listening to the pup and watching the entrance. He hoped the job would soon be over.

That night he caught the four remaining pups. Scarcely would he get one in a grain sack than another screamed in fright. Swiftness of events made the wait easier, and it was wonderful to show the Company five pups, three males and two females, when the boys called for him in the morning. Their admiration and rejoicing helped enormously, but Walter was glad when he left the camp site.

"Did you see the old ones?" John asked.

"No," Walter said, "and I'm glad I didn't. But at least we won't have to buy red foxes this year."

Ginseng absorbed the Company through the spring. Lath arbors were mended or replaced and a new seed-bed put under cover, but before shoots showed above ground the weeds took possession and, with larger bed area, presented a serious problem. Ginseng and farm tasks were a full time job for four, and often one robbed the other.

But the boys still took time to hunt new nursery stock. When they began ginseng culture they had set the round sum of one thousand wild plants as their final goal. But this summer when they reached the figure they realized the goal had been too easy, and they knew they would miss the fun of looting plants from neighbors' forests, and competition with the many shang hunters. So they had lifted the mark to 1,100, an eye-filling number. Now the oilcloth-covered box went forth on quick and furtive forays until they were well advanced in the last hundred. Walter kept the tally. Ginseng had become his department.

The Company's treasury still did not have money for woven wire fencing of new pens. It was useless to ask their father, although the Iowa farm had yielded enough for the purchase of an automobile. He had hesitated before buying a car. It would save hours in deliveries to the creamery or shopping trips to Wausaw, twenty-two miles away, but he said a man whose four sons elected to grub about with ginseng and filthy foxes should save money against the inevitable day when this waste of time and energy must be reckoned. The Company had answered this with spirit; not only would it care for the present but it would provide for the future, and after such a reply it could scarcely try to borrow money for fencing.

Yet by midsummer no one had found a way to raise money. The boys were weeding in the garden when John brought a letter from Funsten Brothers addressed to Henry. Henry was always writing for bulletins, catalogues, and price lists, and the others paid no attention until he held up five new ten-dollar bills. Their picture and fulsome account of "one morning's haul" had won the prize.

Weeds grew unchecked the rest of the day. The Company was too busy choosing a site for pens and making out an order for netting. Lumber and peeled balsam poles were estimated, but roofing and paint were beyond the budget. This distressed Henry, for he wanted the first fox houses to be of special excellence.

The next day, for the first and last time in his life, Henry Fromm became a wage slave. A neighbor agreed that, big for his age and unusually strong, he was worth a dollar a day. Thirty dollars was needed for paint, roofing, and feed pans, and he worked exactly thirty days. When this economic servitude was ended he drove to town and spent the money on ornamentation of fox houses. A white enamel feeding pan at sixty cents, almost a day's work, distressed him, but he had the satisfaction of knowing that no foxes on any farm would eat from better dishes.

When the woven wire netting arrived, John and Henry drove to town and brought it home. The wagonload of rolls seemed some sort of a miracle; they had pitted their wits against the makers of Animal Bait and now had fencing for proper yards of thirty by forty feet — enough space to keep any pair of foxes healthy and contented. The pens were made exactly as the bulletin specified. A ditch was dug and netting sunk two feet in the ground, and a wire overhang was set at the top to prevent foxes from climbing over. The boys changed only one detail.

"There's no reason to build those walls ten feet high," Henry said. "Maybe the bulletin is right about some places where the snow is deep and the foxes could get away over the drifts. We shouldn't build ours over eight feet."

"We'd save netting," Walter said.

"Besides, I've watched 'em," Henry said. "A fox can't jump more'n eight feet without hurting himself." Henry was becoming a fox man.

He and John built the houses. Plans were elaborate after the hollow nesting log and were not exactly forest thinking — or perhaps were forest thinking adapted to man's world. Each house had an insulated nest box and an outside spout or tunnel to permit a fox to make a cautious survey before emerging. The boys followed the specifications. Innovations could come later when they knew more about the home life of foxes, and as they sawed and hammered they talked of the day when these very houses might shelter silvers. It wasn't impossible that one might hold a silver next spring.

A short time later they heard of a silver that an Indian at Star Lake had caught in a trap the previous winter. This proved silvers did appear in their district, and the Company caught fire. The boys couldn't buy it but at least they could see it, could know if it was as beautiful as they imagined. Silvers had become so real to them that they were shocked by the realization they had never actually seen one, and they decided to send a member of the firm to look at it. Henry could not go, with foxes to feed, and Walter was busy with ginseng. Edward was accustomed to dealing with the outside world. Normal school and two months of teaching in a high school had given him assurance, and he was elected.

Henry drove him to Merrill, where he could take a train to Star Lake, and next morning he would return to tell exactly what a silver looked like. The others were still talking of how exciting this would be when they saw Edward coming down the road. The round-trip fare, he said, was three dollars, and when he counted his money he was short sixty cents.

Sixty cents! It had made all the difference between a firsthand account of the color, bearing, and habits of a live silver fox and looking at a picture of pelts.

"I'd have got there if I'd had to walk!" Henry blazed, and he meant it.

When he'd had time to cool his anger and recover from the disappointment, he realized that he might have done as Edward did. Ninety miles was a long way, but he still resented that sixty cents. It was so little, and yet it had been an obstacle to a company which intended to make world history in silver foxes. That morning, somehow, the herd of silvers seemed far away.

The summer narrowed the age gap between Herbert and the four, and Arthur's absence left Herbert the only older brother still at home. His violin helped family concerts, especially when their old music teacher came to spend a few days in a small log cabin Frederick Fromm had built for him. Then concerts lasted into the late evening; with either the two violins and Edward at the piano playing popular classics, or the entire family orchestra — Walter's clarinet, Henry's flute, and John's cornet — in Strauss waltzes or arias from German operas. Even when their teacher was not with them the boys still had music, if only a half hour snatched at noon, and ginseng weeding went the better for the interruption.

The last weeks of the ginseng search were exciting. Early in August they had found the eleven hundredth plant and again success was strangely disappointing. The tedium of a completed mission led John to suggest the change of each cipher to a digit. Eleven hundred and eleven pleased their fancy, but the last eleven plants were hard to find. Aggressive shang hunters had been everywhere, and only just before the first frost did Edward bring in the final plant.

For the first time the ginseng harvest made an impressive pile, so impressive that Walter snapped a picture as Edward carried the last armful to the heap. It was not all first-grade root, but the sale in December warranted a bank account; Walter opened it, and the pass book showed a balance of $175.

The Company was on its way, and it did not need to use bank funds to buy foxes. John and Henry had captured three live females. This raised the fox population; but so many hungry foxes presented a food problem that could no longer be met with game alone. Henry scouted the countryside for old horses. Frederick Fromm scowled when he saw these tired beasts brought home. His farm not only harbored filthy foxes, but now a Fromm went about buying cast-off animals, the final humiliation. When a neighbor asked him to tell the boys he had an old horse to sell, Frederick drew himself up in wrath.

"The boys don't want it!" he said. "If I had my way, they'd never need any man's old horses."

Perhaps the father's uncompromising attitude was a good tonic against the madness which now seized the fur world. Almost overnight the boom started. The boys heard of it from fur buyers and read of it in outdoor magazines and in *Hunter-Trader-Trapper*. Raising silver foxes had become the new and easy way to fortune. The rush of those eager to get in the game sent prices of breeding stock soaring, and pairs of pups brought six thousand dollars. Large companies were being capitalized, and investors were exhorted to get into this newest bonanza before the price of breeding stock went higher. Clerks mortgaged homes, school teachers invested savings, and men and women who had never seen a live fox computed paper profits. Promotion literature made it sound so easy! Each pair of foxes would bear four young. A pair of pups, worth six thousand dollars, undoubtedly would be worth twice that sum next season, and each pair of pups would produce four more foxes. An investor couldn't lose. Silver foxes bought now while prices were at rock bottom might be the foundation of a fortune.

All this meant nothing to the Fromm boys, except as each advance in the price of breeding stock put the possibility of purchase further off. They didn't stop talking about their future herd of silvers, but they began to lean on luck. Henry spent hours studying the markings of their foxes, trying to find some indication of silver blood. When whelping season arrived he made no effort to conceal his excitement, for he was certain there were young in the houses. He was beginning to know foxes.

While the Company awaited the outcome it searched the forest for litters, and because the boys had become skillful they were able to get several. All were red, but no boy admitted his disappointment. Their own foxes, they felt certain, would produce at least a cross, and five of the six females had families, a far better record than that of most inexperienced breeders.

Gradually the mothers began to bring out the young. Each litter was large and healthy. And every pup was red. Not until the very last pup of the very last litter had appeared did Henry give up hope. Even then he couldn't believe it. In spite of the mysterious workings of the silver strain and the lucky breaks of others, the Company had failed to produce a single silver hair.

But at least Henry had proved he could raise foxes.

Chapter Five

Their second failure to get a silver pup, or even a cross, ended the Fromms' hope of obtaining silvers from native stock. They became impatient — or as impatient as a Fromm ever permitted himself to be. It would be years before ginseng money could buy a pair of silvers. Now there was no such thing as finding a bargain in a silver fox. Henry, reading the news of the industry with despair, knew that the price of six thousand for a pair of silvers was already a thing of the past. Walter was not so irked as the others, for he liked ginseng culture; but no matter what the Company accomplished in ginseng, the advance in the price of breeding stock would still carry foxes beyond their reach.

Henry knew this when he answered the advertisement of James A. Kane in *Hunter-Trader-Trapper*. Kane was a dealer in cross and silver foxes. Henry had to talk to someone about silver foxes, and it was the informality of Kane's advertisement in the classified columns of the familiar magazine that led him to hope for an answer, for he feared the large eastern ranches would not bother with him. He did not ask for prices nor pretend to be a potential customer; neither did he mention the existence of a company. His earnest letter told — lest the dealer consider him a young amateur asking idle questions — of the many years he had been planning to raise silver foxes and of his two failures, and it asked if there were any way for a boy with no money to obtain breeding stock.

James Kane answered promptly. The fervor of one fanatic had made touch with another. Kane believed in silver foxes, and he, too, knew failure. His own fox farm had not succeeded. As a buyer of western foxes for eastern ranches he was often absent on extended field trips and the Kane farm, entrusted to the custody of others, had been neglected. Henry's ardor and determination therefore held an appeal.

The two exchanged long letters. James Kane, a man of importance in the industry, was in a position to tell Henry the news and gossip about fox farming. He regularly visited the Canadian ranches, talked with breeders, and knew what fox men were doing; he was aware that fur farming was fast becoming a business ruled by speculation and promotion. Though some of his clients, interested in the future of the industry, were purchasing foxes to experiment with the infusion of fresh blood, others thought only of easy profits and bought for resale. Even at the 1911 high prices, demand for breeding stock had outrun supply, and eastern ranches were building up their herds with importations from the wilds of northwest Canada. There were rumors of ranches where a wild fox might enter the back door at night to leave the next morning as a registered member of the herd. Customers eager to start ranches, and knowing nothing about silver foxes, had been easy prey to such swindles.

But more important to Henry than the shoptalk of the industry were the theories about the silver strain. Kane knew the work of pioneers, men of practical experience who had reached conclusions by breeding foxes. Test matings had proved that a red pup of one silver parent might carry silver blood and in turn, when mated to a silver, produce one, or even half a litter, of silver offspring. These reds, carriers of silver blood, were referred to by Kane as "outcastes"; they were valuable as breeders, and ranchers had even paid five hundred dollars for them. Outcastes, a longer but much cheaper route to a silver herd, suggested a possible means for Henry, and should he want to try it Kane would find him a bargain in an outcaste and a silver mate.

Henry was elated, but he knew that even if they managed the price of an outcaste red there was no hope of buying a silver mate. He refused the offer with deep regret, and still made no mention of a company. It would be too humiliating to admit that a firm organized to raise silver foxes could not purchase even a single silver — and in a year when eastern companies were being capitalized at fifty, and even one hundred thousand dollars. It was absurd for a seventeen-year-old boy with no money to be writing to a leading dealer, and Henry was afraid the correspondence would end there.

But Kane had become emotionally involved in Henry's venture. Something in the boy's letter had caught him. He continued to write and, as a fellow breeder, to discuss problems of fox raising. Henry was delighted to be able to refer his questions to an authority, and he had an important one at the moment. The government bulletin said the male fox should be separated from the litter since he might destroy the young, or his presence might make the mother nervous and drive her to kill the pups. But Henry and John had discovered that both parents grieved when they were separated. They talked it over. Wild foxes lived a family life, and while some fathers might destroy the young, others helped in the care of pups. The matter was referred to Kane and he agreed with Henry; he also pointed out how much the boy was learning by housing reds before he attempted the more costly silvers. When Henry restored the fathers to their families, pen life was again peaceful. But it was just as gratifying that a practical breeder had approved his and John's conclusions.

The autumn of 1911 had arrived when Kane finally suggested an even less costly way for Henry to get silvers. He had found a fine male cross, which he referred to as a "double-cross" because its black coat had a reddish flash only on a flank and shoulder. This, mated to an outcaste, should produce at least one silver pup. He warned Henry that the male was not prepossessing; puppyhood rickets had broken down its front legs. But this defect did not harm its breeding value and was, moreover, the reason for the exceedingly low price of $350. Another two hundred would buy an outcaste female, and with the outlay of only $550 Henry would have a start toward a silver herd. One silver pup was the least Henry might expect, and the male's black coat, showing a predominance of silver blood, justified even higher hopes.

The Company shared Henry's excitement. A double-cross must be almost a pure silver! It was miraculous good fortune — but not within their reach. Apparently Kane had not taken Henry's financial statement quite as literally as Henry had intended it. The Company's funds of earnings from the traps, red fox hunting and a spring sale of ginseng fiber and second-grade root, fell far short of $550. The fall harvest of ginseng could not be dug until late October, and then would take two months to dry and market. But they could not afford to wait. Delay or temporizing would lose the bargain, might even forfeit Kane's interest. It was useless to try to borrow from their father; foxes, red, silver, cross, or outcaste, were obnoxious to him. In the midst of this crisis their older brother Herbert, home from teaching for a week end, offered his savings to make up the deficit. Never was a new stockholder welcomed more warmly.

With the money in hand, the Company now considered its business relations with James Kane, who was under the impression that his sympathy had been extended to one boy yearning for foxes. It was doubtful that this warm interest would stretch to include a whole company of yearners. The obvious course — not to tell him — was hazardous. Should he deliver the foxes in person, he would surely discover the other brothers. The proposed strategies to prevent this became as elaborate, and as diverting, as in the old days when the four had plundered the land of neighbors. But in the meantime Henry's name must be used in making the purchase. Edward argued that this slight deception was really a kindness, since finding out there were four boys instead of just Henry would be a disappointment, if not an emotional loss, to James Kane; the rights of a benefactor were important. Edward had a keen sense of the reactions of others.

But a deal involving so large a sum as $550 had become real business, and company transactions were usually executed by Edward. Older, and already beginning to show ability as a coordinator, he had good ideas that were generally accepted by the others, and he handled correspondence easily. So Edward took over the purchase and managed a fair imitation of Henry's writing, which must have been successful, for Kane continued to address the firm as "Dear Henry." The partners figured that if Edward changed gradually to his own penmanship, the dealer would never notice. The more simple expedient of having Henry transcribe the letters did not occur to them. The Fromm boys liked their obstacles.

Fortunately for their peace of mind, Kane wrote that the foxes would arrive by express. The Company had already started a new block of pens in the woods where shade and trees would give the animals a sense of forest life. The pens would house the new pair and the spring increase, and now the cost of pennage in money and labor must be added each year to increased ginseng gardens.

The pens were finished when the pair arrived. The double-cross male was a disappointment. He looked almost like a silver, but his front legs were worse than they had imagined. The boys were appalled to see that the sire of their herd walked on his elbows. But the red female was a fine large fox, light, with black lips and a tinge of black on the feet proving she was an outcaste, although the term seemed a sorry one for the carrier of proud silver blood.

Now at last, after two years of effort, the silver herd seemed just around the corner. The Company plunged into the rush of the fall season. Not only must a farm be harvested and made ready for the winter, but ginseng seeds were to be planted, roots dug, leaves raked, arbors dismantled, and plants mulched against the winter. When these tasks were finished a log icehouse must be built to provide safe storage for fox food. Sometimes cattle were killed by lightning or Henry was able to buy several horses, and the Company must be ready to avail itself of lucky windfalls. The meat was to be kept in the center of the icehouse, in a hollow square walled with cakes of ice and reached through an ice tunnel. It would be crude refrigeration, but was the best they could devise.

Winter brought another problem. The new pair of foxes must be guarded. In summer both ginseng and foxes could be watched from the beds on the tops of the ginseng arbors, but this comfortable arrangement was no longer possible when the arbors were dismantled. A lookout tent was the simplest answer. They found three trees growing in such a position as to make corner posts. By sinking a fourth post they were able to build a high platform for a tent that commanded a view of the fur farm.

Edward and Henry slept in the tent through the winter. On cold mornings their damp footwear was so stiff and frozen that a barefoot dash to the house was a lesser test of their endurance. But no member of the Company doubted for a moment that this watch should be maintained. Eastern ranches were equipped with day and night guards and often with burglar alarm systems to protect famous foxes and, while the pair of cross and outcaste would hardly tempt a thief, the Company would not have liked to admit this. A secretive boyhood existence, isolation, group allegiance to a goal, and years of struggle, had deepened an instinctive sense of misgiving about outsiders into actual distrust.

The outcaste female was a forthright creature and did not keep her owners in suspense longer than was necessary. In late March her nest box held young; Henry distinctly heard pups whimper. Now the Company was safely past three of the hazards of fox farming — infertility, abortion, and a lost litter. The last is the most maddening to a keeper, for there is no evidence to tell him what has happened to the young. Keepers have learned to recognize the implications when a fox mother drags the straw out of her nest box. They call it "cleaning house" and know it to be the bad sign of a blank, a whole year's work lost. But only the fox mother knows whether a crime has been committed, and she can't be made to tell.

The good news of a litter was written to James Kane. He was as pleased as the Company. No one doubted that there would be one silver pup. Kane, counting on the preponderance of silver blood in the double-cross, was even more sanguine about the number. Edward was inclined to share the dealer's opinion. John held out for one silver. Henry merely waited. And the Company knew now how necessary it was to wait without investigation.

Nervous fox mothers are one of the main griefs of fox farming. Fright will cause them to drag the young from a nest box into the pen yard, hide them, bury them, leave them exposed to damp and cold, or in a complete panic destroy and eat them. Quite as unreasonably a mother, having dined off the litter, may resume her anxious worrying about the lost young. The unpredictability of maternal solicitude is still one of the major problems of fox farming. A fox mother, terrified for the safety of a pup that has escaped the yard, will try to drag it home through the fencing, and in so doing may tear its leg off. Whereupon she is very apt to stop and eat the leg before she returns to her truly earnest and well-meant rescue efforts. Generations of domestication, however, have now accustomed mothers to a keeper's inspection. When the pups are about a week old a good keeper always puts his ear to the outside of the house and listens. If the low whimperings are only those of contentment he does nothing, but if there is continuous whining registering discomfort he investigates, and perhaps saves the litter. In the early days when foxes were much wilder, even listening led to loss of litters. Maternal distrust demanded that a keeper adhere to a set pattern and never threaten intrusion by even one incautious step.

Henry knew this, and resisted the great temptation to find out how many silver pups there were. But at last the period of waiting was over. One sunny April morning Henry saw the family. He stared for a long moment, unable to believe his eyes. Three pups, and all red! To Henry they looked as red as the Wisconsin native foxes. Henry reported the incredible fact to the others, and they, fully as shocked as Henry, rushed out to verify. Everyone had been so confident. Wasn't the sire almost a silver?

The news was written to James Kane, and his reply was filled with genuine astonishment and dismay. Outcaste matings produced silvers for other breeders, and he had made sure this female was an outcaste. Yet she must have been the parent at fault. There could be no uncertainty about the double-cross, for his coat carried visible proof of silver blood.

The dealer made two suggestions. Henry could send

back the disgraced outcaste when her nursing duties were over and he would replace her with another outcaste. Or if Henry, discouraged by the loss of a whole year, had abandoned the idea of a herd of silvers, he could have his money back. Nothing could be fairer than this. The Company did not for an instant question Kane's sincerity and friendship, nor had it occurred to them not to persist in raising silver foxes. But at the moment, still so close to the sudden end of high hopes, they did not want another outcaste. They wrote Kane that they were returning the female and would wait until winter before deciding what to do about a mate for the double-cross. In that fox at least they had a fine male; they had now, in fact, begun to speak of him as a silver. In a way they were justified, for a rusty patch on one flank and shoulder could be considered only a blemish. Kane had truly given them a bargain.

The double-cross was now an even better bargain than when they had bought him, for the price of silvers was soaring. Pairs of spring pups had jumped to ten thousand dollars, and offspring of famous foxes brought still more. The fur world had gone mad in the new bonanza. Companies that had foreseen the sudden rise of prices and acquired breeding stock in the early boom days were reporting spectacular profits. And there were the get-rich-quick stories. A group of clerks had cleared forty thousand dollars in a year, and three sisters had made thirty-five thousand in their venture as fox farmers. Apparently the only requisite for success was capital for a half-dozen pairs of foxes; natural increase and ascending prices would pile up a fortune. Glib salesmanship and specious promises of quick and easy money were finding naive victims, and the silver fox industry was fast taking on all the excitement and inflated values of a land boom or a gold strike. With each week and month hope grew slenderer that the Fromm boys could buy anything but another outcaste. Yet they hesitated. They did not doubt Kane's wisdom, but they could not bear to risk the loss of another breeding season. Their silver male — and now they never referred to him in any other way — deserved a silver mate.

In midsummer luck appeared to nod in their direction. They heard of a silver owned by a farmer named Herman who lived outside the village of Polar, over sixty miles away. The fox had been trapped, and was not only a silver, but a female. Mr. Herman wished to sell, and while purchase by the Company was out of the question, a partnership might be profitable to both Mr. Herman and the Fromms. The Company discussed the possibilities. It decided that representatives should visit Mr. Herman and propose the alliance, and Henry and Edward were chosen. They would walk fifteen miles to Marathon City, take the train to Polar and then walk ten miles to Mr. Herman's farm. The boys wore their best clothes so that Herman's prospective partners would appear impressive. Their best shoes would be uncomfortable for walking, but were an important evidence of prosperity. Alwina packed a lunch of fried chicken, her way of wishing them luck. Frederick listened to the elaborate plans for this partnership in one silver fox and found them humorous. He had gone to the stable when the boys walked toward the gate and he came to the wide door to watch them.

"Go!" he said, and the one word carried his contempt and ill opinion of their errand.

Late that afternoon Henry and Edward arrived at Polar and walked to the farm of Mr. Herman. They saw the fox and stared at it for a long time without speaking. Neither wanted to admit his disappointment. The fox was black, but the unkempt summer coat had none of the glorious guard hairs they had imagined.

"So that's a silver fox," Edward said at last.

"We shouldn't have expected it to look good in summer," Henry said a bit wistfully. "She'll be a different fox when she gets her winter coat."

Mr. Herman said he would sell the fox for three thousand dollars, and he wanted cash. The price was not out of line with the times. Edward began to talk about a partnership. Mr. Herman shook his head, walked into the barn and began the evening milking. Edward and Henry followed and talked about the next spring's increase, which could be halved between them. Mr. Herman did not answer and went on milking. The two boys stood at either side and, as the jets squirted into the pail, argued the benefits of partnership. Never had any promoter of a fox ranch spoken more persuasively of the dazzling profits in the industry of the golden pelt. They summoned every fact they had read or that James Kane had told them, but Mr. Herman remained unmoved. He carried the milk pails to the house and started the separator, a small one of quart capacity.

The separating process lasted a long time, but the boys never stopped talking above the clatter. Mr. Herman was still unconvinced. He remained so through the evening, and when at last he went to bed the boys departed for the barn, where they slept in the hayloft.

They arose early in the morning to resume their arguments. The owner of the fox continued to be obdurate. The price was three thousands dollars.

At ten o'clock the boys gave up. Mr. Herman was becoming irritable. They returned to Polar, so dejected by the failure of their salesmanship that they decided at the station to save the money for their fare. It was sixty-two miles to Hamburg. They walked all day and all night. Their shoes hurt their feet, and when they tried walking barefoot, stones cut their soles. They finished the journey in their heavy woolen socks, and arrived home in time for the morning milking.

When the chores were done the Company held a conference; it had not yet abandoned the idea of the Polar fox. Walter, bookkeeper for the firm, had a brilliant idea. Their father had three thousand dollars in a savings account, profits of the Iowa farm, which he might loan if the Company gave a note and paid bank interest. Walter presented the idea to his father, and to everyone's amazement Frederick Fromm agreed. The note was written that morning. Then Frederick Fromm realized that withdrawal from the bank at this particular time would penalize him for three months' interest. The note was redrawn to cover this loss.

It was noon before negotiations were finally concluded. Henry and Edward had hoped to make up lost sleep during their father's visit to the bank to draw the money, but Frederick Fromm told the boys to get the car. He had sufficient cash on hand to bind the bargain, and no man could be expected to carry three thousand dollars around the country. An immediate departure had at least one advantage; their father would have less time to change his mind.

The three drove to Polar, and again they reached the Herman farm at milking time. The boys showed the silver fox to Frederick Fromm. He made no effort to conceal his opinion; he believed a creature worth three thousand dollars should look wonderful in any season. The boys explained about a fox's summer coat and opened transactions with Mr. Herman, who was still determined but no longer irritable, since Frederick Fromm's arrival had proved the purchasers to be in earnest. The price was argued through the evening, and again the Fromms slept in the hayloft.

In the morning Frederick awoke with deep misgivings. Three thousand dollars was a lot of money. He knew how big the sum was from having worked for it, and the boys would discover how large it was when they had to work to pay it back. Mr. Herman was a hard man in a bargain and besides, this fox did not look like anything a man should pay three thousand dollars to possess. Frederick knew that other fox farmers had paid even more for silver foxes, but fox farming was a wildcat business anyway. He was deeply troubled, and also mystified at finding himself involved in such a transaction.

The boys made a last desperate effort for better terms. Mr. Herman was still obdurate and finally, convinced that it was three thousand dollars or nothing, they turned to their father for the cash to bind the bargain.

Frederick Fromm was not in sight. The boys ran to the car. Although their father could not drive, he might be threatening departure in order to force Mr. Herman to close the deal. But the car was empty. They stared down the road. Large footprints, one so directly ahead of another and so firmly impressed that they meant fixed purpose, led over the hill toward town. The boys feared the worst, but they rushed back to Mr. Herman and told him negotiations would be resumed when they found their father.

They followed the footprints and from the top of the hill saw a stubborn figure plodding down the road. They overtook him, held the car door open. Frederick Fromm climbed into his accustomed seat beside the driver. He said nothing. The boys asked no questions. Everyone knew the episode was finished, and on the drive home no one spoke.

Chapter Six

Frederick fromm's distrust of silver foxes received
wholly unexpected confirmation when news of the Polar
fox reached Hamburg. Mr. Herman had sold it for three
thousand dollars to a Canadian dealer. This news had
been depressing to the Company though no comment
had been made in the family. But later, in the fall fur-
making months when the fox should have emerged a
glamorous creature of beauty, it had proved to be a
Sampson, of no value as a breeder or a pelt. A Sampson
is a fox which does not fur out properly. Such foxes have
been known since the early fur days, when its was assumed that they were merely poorer foxes — inferior
examples of the species. But when foxes were raised in
pens Sampson characteristics grew steadily worse. A
mildly Sampson fox might merely have curly hair. Then
animals would appear that failed to grow guard hairs,
then others with dry and thin undercoats, and finally
foxes with no brushes. If allowed to breed indefinitely,
Sampsons might even become hairless. In any of its
stages a Sampson is a miserable-looking fox, and un-

fortunately it is the toughest fox of all. Nothing kills it except its owner.

Since a dealer had not recognized a Sampson, boys who had never even seen silver foxes could not have been expected to recognize its early characteristics, and their faith in the beauty of the silver fox made them charitable toward summer coats. The skepticism of Frederick, who had no such feeling of charity, had saved them from a crippling blow. The three thousand dollars would have had to be repaid from ginseng profits, thus ending all but the most distant hopes of a silver herd. Shaken by this close brush with disaster, the Company was in no mood to argue with Frederick. His position was unassailable. He might even prove to be right about ginseng.

The Company could only go on working, with the problems of the ranch constantly increasing. Each spring's crop of fox pups required more pens; more pens meant more posts, lumber, and netting; posts and lumber meant more work at clearing; more grown foxes ate more small game. As the ginseng gardens grew in area, more mulch had to be carried from the forest, more sideboards staked around beds, more arbors built. As the number of plants increased, spraying became a problem; the small, hand-driven orchard spray demanded terrific toil. The Company's first change from man to machine power came with the purchase of a gasoline power spray. This more effective weapon in the constant warfare against blight would eventually save many dollars but, like any improvement, it put a strain upon the treasury.

There were difficulties, too, in the scheme to duplicate ginseng's natural environment, for nature sometimes worked against it. The necessity for dry leaf mulch had always been an anxiety. Leaves must fall before tender plants were exposed to cold, and since leaf raking was a long job the boys operated on a timetable over which they had no control. This autumn, 1912, nature contrived a real threat. A heavy snowstorm on October 4th covered the ground and the trees, when foliage had only begun to color. The ginseng gardens, which had been sprayed and weeded and which comprised the Company's entire capital, were without protection.

It looked as though Frederick's dismal warnings were to be justified, and there was nothing the Company could do; one really cold night would wipe them out. Day after day no leaves fell. A week of dreadful waiting and watching was spent, and then all the leaves in the forest let go at once. Leaves red and yellow and glorious bronze worked magic on the white forest floor. The sight was beautiful; the boys recognized its beauty even though it still spelled danger. Through every hour of daylight they worked, scraping the precious mulch from the snow, and at last every plant was protected. They had succeeded in spite of nature, but it had been a harrowing victory.

Washing roots was the hardest task in ginseng culture, for the crop could not be dug before late October when it ripened, and then the washing, which was done in the stream, was an icy job. The water chilled the hands, and the rough roots wore down fingernails until they were sore and tender. Various methods of speeding the operation were tried, such as placing the roots on racks and using a hand-driven barrel spray. Manning the pressure pump demanded a lot of muscle power, but it was less arduous than hand scrubbing. This year, however, there was more root than ever. The first seed-bed, planted eight years before, was ready to harvest. It had been a long time since the boys poked three hundred small flat seeds into holes made with a stick, and the present harvest fell far short of those first brave plans, but it was large enough to increase the dread of the washing and to make it a real problem.

The morning they began Edward noticed the family car standing in the shed, and thought of its motor, idle while they toiled. It should be made to work. He suggested that they drive the car to the stream, jack up the rear end and rig it up with a belt to drive the pump. The extemporized power plant was clumsy, but it was a beginning. They planned improvements. Next year they would buy a better pump and bring the root to the stream in a wagon that had a screen bottom to let the soil escape, thus making a second handling unnecessary. And "Some day," Henry said, "we'll have stationary motors working for us." They were started on the route of planning instead of plodding.

In November the double-cross fox was still living mateless in solitary grandeur when the boys heard of another silver trapped in their own district. That such luck should have struck three times in their neighborhood and yet have passed them by was beginning to seem incredible, for they had trapped dozens of red foxes. The local agent of the express company told the Fromm boys that more than a year earlier Henry Moreland of Iron Mountain had trapped two silvers, a male and a female. He had refused offers from the Dalton Silver Black Fox Company of Prince Edward Island because he intended to start his own farm. But after his first breeding season proved a failure, with no litter or no indication whether a litter had been born and destroyed by the parent foxes, he had reopened negotiations with the Dalton firm. A representative had come to Wisconsin and purchased the male for five thousand dollars. Now Mr. Moreland wished to sell the female. The agent had seen the fox and reported her beautiful, if a three-legged fox could be considered beautiful. She had lost the fourth leg in the trap.

It was almost a duplication of the Polar fox situation, except that the boys now knew it was hopeless to try to borrow from their father. They decided against a personal visit to the owner until they had first sounded him out by letter. Edward wrote a carefully worded proposal of partnership and since Mr. Moreland, through dealing with the Dalton firm, must already be well aware of the profits in fox farming, Edward dwelt principally on the fine qualities of their own silver male and on the Company's success with large litters. The agent of the express company also wrote Mr. Moreland, saying that he had known the Fromm boys for years. The two letters were only the opening guns in the negotiations, and the Company watched the mails for an answer.

To their astonishment the Moreland fox arrived by express. To have been entrusted with the sister of a fox which had brought five thousand dollars, and by a man who had never seen them, was a startling show of faith. The boys were slightly stunned by the ease with which the partnership had been managed; it had been like bracing for a tug at a spike and having a shingle nail come loose in the hand. Moreland's faith put a great responsibility upon them, and two silver foxes, one their own and one belonging to a stranger, demanded vigilance.

They built a watchtower which bristled with an air of threat. The structure was called "Fort Moreland." It had portholes for rifle fire, living quarters for a night guard, and withal a very militant aspect reminiscent of the blockhouses erected in days of Indian warfare. But the Company saw no humor in these extreme measures. Defensiveness was now the set pattern, and the 1913 breeding season must be made a success. Safety, care, and seclusion were the Company's solemn obligations. The rest was up to the foxes. And they couldn't miss. The female was a beautiful silver and the male was almost, though not quite, a silver.

The pair got on comfortably together. Perhaps the cross fox's broken-down front legs made him charitable about the three-legged condition of his consort. Two weeks before the whelping date in mid-April, there was no doubt of an increase; the Moreland female was heavy. In view of her history as a careless, if not an actually cannibalistic, mother, Henry redoubled his precautions for seclusion. If quiet would develop maternal instincts he was determined to provide it, and he tiptoed when he brought the food. Events in the nest box remained a mystery except for one morning after whelping time, when Henry was sure he heard pups whimper. The weeks of seclusion crawled by, and when the litter was about a month old John and Henry made occasional stealthy visits to the pen. The two boys were together when they first saw the litter. For a moment neither spoke. "Mrs. Moreland" was delighted with her family. She suffered no loss of pride whatever because she had mothered two cross pups and two reds.

There was no possible explanation of her failure to produce a silver. She was undoubtedly a silver. The sire showed a preponderance of silver blood. By all known laws of breeding, silver offspring should have resulted. It began to look as though bad luck had fastened on the Fromm boys in earnest; for the second time proper matings had failed them.

John looked at the double-cross sire doubtfully. "Maybe that outcaste red female wasn't to blame for those red pups," he said.

It was the first time suspicion had fastened on the double-cross, and even now it seemed unwarranted. Any fox with a black coat, silver guard hairs and only a slight blemish on the flank and shoulder must be almost silver. John's comment was unfortunate, however, for when the Company considered the grim possibility, they were even more distressed by what Moreland might think of them than by the fact of their own disaster. He had sent his fox in good faith. They had told him their male was a silver. He could only conclude that the Company was concealing silver pups. But the news of a litter of cross and red foxes must be broken to him. Edward wrote the letter, and it required all the statesmanlike tact the Company's "front man" could muster.

Mr. Moreland arrived at the end of the nursing period. The boys exhibited the silver sire and expressed their regret and dismay. They never knew what Mr. Moreland's real conclusions were. He made no accusations — simply departed with his silver female. On one point only he was definite; he absolutely refused to take his share of pups, red or cross. He was through with fox breeding forever.

The fiasco of the Moreland mating cast a shadow on the summer. Henry worried about it. He could not bear to think that a man who had shown such faith in the Company might now consider it dishonest. He brooded until he became really ill. A doctor diagnosed the trouble as a digestive ailment and suggested treatment at Battle Creek Sanitarium; a few weeks of care should put a strong boy of nineteen on his feet. Henry protested at such needless expense, but a thoroughly frightened Company insisted upon it. Although the treasury was in its usual summer doldrums, the poor health of a partner was an emergency.

To Henry the journey, his first into the outside world, was absorbing, but neither the excitement of travel nor the novelty of sanitarium life freed him of depondency. He continued to brood about the litter from the Moreland mating, then finally decided he could never find peace until he himself had made a statement of the honesty of the Company. He wrote a long letter to Mr. Moreland, assuring him it had not stolen silver pups, had none on the ranch, and was still mystified why there were none. When the letter was mailed he began to feel better. Undoubtedly the doctors were astonished at his abrupt recovery.

Completely cured Henry started home, stopping in Chicago for one errand. He visited the fur salon in the Marshall Field store. He'd not known stores had such thick carpets and luxurious appointments, but he did not permit awe to distract him. He asked to see a silver fox scarf. The saleswoman stared at him for a moment and then went to get one. It was priced at nine hundred dollars. Henry examined it carefully, handed it back to the saleswoman, thanked her, and went away. It never dawned on him that he left her mystified. He had seen a silver fox scarf, so much desired by women. The pelt was dark, lustrous, soft, and silky; but Henry thought it should have had more silver to make it brighter.

He returned to Hamburg. During his absence several letters had arrived from James Kane. The dealer was thoroughly baffled by the two unsuccessful matings of the double-cross. He was sure the fox was a western fox, and the term "double" had been his own invention to describe the evident preponderance of silver blood. He agreed, however, that it would be unwise to continue to depend on such a fox to sire a silver herd. Perhaps it was a Jonah.

But the Moreland mating had at least cleared the good name of the outcaste female, and Kane was now more sure than ever of the breeding value of such outcastes. In the previous two years ranchers had discovered many facts about them. Outcastes, mated with each other, produced silvers. And the outcaste offspring of outcaste parents might in their turn produce a silver pup in a litter of mixed foxes. Kane was so sure of their value that he did not hesitate to urge this method on Henry, and it seemed the only way for a boy with no capital to get silver foxes. To make this route possible he offered to find Henry a pair of outcastes for $450. The offer was intended to make amends for two years of disappointments and to encourage a boy who had become his friend. But nothing else could have made more vivid the contrast between the Company's fortunes and those of other ranchers.

Now in the fall of 1913 — when the Company had barely started, and did not have the money for the purchase of a $450 pair of outcaste foxes — the silver fox industry had reached new and dizzy heights. Pairs of pups were selling at fifteen to thirty-five thousand dollars, with options selling even on the next spring's pups. Ranches on Prince Edward Island were heavily capitalized; one hundred thousand dollars was not unusual, and the two largest were capitalized at more than six hundred thousand. Dividends to stockholders were astounding. One ranch had announced a dividend of 500 per cent, another of 300 per cent, several had paid more than 200 per cent, and investors could be assured a profit of from 10 to more than 100 per cent on their money in a single year. The boom foretold in 1910 was now on in full force, three years later. The industry had spread to the Eastern states and scores of new ranches were being started. Demand for breeding stock was at a peak and had almost ended the sale of ranch pelts, for no breeder would pelt a fox which could be sold to eager customers at a fantastic price. Fox farming, begun as a pioneering effort to domesticate and produce fur-bearing animals, had become a highly speculative, over-capitalized, stock-selling scheme. Blatant promotion, illicit methods, and even misrepresentation had permeated the industry, and were now a far greater hazard to the new investor than the difficulties of raising foxes. Animals — mixtures of every variety that could be imported — were being sold as standard, the term now used to describe the eastern purebred; and a rusty color had cropped up on many ranches which were supposed to have a thoroughbred herd.

For some time eastern ranches had been importing the western fox. Ranchers had become aware of the special quality of Peace River foxes, native to the district lying between the British Columbia border and Edmonton. These foxes had larger size, bone, and sinew, and they were brighter in color, while the eastern standard foxes were being bred smaller and darker. The lustrous dark eastern fox with delicate silver markings still ranked first in desirability, but breeders were hoping to add stamina and virility to their herds with the infusion of Peace River blood. Foxes from this district had become so valuable that a fine female silver, dug from a den by a Peace River trapper, had been bid for by eastern ranches and finally sold in Montreal for ten thousand dollars.

When James Kane proposed to sell Henry a pair of western outcastes for $450, he was offering a bargain. The Company realized this, and now that faith in the double-cross was shattered, they were more eager to try the mating of outcastes. But they were faced by a depleted treasury. Funds had been eaten by expansion. Every year they had had to build something. Wire for pennage, milling for arbor lumber, the purchase of sprayers, hose, and hardware, had kept them on a precarious footing. But they knew if they were to become breeders of silver foxes they must soon make a start, and somehow they must raise $450.

Edward suggested expansion of the Company, the usual method of handling a firm's financial crisis. Their cousins and neighbors, the Niemans, had money and might be persuaded into partnership. The Company paid a call on the cousins and Edward presented the idea, but before he had even finished his carefully prepared arguments he was refused, and with vehemence. Mrs. Nieman, who was planting beans, said she would make more money from the beans than the Fromm boys would ever make from "stinking foxes." She was as violent on the subject as Frederick Fromm.

Henry, even more than the others, resented his aunt's vivid vocabulary. He admitted foxes had a distinctive odor, and one which clung to the clothing of keepers. Being aware of this may have made him more sensitive, but he felt his aunt's description did his foxes an injustice. He was still fretting about the matter several days later as he and John rode their bicycles to Rib Mountain.

The expedition had been planned for a long time. Rib Mountain, or White Hill as it was called locally, was a geological curiosity. Almost eight hundred feet above the plain, and the highest point in the state, it rose abruptly from the surrounding country, a great jumble of white quartzite left by eroision. A few years before a fire had killed the Norway and white pines that grew on the bold shoulders of the hill, and now blanched tree skeletons and quartzite in summer, or shrouding snow in winter, had earned it the name of "White Hill." John and Henry had never visited the mountain, but eight years before, when Walter and Edward were in school in Wausaw, they had cut their names on the top and had boasted of the feat. It had required a chisel, hammer, determination, and real labor to cut letters in the stone. Now John and Henry were determined to outdo their brothers and leave their names on an even higher point of rock. They went equipped with tools, food, and blankets, because the job could not be finished in one afternoon. John was prepared to spend the night. But Henry had to return to feed the foxes.

Pedaling a bicycle over twenty miles of soft road was hard work, and their spirits were low. After four years of effort they still did not have a silver fox on the ranch, and they might not have one next spring if they couldn't manage to raise $450. Henry was nineteen, John twenty-one, and four years seemed a lifetime.

Their wealthy, scornful, cousins had not only refused them but had jeered at foxes. Henry recalled his anger, and at that moment the Nieman automobile passed them. The car looked powerful and prosperous, and the tires sent sand and pebbles flying out behind. John and Henry stared after it. The car seemed the final insult. The boys flared into a sudden rage and vowed that some day they *would* have silver foxes, cars, and everything else they wanted. They wished they had said this to the cousins. But saying it to each other made them feel better.

When they dismounted from their bicycles at the foot of the mountain John asked what they should carve at the top. Henry considered the question as they climbed. The inscription was important. It must be as enduring as the mountain itself. Undoubtedly someday roads would be built up the steep hill and people would come to see and marvel at so strange a geological formation. In itself, this idea held a challenge which made mere names seem trifling, but in another way Henry felt that what they carved that day must be an answer to their circumstances. Invincibility was in his thoughts.

They found the high point of the highest rock. It was only a few feet above the one that held the names of their brothers. John unwrapped the chisel and the hammer and prepared to carve. He looked at Henry And Henry had thought out the answer. He tore a page from his notebook and wrote:

John and Henry Fromm
Pioneer Breeders of Silver Foxes
1913

Chapter Seven

THE NEXT MORNING HENRY WAKENED WITH A SCHEME
to raise the money to buy the pair of outcaste foxes.
They might be able to sell the double-cross. The male
fox had lost in prestige, but Henry did not permit doubt
to creep into the advertisement for the October issue
of *Hunter-Trader-Trapper.* He considered using the
adjective "fine," but decided this might be unwise. The
advertisement read only, "For Sale — Silver black male
fox with rusty ear or neck, and shoulder flank. Henry
Fromm, Hamburg, Wisc."

The fox sold, and almost immediately. Even more
astonishing, it sold for the asked price of $650. The
Company had been prepared to dicker. Moreover, the
purchaser wrote how pleased he was with his bargain.
But apparently the career of the double-cross was ill-
starred, for after the next breeding season he was offered
back to the Company at a reduction. The new owner
was equally bewildered by a litter of red pups. No one
understood the mystery.

Not until years later was a genetic law formulated

by Karl B. Hansen which might explain the enigma. Hansen carried on experiments in mating Alaskan and eastern silver foxes to discover that both were recessives, but different recessives. And since the behavior of different recessives, even if similar in appearance, is, when mated, the same as that of a straight strain, the recessive is lost and offspring tend to return to the normal. Litters of cross foxes would be the expected result. This outcome had been the more bewildering because no one had known the exact geographical boundaries of the habitant of the Alaskan fox. It comes from the interior of Alaska, and the Peace River District silver foxes are apparently not of the Alaskan variety, since they had always been mated successfully with eastern or standard foxes. The boundary between the two strains, eastern and Alaskan, lies somewhere between Peace River and Alaska, and it is barely possible that the famous double-cross that cost the Fromm boys two breeding seasons might have been a real Alaskan silver.

James Kane, in wishing to befriend Henry, had found for him a black fox with only two rusty tinges for $350. Quite unwittingly he might have selected an Alaskan silver which, when mated to a standard, could never produce silver pups. It had been the Company's ill fortune to be involved in a genetic mystery when geneticists had not yet given their attention to silver fox breeding, and fox ranchers were not even aware that fur farming was a genetic problem.

In the middle of November the pair of outcastes arrived by express. Kane, by now quite as eager for a successful breeding season as the Company, wrote full instructions. Especially he warned Henry against over-feeding. Too fat a fox would not breed. The male was a big fox, greyish red and wolfish, undoubtedly from Peace River, and he had an aggresive bearing that delighted his new owners. The female was finely molded. The' pair was installed in its quarters and Henry, with Kane's warning fresh in his mind, took care not to feed a large supper. He was determined to make no mistakes in this breeding season.

The evening was a happy one. It seemed almost too good to be true that at last the Company was prepared for silvers. The double-cross would never again confound them, and as fine a pair of outcastes as anyone could wish were now members of the herd. Even the night guard in Fort Moreland slept the sound sleep of achievement.

Early next morning the Company went to inspect the new foxes. The male appeared to be in even better spirits. A moment later they saw the tail of a fox lying on the ground. It was all that remained of the female. Half of $450 had gone down the male's gullet.

The crime might have resulted from a scanty supper or a quarrel, or the Company might have bought what fox men call a "killer." At the moment, however, the explanation seemed irrelevant, even trivial. It could not change the fact that the Company was again the possessor of a single fox. The boys wrote Kane of this fresh disaster. His dismay matched theirs, and by this time he must have been as determined as the Fromms, for he wrote at once offering a second female, and for only $150. Any female outcaste was worth more, and when the boys saw the fox they realized how generous the dealer had been. She was finely drawn, and had a sharp red dark coat almost the color of the Kamchatka red fox. She arrived with careful instructions for the introduction. Neither the Company nor Kane could continue to feed the male with expensive mates.

The dealer directed that the two foxes should first be sprinkled with alcohol to make them smell alike, and then kept for several days in a wire cage three feet square, with a dividing netting in the center. This would give each fox living quarters of a foot and a half and a constant awareness of the other. When the boys read the instructions they doubted Kane's wisdom for the first time; if their male were a killer, such imprisonment would only aggravate his disposition. But they carried out the directions faithfully. The male seemed somewhat baffled by the barrier and intrigued by his companion, although the boys had no way of knowing whether he was regarding her as a mate or as a meal. After four days the foxes were moved to their pen and Henry, even at the risk of jeopardizing breeding season, pressed large meals upon them. But the foxes were already friends, and by breeding season they were devoted to each other.

Henry knew the pair had bred, and wrote the whelping date in his notebook. That event passed off successfully, for later Henry heard the pups. The weeks ahead would be a period of anxious waiting, but they had worked too hard and through too many years to risk disaster now. Henry stopped beside the pen only long enough to slip in food and water. The litter meant so much that not a member of the Company was even tempted to investigate. They hardly dared think of the outcome. The results were already decided, and only those most concerned did not know the answer.

Henry had caught not even a glimpse of a pup when the litter was a month old and a three-day May snowstorm covered the ground with two inches of fluffy snow. Then the sun came out. It was a lovely morning. Henry gave breakfast cereal to the outcaste pair, and as usual the mother picked up food to carry to her young. Then, as she went toward the house, she called her family. It was a strange little sound, half sigh, half grunt, because her mouth was full of cereal. But the youngsters heard it, and a red pup came to the opening of the funnel and started down the ramp. Henry stood motionless, his heart beating so hard he could feel it thump. A second red pup followed, then a third, then a fourth, and Henry was beginning to fear there were no more when a fifth pup appeared and came down the ramp.

Its blackness against the snow was unforgettable. After five long years of effort at last they had a silver! The puppy fur glistened in the sunlight. Henry knew that never would he forget that moment of delight. Then he thought of the others, started for the house on a run and burst through the kitchen door to shout the news.

And it was the happiest day the farm had ever known.

Chapter Eight

THE COMPANY HAD WORKED FIVE YEARS FOR THIS PUP, had been planning silver foxes more than ten. Henry was twenty, John two years older, Edward twenty-four, and Walter twenty-six. The little progress they had made was frightening.

The Company considered its position. Silvers could be obtained from outcaste reds, but the process was slow. One breeding season, though successful, did not guarantee another. If the partners tried to build a herd by the addition of a single pup each year, they faced at best a long period of sluggish growth, plus the hazard of an annual chance of failure. They did not even know whether outcaste matings were certain.

Genetics was an unknown word to the Fromms, and only a few ranchers, far more experienced, realized the import of the Mendelian law. Geneticists had but recently established the fact that the silver coat character was recessive to the red, and followed Mendel's rule of the recessive's three-to-one ratio, a proportion based on averages. In a thousand matings it would work out with accuracy, but a single mating, or half-a-dozen, always held the possibility of misses or departures from the average. The Fromm boys had been lucky that in a single outcaste mating the hidden or recessive silver characteristics of the parents had bred true in one pup in the litter, and there good fortune ceased. Undoubtedly others of the offspring were half silver, but this did not show, the silver color being recessive to the red. Thus, even had the boys known they had half bloods in the litter, it would have been difficult to differentiate except by breeding, and that would take another year. The fox's annual reproductive season was an inexorable time obstacle. Another year, with its risk and uncertainty, was out of the question in their minds.

This left one way out — the purchase of breeding stock — and now, actually possessing one silver pup, they felt anything less than bold, aggressive action would be a sellout of their dreams. They determined that before the next mating season they would have, not only a mate for their silver, but a second pair of silvers as well. The farm they had envisioned could not be started with less. They had no idea what breeding stock would cost or how they would get the money, but they took the first step and wrote to James Kane. He had adopted all the Fromm boys after learning Henry was the youngest of a firm of four brothers, and if anyone could help them, he was the man.

An answer had not come from Kane when Frederick Fromm departed for his annual visit to his farm in Iowa. A few days later after his departure Kane's letter arrived and offered three silver foxes for $6,800. The boys had hoped the price would be less, but even so it was moderate, and the company knew these foxes would be the three best Peace River silvers it was possible to buy for the money. Kane wrote as a friend. He was delighted they had at last decided to buy breeding stock, the sure and speedy way to a silver herd, and he knew they would not regret it. He would hold the foxes for their answer.

It was now or never for the Company. There was no money and nothing on which to borrow. The first large ginseng crop, the half acre of seed planted so many years before, would mature in 1915, the following year. The neighboring Nieman cousins would never consider a loan against the crop or an investment in silver foxes. That embraced the only possibilities. Then one of the boys said quite suddenly that their mother was the one who owned the farm. The quarter section had always remained in her name.

The Company went to the kitchen to see Alwina. The boys knew the farm had never carried a mortgage and that their parents' ways had been slow and thrifty. They had never spent more than they made, had always waited until they could afford a purchase, and in the early years they had contrived to produce food, shelter, and the family's clothing. Even the boys' suits had been made of homespun because Alwina's fingers could save the cost of woolen yardage. The boys knew of those years of work, knew too of their mother's boundless faith in her sons, but they had never quite taken the measure of her courage nor her spirit, for now Alwina did not hesitate.

"What good is land unless it gives a family a start in life?" she asked.

The Company had intended to be persuasive.

"Fox farms are making money," Walter began, "and—"

Alwina looked at him reproachfully. "What makes you think I wouldn't mortgage my farm to give my sons a chance?" she asked.

Suddenly the Company was sobered. It had not been prepared for the burden of such faith.

"Look at all the things that can happen to foxes!" John burst out. "Ma doesn't know anything about them. We got no right to let her mortgage the farm. She ought to think about this." He had said more words in a few moments than he usually spoke in a day.

Alwina wiped her hands and hung her apron on a peg. "But you boys would have had your chance," she said.

"Next year we can dig a half acre of ginseng." Walter said. "It isn't as though we were depending only on silver foxes."

Henry was troubled. Youngest of the boys, he had been his mother's baby, closer to her than the others, yet no one desired a silver herd more ardently. He had thought about nothing else for years. Now a path which had opened was closing before him.

"But Ma believes we can raise silver foxes," Edward said. "She knows we've got to buy them when we have the chance."

The Company and Alwina drove to town to see the banker. Mr. Gruett had known the Fromm boys since they were youngsters, had admired their perseverance and capacity for work, and he had watched the ginseng gardens grow from the first small bed. But every instinct of a conservative country banker was aroused by the Company's proposal.

"A mortgage on your mother's farm for sixty-eight

hundred dollars to buy silver foxes!" he said. "And your father doesn't even know about it!"

This was only the beginning of his protest. The mortgage was too large even for a legitimate purpose, was poor banking practice, but more important, he had no right to countenance such an action. A banker held the same community responsibility as a doctor. He was a family adviser.

"This is more than business," he said. "It is a moral question."

The Company argued passionately, but failed to convince him that silver fox farming was an established industry with an assured future. Then it fell back on ginseng, the real guarantor of the loan. Even if Mr. Gruett could not believe in silver foxes he must believe in ginseng.

Here the banker was on familiar ground. He had discussed loans with other growers and he knew how seldom the golden dreams of ginseng were realized; as yet no one had succeeded in harvesting a ten thousand dollar half acre. The Company acknowledged it wouldn't, but was sure the crop would run to five thousand dollars. Mr. Gruett conceded this possibility, but spoke of the costs of growing, which the boys knew well. On the firm footing of a practical discussion of ginseng culture it was finally agreed that even if silver foxes proved a failure, ginseng could in the years ahead pay off the mortgage.

Alwina's signature on the mortgage had a new-found boldness. The banker alone was troubled. He must explain this loan to the directors and he knew inner doubts would nag him, but for better or worse he was involved in the hopes and fears for three silver foxes.

Before the boys left town a check was mailed to James Kane. It was wise, the Company felt, for the purchase to be finished business before their father's return. The money passed through their hands so quickly they had no time to get a sense of grandeur. The three foxes arrived ten days later.

The Company would not have admitted it, but the foxes were a disappointment. The magnitude of the investment had given the boys a vision of glorious creatures, and they'd forgotten that it was summer and foxes eight weeks old would still be in puppy fur. The pups should be more impressive, if only to soften the impact of the news to Frederick Fromm. No one had written him of the mortgage, and he was expected home a few days later. If Alwina dreaded the coming interview — for her action had challenged the ways of a wife of her time and among her people — she did not show it. When Frederick arrived it was she who told him that the three big-headed long-legged timorous creatures had put a mortgage on the farm.

Frederick Fromm said almost nothing. Argument was futile with the catastrophe already an established fact, and perhaps he recognized in Alwina that same unalterable determination that years before had marked her refusal to leave the forests of Wisconsin. But he knew that life was altered. From now on tilled fields must be given to fox pens and ginseng arbors, for one or the other of the ventures would have to repay the loan. The mortgage had forced the conflict to a decision.

As the young silver foxes grew and thrived, the Company felt that they demanded names. Eastern silvers bore proud titles befitting aristocracy — Sir Wilfrid, Sir Cecil Frederick, Lady Evelyn, Queen Anne, King

Charles, Count Otto, Pride, Glorious, and Incomparable. The partners chose "Kaiser" for their own pup because of his arrogance and proud bearing. Names of the others were everydayish, almost homely, which was right for creatures who were practically members of the Company. The male was called Tom after James Kane's son, who had brought him. The more quiet of the two females, a large, light fox, was christened Toynette because this seemed a good name for a gentle animal. The smaller female, a wild and excitable creature, was called Alaska despite her Peace River origin, because of the untamed nature of that land. They considered that a name for Kaiser's mother should honor her achievement, but since she had already brought renown to the term of outcaste, they decided not to change it. And in the years ahead, as she became almost a cornerstone of the ranch, producing each season a large litter with one or two or even three silver pups, she was always known as the Outcaste Mother.

Mating the foxes was decided by color. All four were bright, ranging from one-quarter to one-half silver. These terms were used by fox men to describe, not the purity of the strain, but the amount of silver guard hairs in the coat. The wide variation of the silver fox, from black with a white-tipped tail to an all-over silveriness, demanded definite description. The black might have no silver, or a faint suggestion of silvery hairs on the posterior; the extra-dark silver, a faint scattering of silver hairs on the hind quarters, and the dark more silver; the quarter-silver had silver hairs only on the rump and forehead; the half-silver carried the silver toward the middle of the back. The black was rare and had been prized by the Russian nobility, but some fur men argued that the skin could be imitated, in color at least, by dyed red fox, whereas the silver guard hair defied imitation. Its design, unique with the silver fox, consisted of color bands. Close to the body the guard hair was the color of the underfur, followed by a band of sharp black, then by a narrower one of silver with a long black tip. The silver band should be truly metallic, beginning and ending abruptly, since if it were shaded it gave a brownish cast. The long black tip of the guard hairs formed a veiling for the silver.

The Fromms' four Peace River foxes had more silver than the eastern fox. Toynette and Kaiser, brightest of the four, were half-silvers, and so would have the most silvered and, to the Fromms' notion the prettiest, pups. The Company's idea of mating to develop more silver differed radically from the accepted method. In the opinion of the fur world the small dark or extra-dark fox with a limited area of silver was the most beautiful, the most distinctive, and the most becoming to the wearer, hence this pelt brought the highest prices. Eastern ranchers believed that if two light foxes were mated, not only would the silver be too predominant in the offspring, but the black fur would tend to lose clearness and become rusty. But the Fromm boys liked silvered foxes, and the brightness and the life that silver guard hairs imparted to the pelt, and they bred to bring out silver.

This decision was of tremendous importance, both to the Company and to the silver fox industry. At the time it was incredibly presumptuous; it went against beliefs of older ranchers, rulings of fashion, and financial advantage in the face of a heavy mortgage. Farm boys who had never seen a fox scarf on the shoulders of a woman could scarcely judge what would be becoming, and certainly had no reason to believe they could change a trend in fashion. Since the silver fox had first aroused awe and wonder in the courts of Europe, the dark silver had led in favor, and now youths in a Wisconsin wilderness challenged the whole world's opinion. But this fitted with their dream. Years ago they had vowed to raise the most beautiful silver foxes in all the world, and they believed silver was the key to the real beauty of these glamorous creatures. They stubbornly set out to prove it.

Chapter Nine

IN THIS YEAR, 1914-15, GINSENG AND FOXES TOOK TURNS
in confronting the Company with new problems. By
early autumn it realized that the days were not long
enough to accomplish what must be done. Home supply
of man power could no longer keep up with the demand
of the two enterprises, and the boys who had once
worked for their neighbors now asked neighbors' sons
and daughters to work for them. Committing themselves even to this small pay roll through the rush season was a big decision, but they had already taken a
bigger risk — the mortgage. Ranch output must be
speeded up to meet the obligation.

Girls could rake leaves, transplant ginseng, drop seeds,
and gather ginseng root. Men could bring leaves and
loam from the forest, work the soil, make trenches,
and dig roots. Work could be done in crews of a man and
a girl; team work occurred naturally to the Company,
since for years the boys had instinctively resorted to it
for effectiveness and speed. Now they were ready to
show others, and their neighbors — rural folk who usual-

ly do not take kindly to instruction — were willing to be shown because large production in ginseng culture was new, the assembly-line idea exhilarating, and the Fromm boys worked even harder than their employees. A man moved the soil; a girl dropped seeds. A man dug a trench and drove two stakes at either end; a girl fastened a guide line to the stakes and transplanted ginseng, using knots tied at seven-inch intervals to mark the position for each plant. A man dug ginseng roots with a handfork; a girl picked up the roots, shook off the soil and tossed them to the pile. Two men washed roots beside the stream with the new sprayer and pressure pump; the Fromm car supplied the power. With every task in ginseng calling for speed, with a new job pressing for attention before each one in hand was finished, no one had time or energy to consider whether he was the hired or the hirer; it made little difference when there was so much to be accomplished. Ginseng work took on the communal excitement of a barn-raising, and a crew's pay roll, which might have been the first dividing sign of a new success, brought about instead a fuller sense of neighborliness.

The harvest, the largest yet, was dried in an upstairs bedroom and strained the room's capacity. Racks were needed, and many of them. Then someone remembered the sections of the arbor roofs which, placed one above another like a multiple-decker bed, would increase the drying area. The movable arbors, John's suggestion of so long before, now paid a second dividend.

But while they were succeeding with ginseng the boys heard disturbing rumors about the silver fox industry. Prices of live silver foxes had declined. At first the boys refused to believe this, but as reports of distressed fur farms increased they realized the Company had waited for years only to buy breeding stock at the peak of the market. For a long time men had been saying the silver fox boom could not last, yet it had continued to soar higher. Now values were deflating. They reached bottom with the collapse of the London market. For centuries London had been the center of the fur industry, setting fashions, fixing prices, and establishing values. Since the most remote outpost was attuned to the news of London auctions, this break rocked all fur land. Fox ranchers, really frightened, frantically sold stock; foxes purchased at fabulous prices were offered for whatever they would bring. Over-capitalized companies, with inventories now fictitious, ceased to be, and promoters fled the wreckage. Stockholders tore up paper calculations of a fortune and knew their dream was over. The bubble had burst, as wise fox men had always known it would.

One of the bigger shocks to the Fromm boys was the letter from James Kane telling them that he was ruined. He had returned from a western buying trip with a carload of foxes to discover a market being unloaded in panic. Kane surveyed his losses with equanimity. He'd had the excitement of sharing in the gaudiest era of any fur in all the world, and now had plenty of company in adversity. But he still believed in silver foxes, and he was sure once the industry was rid of speculation and inflated values, real fox men would build ranched foxes into an important business. But the process of getting on a sound footing would be tough for many fox farms.

It would not be tough for the Fromms. The Company had no stockholders to appease, no promotion schemes to justify. Though their breeding stock had shrunk in value — the three silver foxes were now worth only a third of the purchase price — they did not have to sell. Edward was inclined to regret their earlier conviction that it was now or never; patience for a few more months would have repaid them.

But Henry said, "At least we got our foxes. And we like them. Some day they'll be worth every cent we paid for them."

Actually, Alwina Fromm was the one who should have been the most concerned about the collapse of the market, but she only became more than ever a partisan of silver foxes. The three Kane silvers were still worth a mortgage, in her opinion. Frederick Fromm did not say, "I told you so" — he never spent words unnecessarily — but his manner was that of a man whose judgment had been right all along. Mr. Gruett, the banker, was the most troubled. Every Saturday through late summer and fall he had driven to the Fromm farm to make sure the foxes were still alive, and now the collapse in prices renewed his earliest misgivings. The Fromm boys were saddled with a debt that would absorb ginseng profit. Ginseng was their only hope.

In midwinter the ginseng was finally ready to go to market. Weeks had been spent in the tedious job of stripping fiber and prongs from the root and sorting the products — fine fiber, coarse fiber, prongs, second-grade root, and that of the first quality. Each brought different prices. The kegs of ginseng were packed for shipping when the Company learned that this market, too, had suffered. First-grade roots, for which they had expected seven dollars a pound, were now worth only five. Ginseng, as well as silver foxes, had let them down.

But the boys managed to meet the interest on the mortgage, and even to make a token payment on the principal. After this heroic gesture they deposited the remaining five hundred dollars in the bank. Those dollars would have to be spread thin.

Breeding season followed soon afterward, and in late April it was evident that the excitable Alaska had lost her litter — or never had one; it was difficult to reach conclusions about a fox household which was in a constant state of nervous panic. There was no doubt, however, that the Company faced a 50 per cent loss in the year's production of silver foxes. They had not been prepared for a miss. In other seasons they'd always had large litters even though the pups weren't silvers. Apparently fox ranching never lacked a new grief to spring on owners. Henry read everything he could find on the subject of lost litters. He had followed the rules, had not overfed in breeding season, had kept his foxes quiet and secluded through the critical months until whelping time. The bulletin offered no further suggestions. He was on his own, and he brought in a one-man report to the Company.

"There's only one thing to do," he said. "After we've read the bulletin and got the general idea, we'll have to watch our foxes and find out what each one wants. We've got to get along with the nature of each animal."

Asked if he knew what Alaska wanted, he said she was an unusually shy creature. Most of all she needed a sense of security, which might be possible if her pen were made to resemble a forest, with enough brush so that she would never lack for cover. They couldn't eliminate fencing and meals, but they could make her believe she was living the same existence as her wild forebears. Henry's scheme was a radical departure from instructions in the bulletin, which had especially warned against the dangers of brush-cluttered yards. But any scheme was worth trying. A pair of foxes costing $3,400 would be worthless except as pelts unless they could be persuaded to become parents. John and Henry camouflaged the pen so thoroughly that even they could scarcely see the netting, and the tenants could live a practically concealed existence. After a year in this retreat Alaska's fate would be decided. She would be a mother or a scarf.

Toynette presented no psychic problem. She brought out her litter even earlier than seemed wise to the keepers, but she was a natural mother with no hysterical anxieties, and her five silver puppies seemed to thrive the better for her easy ways. The Outcaste Mother, mated to her son, presented the Company with two silvers, and her year-old daugthers added three more silvers to the herd. The outcastes had become an eminent family.

The Company could scarcely believe its good fortune. Fourteen silvers on the farm — vastly different from the year before, when a single silver pup caused a celebration. And the boys prepared to back their luck. All energy, every dollar, must be expended toward one purpose. Though silver foxes were a long-time gamble and the fox farm could not now pay its way, it fortunately did not have to, since there was a second source of revenue. Ginseng must be expanded to carry the foxes, and capital for this expansion had to be dragged out of the ranch and out of themselves. No economy was too small to be practiced. Even personal wants were curtailed. They patched work clothes until patches overlaid the original garment; they knitted socks on the knitting machine and, because time made the hand-turned heels precious, they patched these with cloth to make the heels last longer. Similar rigorous economies were carried out in ginseng and with foxes. There was no choice but to pay money for wire, sawing, netting, nails, new equipment — even outside labor. Extra help had been necessary for the large spring arbor, a crew was needed for the fall season, and occasionally in summer they hired girls to keep down the rampant weeds. But all this outlay was held to the barest minimum. An almost fanatical zeal drove them, bringing the members of the Company very close together.

At long last the first half acre of ginseng was ready for harvest. The boys remembered the autumn of its planting in 1909 when they had talked of a ten thousand dollar crop within five years. It was now 1915, and in those six years, what with plant blight, root rot, slow maturity, production costs, and unstable prices, the crop at the present market value would not bring four thousand dollars.

This year the fall crew was larger, ten men and ten girls. Twenty extra at the table, beds for those who lived too far to go home, heavy cooking, and piles of dishes — the growing business had invaded the small farmhouse. Alwina could be of little help, for she had begun to fail; often the care of her own family was now beyond her. Edward and Henry, both proficient in the house, had learned how to take over, and since a cook for the crew was a job that could be supplied by home labor, they added this to their other responsibilities.

The larger harvests demanded changed methods. Assembly-line systems must be kept flexible so as to adjust to the problems of greater loads. Also increased production could magnify small mistakes into material losses. Last year's crop had run too heavily to second-grade, and they knew that bruises on the tender roots had permitted rot to find a foothold. This fall they built "digging tables" with canvas beds on which diggers threw the forkloads, and girls sorted the root from the soil. Drying, too, was improved through experience. The drying racks were carried to the attic where, with the windows thrown open, there was space and air. The confusion and work involved in carrying a ton and a half of green root up the steep stairs should have reassured them as to its safety. Only a super thief or a phantom could have managed a raid, but robbery was now an accepted danger, and one of the Company always slept within sight of the treasure.

The half acre yielded $3,564.09. The Company had earned it down to the last nine cents.

The check seemed magnificent, but it was not affluence. A payment of fifteen hundred dollars on the mortgage cut the sum almost in half and the remainder had to be put aside for expansion. A stationary engine must relieve the family car, much too clumsy a power plant for washing the larger harvests, and a galvanized wire netting was needed to lay on ginseng beds as anchorage for dry leaves. Leaf mulching had always been a major grief because of tricky timing; if the mulch were spread too early fall winds carried the dry leaves away; if it were delayed plants were in danger of a sudden frost. In the early years of smaller gardens the Company had been able to cover quickly and to patch after each stiff wind, but this was not possible in plantings of three acres. Sufficient netting to anchor leaves on all the beds was a must, no matter how big the investment. Another constant cost from now on would be labor. Arbors were now too large for home manufacture. A supporting structure must be built around three acres, innumerable lath sections for walls and roofs made and set in place, sideboards staked around four sides of 144 beds, each 143 feet in length. In the coming years they must build even bigger arbors. And each year they must build until they had a sufficient inventory of posts or lath sections. Now an enterprise begun ten years before with a few plants brought from the forest was a lusty youngster, taking much and giving little.

Even forest loam, once a free natural resource, had slipped into the cost column. They had scraped their own forest floor and turned to their neighbors. During that summer Edward had beguiled Mother Roehl into selling an acre of forest loam for fifty dollars and the promise not to destroy any growth of young trees. Obviously that was impossible; some young saplings had been uprooted, and the boys had concealed the evidence under piles of brush in a deep ravine. This had seemed more practical than regrets, but unfortunately Mother Roehl's counselor in farm matters must have possessed X-ray eyes, for he went unerringly to the caches. Edward made the firm's apology and promised to do better, and Mother Roehl reluctantly agreed to give them one more chance. The Company had to have that forest loam. But they knew sapling accidents were bound to happen, and if again they were unsuccessful in eluding the snooper, they might have to go farther away and pay even more to some other owner of forest loam.

Walter was already searching for a solution, a man-made substitute for forest soil which contained humus, was light and porous, and had the necessary qualities of decayed forest vegetation. He had planted peas, plowed them under, and set out an experimental garden. But an experiment in ginseng was a long-time process. A year of vigorous growth proved nothing; a healthy maturity was what counted. Even thriving transplanted ginseng could not immediately prove that seeds might be entrusted to anything but natural loam.

In the spring the fox farm had expansion trouble. Now that the herd consisted of fourteen silvers and eighty cross and red foxes, neither John nor Henry had time to hunt nor to set out snares for rabbits. Fox meals, even of ground horse meat, entailed a big job. Where once a kettle from the kitchen had been large enough to carry fox suppers, now a tub was taken to the pens on a hand cart. Henry cut horse meat from the bone, ran the meat through a grinder and baked corn cakes in the oven of the kitchen range. Cereal and horse meat was the unvaried diet. The foxes liked it and seemed to thrive, and Henry believed he'd solved the feeding problem.

Suddenly there was an outbreak of rickets. There was no danger of deaths, but no one wanted to build a herd with broken-down foxes. Henry consulted a druggist, who suggested limewater. This helped the foxes but not Henry; he had to know why healthy animals suddenly had rickets, especially when he knew that horse meat was good food. Then he realized that foxes which had once been fed whole animals now had no bone whatsoever. Wild foxes never lacked for calcium because they ate what they caught, bones and all. The Company bought a hand-operated bone grinder, installed it in the cellar of the farmhouse, and every day Henry ground horse bones into rations. The din of clashing gears and splintering bone, punctuated by loud explosions in particularly heavy going, was frightful and hard on everyone. The man power required to turn the grinder was appalling, but the legs of the foxes stiffened and they walked as foxes should walk, with pride in their bearing.

Chapter Ten

By the spring of 1916 the silver fox industry had purged itself of the evils of its boom time period. Fox farming had paid heavily for its prodigal years, and now the sobering-up process brought about a spirit of reform. Ranchers who thought only in terms of an easy fortune had departed. The real breeders, anxious to see fox farming become a sound enterprise yielding justifiable profits, knew that never again would foxes like the famous Sir Wilfrid and Lady Evelyn make owners wealthy. Sir Wilfrid was reported to have earned almost a hundred thousand dollars, and Lady Evelyn had repaid the five comparatively poor men who had clubbed together in her purchase not only with a sizeable fortune, but had financed a plant of 100 pens, a dwelling house, a barn, and all the necessities of a ranch. Such returns could no longer be expected from silver foxes, but with good foundation stock costing two or three thousand dollars a pair, with wise breeding and good management, a fox farm could be built into a highly successful business.

The ranch bred fox was no longer an experiment; in the estimation of fox ranchers it had earned its place as the equal if not the superior of the product of the wilds. But the fur trade was still prejudiced against the domesticated silver fox. Ranchers realized this was largely their fault. In the speculation era, when prices of breeding stock were at the peak, only the poorest pelts had been sent to market. Poor quality and misrepresentation had done the industry a great disservice, and fox men must now reestablish the reputation of the ranch bred fox by setting a standard for the quality silver fox and uniting to produce only such animals. And, as always, new beginnings went hand in hand with deep convictions. One of these was the belief that the small dark silver should be the goal of all selective breeding. The black must be clear and glossy, the silver truly metallic, never chalky, too extensive, or too conspicuous. This was the idea of silver fox at its perfection. By breeding for and achieving this quality, fox farmers could supply the fur trade with what it wanted and at the same time prove that more and better foxes could be produced on ranches.

The Fromm boys read in bulletins and in the *Silver Black Fox Magazine,* published in Canada, of the vigorous stand taken by the fox industry. But their ideas continued to be as home-grown and individualistic as the Company's entire enterprise had been. They saw their problem as that of any farmer. A successful crop, whether wheat, oats, or silver foxes, depended on both quantity and quality. Quantity in pelts demanded a herd of strong, sturdy prolific foxes, and they knew that a fox with body length and good cavities was bound to be a better producer than a short, stubby animal. Therefore Fromm foxes must not be small. Quality in fur was a matter of texture, gloss, length, and color. And the Company liked silver, hoped to make its foxes even brighter in the future. Peace River foxes had the qualities that the boys admired — size, bone, and sinew — and the coats were strong in silver. So inevitably these foxes conformed to the Company, standard as the beginnings of their herd of prolific and lovely foxes.

The breeding season of 1916 was a success. The female Alaska proved the wisdom of a year's retreat by presenting the Company with a litter of four silvers. After this happy event the screening brush was removed, a little at a time, to accustom her gradually to the normal life of a farm fox. Toynette produced her usual five silver pups, an astonishing record in fertility for so young a mother; she promised to be as hard-working as the Fromms themselves. Henry was sure that in time she would be tame enough to eat from his hand. She evinced a passion for dried raisins, and already she had considered proffered tidbits. The outcastes maintained their standing as a distinguished family by producing even more silvers than the Company had expected. Except for one pup they were all fine animals, quite as fine as the offspring of the purebreds.

The one pup was sickly and spent the greater part of the summer in a corner of the pen, practically immobile, but when he lost his puppy fur and grew the coat he would wear in winter, the Company was astonished to discover than an outcaste mother had thrown an extra-dark silver considered particularly rare and desirable. But even ownership of such an animal did not change the Company's opinion about the color. Knowing the pelt had some value, although it was lusterless from ill health and worn by the fox's lying on the ground, the partners sent it when fur was prime to Funsten Brothers, who bought it for $450.

This amazing check aroused curiosity as to the market value of their silvers. St. Louis was now, since the collapse of the London market, an important fur center, and pelts from the entire country would be offered at the midwinter auction. Silver fox was expected to bring good prices. Matched pairs should sell for at least fifteen hundred dollars and fine singles might command a thousand. The Company decided to try out its silvers, and in order to make the investigation conclusive chose three foxes ranging from one-quarter to one-half silver. They were beautifully furred but small animals, and the body structure did not promise prolificness. Henry consented to the pelting only for this reason, and even then the hardest thing he'd ever done was to kill three fine creatures. But when the fur was finally ready for shipping he was as excited as the others. The Company's first crop of silvers was going to market.

Dark silvers sold well at the January auction. A New York furrier paid $1,650 for a pair of matched dark silvers; a single pelt brought $910. But the Fromm pelts sold for $160 each — the three bringing little more than they had received for the damaged skin of one dark fox. If ever a company had a warning it was embarked on a precarious course, this was it.

The most stubborn individualist might have paused and pondered, but the boys did not even reconsider. They knew the silvered pelts were more beautiful; anyone with a sense of beauty must see what the silver did for black, picking it up, giving it life, making it shimmer. If anything, the price of those three pelts only made the Company's faith in silvered foxes the more fanatical. It was sure that bright silvers must some day become the world's preference, once there was a real opportunity to judge.

The effect of the midwinter auction was quite different in the fur world. Ranchers read the prices in *The Black Fox Magazine*, a new American publication for fox farmers, saw that dark foxes topped the list with quarter- and half-silvers trailing at the bottom, and decided that without a doubt the small dark fox was solidly entrenched. Authorities in fox farming began to urge an even more selective breeding to produce such a fox, and gave scientific methods for the procedure. It had been proved in practice that if a dark silver male of 25 per cent or less of silver were mated with a female of 25 per cent or more of silver, a majority of the offspring would be dark silver; and if the ancestors of the pair had been bred with the aim of producing dark or extra-dark silver there was a strong possibility that the offspring would continue to produce dark silver. By this method ranchers might attain a fixity of type.

Although none of these developments altered the Fromms' opinion, they did realize that it was to be a long battle. Their herd was still so small as hardly to deserve the term, and their foxes were far from as bright as they intended to make them. It would take years to achieve the color they desired, and more years to convince the public that the brighter, more silvered, foxes were beautiful. But it had taken years to grow ginseng in order to get a start in foxes; they were accustomed to a long-time gamble.

Since they had formed the habit of keeping their own counsel, they did not write to fox men in the east or argue the merits of accepted beliefs in breeding. With the whole fox industry arrayed against them, they were on the defensive — but a belligerent defensive — and the boys who had carried ginseng in covered baskets, strung a homemade burglar alarm around their first ginseng beds, lived in a lookout tent through a winter, built the militant Fort Moreland, and who still slept where they might watch both ginseng and foxes, now began an equally secretive existence as fox farmers. They were unapproachable to other fur ranchers, did not show their foxes, did not discuss breeding procedure.

They were not at all sure that their highly selective breeding for brighter foxes would be successful. It was the universal belief that mating lighter foxes must inevitably sacrifice the greatest attraction of the pelt — the sharp contrast between clear black and metallic silver. The Company was pursuing a dangerous course when it assumed this was not true, and the experiment demanded a good eye for clear color, sharp contrast, and the first warning tinge of rust. This required, even more than keen observation, an almost instinctive reaction to scarcely discernible gradations.

Fortunately for the Company, John had this gift; it must have been an aesthetic heritage, a feel for color, and it might perhaps have been fostered by days and weeks spent in watching the changing hues of the forest. Some artists claim that an extreme sensitivity for color is developed in the out-of-doors, where tints, shades, and tones change from one moment to another. Perhaps this was true of John Fromm. More and more he became the partner who made the selections in the matings, who knew how far the Company might safely carry its search for silver. Whatever the explanation of his peculiar ability, it has been of enormous value to the Fromms.

Until this day the clear brightness of Fromm pelts has been in great measure due to John's unerring recognition of color gradations.

Gradually, and without discussion, the members of the Company had slipped into their special jobs. They teamed on every project, but each did one thing better than the others. Walter had taken charge of ginseng. Edward handled business matters, was idea-man and coordinator of all their efforts. Henry had a way with foxes that made for healthy animals which would produce large litters. And John fitted in with Henry in breeding a special type of silver. The Company's welfare was the tyrant that drove them all.

To Henry, the keeper, raising foxes had always seemed natural and easy. In the summer of 1917 the Company had sixty-five silver foxes and, counting the reds and crosses, 150 in the herd. They had never lost an animal through sickness. This was an amazing record when other ranchers reported seasons of whelping deaths, seasons of abortions, high mortality in litters, losses from gastric diseases, and whole ranches cleaned out by distemper. None of these things had happened at the Fromms'. So it was the more incredible when their foxes suddenly began to have what Henry could only describe as "fits," because the seizures resembled those he had observed in dogs and cats. He could find no explanation. Food had not been changed nor care lessened, nor was there any apparent reason for hysteria or nervousness in the herd.

Henry was appalled the morning he found three dead foxes, two silvers and a red. Since summer pelts were valueless he buried them, and as he dug the hole he hoped there would be no more; the herd could not stand such losses. Next morning four more foxes were stretched lifeless in their yards, and Henry knew this was an epidemic. He was sure it was not distemper, but his inability to guess the identity of the killer only made it the more terrifying. As he cut the animals open he wished he knew how to perform a real autopsy. He was aghast at how little he knew of fox diseases. No special knowledge was necessary, however, to decide what had killed these foxes. The digestive tracts were lined with worms.

Parasites, the great foe of ranched foxes, had caught up with the Company and the infestation had gone unnoticed until the whole herd was infected. Henry called the others. Vermifuge capsules were needed at once, and a lot of them. They were quickly procured and, as the boys dosed their foxes, they hoped that the promising claims of the makers of the medicine were justified. But the remedy had come too late to halt disaster. Each day they found more dead foxes, and it began to look as though they were losing the fur farm. A thoroughly frightened Company, counting up appalling totals, now learned — the hard way — that fox farmers can never afford a sense of security. So long as they own foxes they are vulnerable.

Finally the parasites were defeated. But by the time the seizures stopped and survivors began again to look healthy, the Company had lost half its foxes. This was a fearful setback, but even so the Company had fared better than it had believed possible. Never again would any member of the firm think fox farming was so easy. The fright of what might have happened lasted through the years.

Chapter Eleven

Later they spoke of that summer as "the bad year." They had lost thirty foxes but they had not yet discovered how extensive disasters could be, nor had they felt the full prod of a fast-growing business.

The real strain on the Company began the next year, 1918. The spring's increase in silver foxes was larger than in any previous breeding season. Pups of one year are parents in the next, and early efforts to establish a strain of prolific animals began to show results. More foxes required more pens, and this gave the Company an opportunity to try new ideas. It abandoned the woods, originally believed necessary for a natural environment but where construction costs were heavy, and tried blocks of pens in the open. These had alleyways wide enough for a food cart, and Henry no longer had to carry meals from the outer fence.

The new houses differed from early models, for now the Company dared to disagree with the government bulletin. The first departure was in the outside spouts or tunnels. These were an important feature, for they gave foxes the sense of a burrow, but weather was hard on exposed woodwork.

"The foxes don't care whether those tunnels are outside or in," Henry said. "All they want is a chance to make sure it's safe to go out."

"Why don't we put the passageways inside, then?" John said. "The door would be like an opening to a burrow. I bet the foxes will like it better."

"And if we put two nesting barrels in each house, maybe the mothers will stop dragging pups outdoors," Henry said. "Remember how, when we were hunting wild litters, a mother would carry her young from one hollow log to another?"

It was a new idea for nervous mothers. The barrels were identical, but a distraught female could move her family. Fox mothers' unalterable determination to move litters had for years baffled and enraged fox men. Ranchers referred to these stubborn females as "draggers," and had tried all sorts of deterrents. Some ranchers imprisoned mothers with their litters and thus added frustration to hysteria. Others tried distraction. One kept a flock of chickens and threw one into the yard to engage the attention of a mother absorbed in finding a safe place for her young. Now the Company gave its mothers a choice of nests, and freedom to carry out their whims in two homes wholly their own.

Meanwhile the controversy about dark and silvered foxes became thoroughly defined. Fifteen well-known fox men organized the American Fox Breeders' Association. Charter members were from the East, although ranchers in the Middle- and Northwest, unable to attend because of the breeding season, wrote of their enthusiasm and support of measures to encourage the raising of choice breeds, to improve methods, to disseminate and exchange information, to maintain a registry of thorough-bred animals bred in captivity, and to promote and enhance the ranched silver fox.

Requirements for registration were a pedigree of four generations of black silver ancestors, and a rating of at least eighty-five points out of a possible hundred. Color of coat counted heavily in point total and gave dark-silvers a great advantage. Silver foxes were classified by color as black, extra-dark, dark silver, pale silver, and extra-pale silver. Each class was described. The black must be black all over except for a white-tipped tail. The extra-dark must be black except for a small area of silver on the hips. The dark might have a larger silver area on the hips, which could continue to the lumbar region. The silver must be black on the anterior and middle body, shadowing to silver on the posterior, and the forehead might show silver. The pale silver must be black on the top of the neck and sides of shoulders, but the remainder of the body might have a slight sprinkle of silver. The extra-pale silver might have silver all over the body, except that the neck must be black. Point value was graduated down from black to the extra-pale silver, and in this and in size, Fromm foxes would make a poor showing indeed.

New terms crept into common usage among ranchers — "the eighty-five point fox," "proved breeders," "a system of selection and matings," "the elimination of inferiors and culls," "the quality fox." With foxes of approved quality as a weapon, the Association was fighting a necessary battle against a very real prejudice; the previous fall a prominent New York fur house had bought space in a daily paper to tell the public the difference between wild and ranched foxes, and there had been a poetic note in the advertisement: "One is a highly prized animal, upon whose trail an Alaskan or Siberian trapper has spent many weeks. The other is a 'domesticated wild animal,' fur raised on a farm in Canada. There is as great a difference between them as between the genuine and the synthetic ruby or diamond." Fur ranchers, aroused by this threat, had united for defense, and quickly there grew up the belligerent belief that any breeder who failed to make his goal the production of the "quality fox" up to accepted standards was doing a disservice to all fox ranchers.

The Fromm boys did not join the Association nor apply for registration of their herd. Rather, the standard "quality fox" and the point system stiffened their obstinate attitude. They knew that other fox men, even neighboring fox ranchers, said Fromm foxes were no good, and they made no effort to conceal their resentment of chance visitors. But on one point they enjoyed a quiet triumph. Their record of large litters had become known, and a few ranchers who wanted the infusion of so prolific a strain came to buy foxes. The bargaining never had the friendly give-and-take of the usual rural transaction, and although the Company was in desperate need of capital, few fox men were allowed to visit the pens and none were told breeding secrets. Often the member of the Company who conducted the sale carried a gun so casually as to appear that he was never without one, and usually the purchaser was glad to take his foxes and depart. The Company had the satisfaction of knowing that no matter what other ranchers said about Fromm foxes, they were willing to pay more than a thousand dollars to own a pair.

Need characterized the entire summer. The partners needed loam for the larger gardens. Urgency drove them to risk using green mulch from plowed-under peas and rye in the transplanted beds, but they dared not trust seeds to anything except a natural habitat for fear the tender young shoots could not push through; seed plantings were the very lifeline of ginseng culture.

They needed capital. The brothers had received some help when Herbert also abandoned teaching and came home to join them, but now they needed real capital to purchase supplies for an expanding business.

Even more desperate was the need of land. They were fast reaching the end of the cleared fields in Alwina's quarter section. Other growers had experimented with various methods to restore ginseng soil, but not even an elaborate steaming process had killed spores of blight left from the previous harvest. Nevertheless the Company decided to try rested land, and made a transplanted garden in a plot that had been idle for several seasons and might be safe. For a time the boys thought they'd hit on the solution. The plants came up in spring and looked healthy through the early summer, but one morning Edward, who as night guard was using the arbor for a bed, looked down to see red leaves. This meant rotting roots. Later, red splashes appearing all through the green told them the garden would be gone before another season. A whole year's transplantings had been lost, to prove that using land for ginseng a second time was futile.

The most vital need of all was a drying house. In previous years the root crop had crowded the attic. The root's extreme vulnerability to mildew in the final process of drying added a last-minute hazard to ginseng culture. By experimentation the boys had found the safety point in loading racks; the top racks in a tier of ten could carry a larger load than the lower because hot dry air rose; top racks would dry 150 pounds, middle racks 100, and the three lowest no more than 75. But this capacity was already reached and there must be bigger quarters for the fall's larger harvest. A crop that had taken years to grow could not be endangered in the final two weeks.

A drying house with a central heating plant would be costly. Yet the expenditure was necessary, and immediately; this crop of root would buy so many essential things they could not afford to risk its loss. And then Frederick Fromm surprised his sons with a magnificent apology to ginseng. The threat to a harvest had aroused his farming instincts, and he offered an extended loan of fifteen hundred dollars.

The Company began the new two-storied building the next day. The loft would be used for drying ginseng, the first floor for store equipment and stock feed, and the basement, with the heating unit, had room for fox food grinders. No longer would Henry have to thaw out frozen horse meat in the kitchen, and the peace of a household would not be shattered daily by the noise of the bone machine. The heating unit was a hot-air furnace, and an elaborate system of pipes to carry off moisture was designed by a local plumber for the special needs of ginseng drying. It was installed, and the Company began to dig the ginseng harvest with a considerable sense of satisfaction. Drying troubles were now behind them. The crop outran expectations, and at the current high price of eight dollars a pound this was wonderful. But misgivings began to nag as digging teams heaped roots beside the beds and washing crews worked extra hours to keep abreast. Even three-quarters of the crop would push the capacity of the drying house into the danger zone of mildew. The Company was being threatened by success!

Tiers of racks filled the loft and overflowed to the first floor, and still wagons full of washed root drove to the door. All the rules of safety were abandoned; the roots had to be dried. The boys needed the harvest money desperately, but as they heaped the piles of green root they knew they invited trouble. Mildew, final and greatest threat of all, could bring disaster in from thirty-six to forty-eight hours. Only vigilance and the elaborate system of pipes to carry away the moisture could save them now.

After a day they knew the pipes wouldn't save them. Moisture was everywhere. Roots, racks, and even the walls of the drying house were dripping, so now they depended on vigilance alone. They watched the root, brooded over it, turned it, changed racks from bottom to top, did everything they could to give each part of the harvest its chance at warmth and air. John worked hardest of all. He could not give up and each night, long after the others had gone to snatch some sleep, he remained in the drying house moving roots from one rack to another, changing racks from floor to ceiling, trying to find some way to arrest the swift spread of rot.

Before the first five crucial days were over the Company knew it had lost the battle. The boys learned the habits of mildew in a way they could never forget, learned to recognize the cold and clammy feeling of roots in which mildew was about to start, learned mildew's distinctive smell. Its dank odor struck them as they entered the door; it polluted the air, clung to their clothes and skin, and always it was a dreadful reminder of defeat.

They knew they had lost a large part of the harvest, but they did not realize the full extent of the disaster until in sorting they found that half the roots had black spots of rot. Their first major improvement, a drying house equipped with furnace and an elaborate system of ventilating pipes, had cost the Company ten thousand dollars.

And this was to have been their big year!

Chapter Twelve

Edward took nine pelts, good skins ranging from quarter- to half-silver, to the 1919 winter auction in St. Louis. The Company felt it was time the fur trade became aware of the Fromm strain of foxes. Edward was proud of them in the wareroom of Funsten Brothers, where buyers from all over the country gathered to examine offerings, to choose those they intended to bid on, and to decide the limits of their bids.

St. Louis had become the largest fur selling market of the world. It had occupied a unique position in the early days because of its geographical position at the juncture of the Missouri and Mississippi Rivers, where early trappers and buyers had brought their furs by flatboats and barges. Now it had become the big auction center. Its first winter sale in 1916 had totaled less than a million dollars, and three years later the winter sale yielded almost eight million. New York was close behind with a winter sale of six million dollars. Fur was becoming an important industry in America.

Offerings in ranched silver fox commanded general

interest this year, and the number of pelts was larger than in any previous one. The sale opened with the finest pelts, sold singly. Bids were silent as in all fur auctions, which had established their own particular pattern. Since a bid was always for a stipulated amount, a raise could be indicated by the merest gesture, a lifted eyebrow, an almost imperceptible nod of the head, the slight movement of a pencil. The auctioneer knew the gestures, and was able to take quick advantage of competition. The silence was broken only by the auctioneer repeating the latest bids, or by the voices of his "callers," assistants who stood on either side to scan the outer fringes of the crowd and cry "up" when they caught a signal.

The room held a sense of deep excitement. Bidders cloaked eagerness behind blank faces and guarded gestures. Ranchers sat forward tensely when their pelts were offered; for them the profits of a whole year of fur farming would be decided in a few moments. Lucky ranchers who had produced a silver pelt for which the trade competed, were jubilant. Others who sold for only an average price were merely philosophical.

Edward had no reason to be jubilant or philosophical. As he recorded the prices on his fur sheets, he saw that all the first and finest silver pelts which sold well — one for almost eight hundred dollars, several for seven hundred — were skins from ranchers known for their dark silvers. Then the Fromm pelts were offered in pairs, and finally in a trio. The nine pelts totaled only $1,826, an average of $200. Again the fur trade had passed judgment on bright silver foxes.

Edward took the unhappy news home to the Company. The partners had expected it to be better, despite the opinion of the Fox Breeders' Association. It seemed incredible that the easily apparent beauty of the brighter silver fox was not as evident to the trade as it was to the Company, and some day, it was convinced, this beauty must be acknowledged. But its belief in silvered foxes had been costly. The four or five hundred dollars of difference between silvered and darker fox pelts was no loss to be written off lightly. Fur could not be counted on to underwrite the years of expansion. Ginseng must be made to do so.

In October when time came to dig ginseng root, the Company still was not sure it had solved the problem of safe drying. It had not been able to afford an enlargement of the drying house, and this year the ginseng crop would be larger than ever. The safest plan was to dry half the harvest and burn the rest, but no one even suggested this. Too many years had been spent in growing it. The only other possible method was to dry the root in two shifts. This meant an extension of digging time, which was risky. In early October the root was still green and in November a frost might ruin it, but they had to take the gamble; and when the root was ripe the digging and washing crews were started on half the garden. The drying house became a place of tension. The elaborate system of piping out moisture was ignored. Instead the Company installed electric fans, opened windows, and observed the rules of safety for rack loading. As the work progressed it was discovered that even partially dried root could be doubled up, as the long fibers dried most quickly and kept the roots from packing together. This enabled the workers to speed digging, and before the first threat of frost, the drying house was crammed with roots — clean, sweet roots without the slightest taint of mildew.

Unless the ginseng market betrayed them or the process of stripping and sorting developed griefs they had not yet encountered, the early months of 1920 would bring a real ginseng profit. The boys had a sense of triumph as they looked at the great heap of roots in the drying loft. Sixteen years had passed since they had brought those first 150 plants from the forest. It did not seem so long. They had been so busy.

The year had brought many changes in the Fromm family. In June Edward had married. He was twenty-nine and Alice Fredericks was twenty. This marriage was the first break in the almost monastic four who had been too much occupied for girls or romance. Edward had moments of misgiving when he questioned his right to ask Alice to share the confusion and hard work of a life in which farm and industry so overlapped, or even to face the uncertainties of his own future. But Alice had the easy courage of the very young, and had remembered the Fromm boys since a school festival years before when she had looked up to see four youths standing in the doorway. She had known instantly they must be brothers because their bright blue eyes had the same unusual intensity, and she had asked their names. At that time she was a youngster in pigtails and Edward seemed grown-up. Now it was wonderful that she could help him; his was a home that needed a woman. An invalid mother, meals for a crew of twenty, beds for workers, heavy cooking, piles of dishes, an apple orchard, a dairy herd, milk pails, pans, and separator to be cared for, a daily trip to the creamery, a flock of chickens, water brought from a well a half mile away — it was a case of everyone doing all he could and of long, long days of heroic work. The Company was gambling time, energy, and all its money against a future which still depended on changing the world's opinion of bright silver foxes. But it was a challenge, and Alice was eager to be in the adventure.

That summer Herbert left the home farm. He had not shared the early dreams of his younger brothers, and now his interests were in music and inventions rather than in fur farming. He wanted more time for them than was possible in a Company confronted with such major problems, and he took his share of ginseng and foxes and began his own venture down the road.

That winter Henry also married. He was twenty-six and Mary Jacobs — or Mamie as everyone called her because this name seemed to fit the warm radiance of an outgiving nature — was eighteen. She was aware of the big job she had undertaken. Like Alice she was a neighbor's daughter and knew farm life, but she had been associated with the enterprise and had watched it become something that was neither a simple farm nor yet an established industry. Also, she had a sense of humor to balance the fervor that drove Henry.

The small farmhouse now held three families. With ginseng crew and fox workers, housekeeping might well have appalled young wives, but Alice and Mamie backed the Company's efforts. It was a life, too, in which first things must come first, and company needs were automatic firsts; but if the girls ever thought their lives were harder than those of other farm wives, they remembered that the goals were higher.

The Company itself made the most revolutionary change of all. The four brothers, who from the beginning had carried on a business within a citadel and had avoided contacts with fellow growers, suddenly became part of another enterprise to grow ginseng and raise silver foxes. This was in some measure the outcome of a sister's marriage. Erna, the last Fromm daughter to leave home, married her cousin Edwin, from the Cedarburg branch of the Nieman family. The Fromms knew Edwin well and liked him, and since he shared their enthusiasm for silver foxes, the Company gave Erna several pairs for the beginning of a fur farm. Edwin's father, a banker and pea canner in Thiensville, near Milwaukee, gave his son money to buy more breeding stock, and the young couple began their own fur farm in Thiensville. Through this the elder Nieman, John F., became interested in silver foxes. Eventually a new firm was formed, Fromm Brothers-Nieman Company, and this was a partnership in a southern ranch at Thiensville. Double cousinship, Nieman holdings of land, Erna's marriage and common interests, led to its organization. The Fromms invested foxes and ginseng, of which they had plenty; but not money, of which they had none; and John F. Nieman bought his share of breeding stock from the Company. This made the strains of the two herds identical.

The Company at Hamburg continued wholly separate from the Thiensville venture and remained so through the ten years in which the enterprise existed. Nothing could have tempted the Fromms to share Hamburg or the original Company with anyone.

On the home ranch the care and feeding of two hundred pairs of foxes had outgrown home labor, and Henry Czech, a lad from the neighborhood, became a full-time employee. This was a real innovation in Fromm fur farm affairs. For eleven years Henry Fromm had fed the foxes. It had been a long, hard grind, and only one of his strength and endurance could have stood it. He had not only strong muscles but an indomitable will to drive them, and his weight-lifting exploits had become a legend in the township. It was time, however, for a full-time assistant. Czech liked the care of foxes and the two Henrys worked well together, but when Czech became an assistant keeper he had no idea that over the years he would prepare more meals for fur bearers than any other man in the world. Czech was not considering world's records. He was looking for a job he liked, and housekeeping for foxes happened to appeal to him.

Housekeeping meant more than meals. Foxes had a genius for digging, and their ability to move earth was astounding. They not only tunneled underground but excavated antechambers along the tunnel, and while depths of four or six feet satisfied the ordinary fox, more enterprising diggers achieved ten and even fifteen feet. These excavations held a menace. Foxes, even those not intent on escape, emerged to find themselves outside the yards. Animals were lost in cave-ins if the ground were loose. Often a whole day had to be spent in digging out a family and filling in the underground retreat. The rocks which the boys had carried to the woods so long before to earn a ginseng garden became invaluable as filler to discourage further digging. The Company exhausted its own pile and carried rocks from the land of neighbors.

The larger herd had brought the problem of identification of many pups. In the early days Henry and John knew each fox, its parents and grandparents. Now that this was no longer possible each pup must be marked when the young were taken from the mothers. Tattooing the ears with a serial number had become the usual method of fur farms. Tattooing, except for a short moment of terror, was painless, and could not be chewed nor shaken off as could a leg band. The right ear carried the year of birth and a mark to distinguish one pup from others of the litter; the left ear had the pen number, which held the key to the history of forebears. It was an ingenious system, but time was required to catch a pup, tattoo each ear with an electric needle, enter the record in a book, and rub vaseline on the tattooing. This, like so many other tasks, was the result of expansion.

Meals for two hundred pairs of foxes provided almost a full day's job. Food was mixed in large flat boxes with a hoe, much as workmen stir cement, then taken to the pens on a stoneboat drawn by oxen. Horses and wheeled vehicles were costly and required roads. The need for roads was already coming over the horizon — roads to the ginseng gardens, roads to the forest for leaf mulch, roads to the pens, and roads in the aisles between the rows of pens. But like land, machinery, equipment, buildings, and wire netting, roads must wait until products paid the way.

When pelting time came in November no one expected the ten-skin crop to bring much revenue. These pelts had even more silver than those of the previous year, but it would have been an admission of defeat not to prepare them for market. Nor would fur houses ever discover the real beauty of silvered foxes unless buyers had a chance to see them.

The Company's was a small voice from a Wisconsin wilderness, hardly a whisper. It owned two hundred pairs of foxes, while in the United States there were between twelve and fifteen thousand silver foxes on four hundred ranches representing an investment of eight million dollars. The position of the American Fox Breeders' Association had grown stronger. Publicizing the ranched "quality fox" of approved standards had raised the value of breeding pairs, and even the price of pelts. In the fall dark silver pelts had sold for fifteen hundred dollars, and ranchers expected these to bring two thousand in the midwinter sale. Now the Association was working for even higher standards than those of eighty-five point foxes. A second classification, advanced registration, had been opened for superior foxes, and these animals scored ninety-three, ninety-four and occasionally even ninety-six.

Points had become the accepted measurement of quality. Originally the point system had been introduced as an educational device in an effort to set a definite and scientific fur evaluation. Points were allotted to various features — general appearance, clearness of color, texture, length and gloss of the king or black guard hair, makeup of silver guard hair, undercoat, and brush. The texture of the fur must be fine and soft, the king hair impart sheen to the pelt, and the undercoat be dense and strong to hold guard hair away from the body. Also the brush must be of good size and the tip a clear white.

This new classification of superior foxes with advanced registration promised a great improvement in ranched fur. Progressive ranchers looked forward to the time when only high-scoring foxes would be produced. Unfortunately, however, the total score gave no indication of the history of the forebears, and a fox that scored in the high nineties might conceivably be the parent of a litter of scrub pups. Obviously the Association was ignoring the whole matter of selective breeding. Another serious defect in the scoring system was that it gave rise to a new profession. Ranchers engaged a professional scorer for a fee, and since such terms as "long," "thin," "dense," "glossy," or "dull" were somewhat undefined, decisions depended entirely on individual opinion. A professional scorer even with the highest motives might be variable in his judgments. Furthermore, since some ranchers were not willing to pay money to learn that no fox on their farms warranted advanced registry, scores were apt to be misleading.

Another unfortunate result of the scoring system was that in the rehabilitated fox farming industry breeding stock had again become the important product. This was inevitable with a fresh impetus behind fox farming, and fox ranches increasing rapidly. Scoring figures, which carried authority, were easy handles for the speculator or dishonest dealer, and the industry which had so recently entered a period of reform was again threatened by the very elements that had once before brought about its ruin. Fox ranching was becoming a game of numbers and the Association, quite unwittingly, was serving the unscrupulous by emphasizing the value of a score. Association members bought pages in fur periodicals to advertise scores and to assure prospective customers that only with such high-scoring foxes could a herd of quality be built. And since a ninety-five point fox was claimed by the Association to be an animal of distinction, men who had never seen a good fox, alive or dead, felt protected in their purchases.

Scores did, however, entrench the position of the dark and extra-dark fox. At the December 1919 Silver Fox Show in Boston, the first to be held in America, the black and extra-dark captured all the prizes. Points justified the fairness of the awards, for in competition with all other foxes these scored the highest. But the triumph of the dark fox worked one advantage for the Fromms. In the Middle West, fast becoming one of the important fox ranching centers, were many new ranches that needed breeding stock. They wanted dark silvers, the very foxes the Fromms wished to get rid of. The Company had now reached a point where herd replacements by younger foxes must be heavy in order to evolve a special type of silver fox. Each year's crop must be an advance, a step further, with offspring carrying the desired traits. In nine generations the color of a silver herd could be changed, but to do this older foxes, which had served their usefulness in establishing the fixity of the strain, must be weeded out to make way for younger pairs that would breed still larger, brighter, better foxes. The quality of a herd depends upon careful mating for the elimination of the inferior, and this procedure is the very heart of fox farming.

No one in the Company called these decisions genetics, and John and Henry would have been astonished to discover they were working along genetic lines. To them it was merely the job of breeders. Foxes must become larger, sturdier, more prolific. Coats must become brighter without sacrifice of texture or clearness of color. Quality must always be the first consideration, for it was future capital. With these ends in view they examined foxes, decided which ones still held value for the Company's aims, and which might better be sold to other ranchers.

In late January Edward took ten pelts to the auction in St. Louis, but he did not intend to sacrifice them as he had the skins of the previous year. He took the precaution of arranging a signal with the auctioneer should the final bid on any pelt be unsatisfactory, so that the Fromms could buy it back. This protection, called "buy-backs," is a common practice in fur auctions.

The silver fox sale was lively, despite the drop in price of other furs. This was the auction that did more to establish the value of ranched silver pelts than any so far held in America. Important fur houses competed for the dark silvers, and while a few of the Fromms' pelts were bid higher than in the previous year, they were still far below the prices of others. Each time the bidding drew to a close and Edward saw their pelts being topped by skins he knew to be inferior, he signaled his own bid. At the end of the sale the Company owed the 5 per cent cost of auctioning $3,510 worth of foxes, and still owned the ten silver pelts. When he returned with the news the Company applauded his decision. Thirty-five hundred dollars would have accomplished a great deal on the farm, but nevertheless it was far better invested in the battle for bright silvers. Perhaps next year the tide would begin to turn.

Other fox men read the news of the St. Louis auction and drew their conclusions. Dr. Samuel F. Wadsworth, a pioneer in the industry and one of the first fox men to call attention of other ranchers to the value of the Mendelian law, wrote in an issue of *Black Fox Magazine:*

"If all blacks [black silvers] were destroyed, and all blacks were never used in breeding, we would soon have nothing but pale silvers, and before long we would be getting rusty silvers. The problem is how to keep from getting too much silver and how to produce silver that has the correct blend with black.

"Undoubtedly as time goes on a strain of pure black foxes will be produced which will not become silvered even with age, and when the silver coloration has been eliminated we shall see a wonderful animal from a strain of black ancestors whose value as breeders will be difficult to estimate.

"For this reason I hope to see all fox breeders' associations recognizing the pure black fox as the firm foundation for fox breeding associations."

Dr. Wadsworth had given much thought to the genetics of fox breeding, and if anything could have discouraged the Fromms' dream of a herd of bright and shimmering silvers, that article should have done so. But even the threat of rusty silvers left them untouched.

And then the Company was suddenly confronted by a new and very different hazard and one, moreover, for which nothing had prepared them. The ginseng harvest brought a check for forty thousand dollars, and this was the most dangerous event in its career.

Chapter Thirteen

THIS CHECK CAME TO A GROUP VERY DIFFERENT FROM
the four boys who had planted those first ginseng seeds.
The close unit had been broken. Two brothers had married. Edward's first child had just been born. Henry was
to become a father. The Company had rivals, family ties,
and rights of individuals to a life of ease and relaxation
from the urgencies that had driven them.

"Forty thousand dollars after years of counting pennies!" Edward said when he told the news to Alice in the
hospital where for the second time he had seen his small
daughter. "It's frightening."

"What's frightening about forty thousand dollars?"
Alice asked.

He hesitated. He was elated, and yet strangely fearful.
"It's the first real chance the Company's had," he said.

Edward, at the center of a project spreading out in
all directions, was in a position to recognize how critical
was the position. That evening when the brothers talked
after supper he was still sobered by a sense of danger.
It was the first time they had all been together since the

check arrived. In the past they had often talked of what the Company could do with money, but would forty thousand dollars, theirs in the bank, bring a change of opinions when so many paths were open? But the other brothers, too, had been thinking.

"The Company's got to have more land," Walter said. "It's got a chance to get into real ginseng production. It ought to buy the Roehl farm."

The boys had always called this the "old homestead" because it was the original farm of their grandfather, Joachim Nieman and, more important, it adjoined Alwina's quarter section. It was cleared, had good land for ginseng, and was the logical first step in expansion.

The others nodded. To have the old homestead had been their secret wish. John asked how much the farm would cost.

"Whatever it costs, the Company ought to have it," Henry said. "But we've got to buy some breeding stock. The eastern strain could improve the texture of our herd. It's a crime that a Company with two hundred silvers hadn't added some standard blood before this. That's what John and I want to do with part of that money. This Company's got a chance to go somewhere with silver foxes."

"And we have to enlarge the house," Edward said. "We need quarters for a bigger crew and a place to feed them. We need a well, and that will cost a thousand dollars. But land and foxes must come first."

The remainder of the evening was spent with pencils and paper and long columns of figures. The Fromms were as poor as ever, still absorbed in devising ways to accomplish the impossible. In the following weeks it developed that the Roehl farm could be purchased for

$18,500. This was the highest price ever asked for land in their vicinity, and the entire countryside was amused that the Fromm boys had so lost their heads over one successful season as even to consider the purchase. The price did not amuse the Fromm boys. They were staggered, but still determined. The deed was signed a year later. Purchases of farms move slowly since a sale must dispossess both crops and family, but the Company was grateful for delay. This permitted digging the well, building pens, and enlarging the farmhouse on money from the Roehl farm fund. All this required management, and meanwhile the Company sold breeding stock and the boys continued to take a mere subsistence wage from the business.

With $18,500 allocated to the Roehl farm, $21,500 was left for the purchase of breeding stock. The boys intended to select the eastern foxes personally, and the buying trip must be postponed until after the fall ginseng rush, but this was an advantage. The purchasing committee could choose from foxes nine months old and in their winter fur.

Not a dollar was spent on ease and comfort. Even the idea had not occurred to one of them. The enterprise in its first comparative success had become even more rapacious of energy and toil than before. The Company and its needs still came first.

This era of even fiercer effort won a convert. Perhaps it was the enlarged dwelling house which Frederick Fromm had always planned to build, or the well, which ended forever the need of hauling water barrels on a go-devil, or possibly an older and more understanding recognition of the drive of youth, but Frederick ceased to frown on silver foxes. Pens and arbors would never have for him the beauty of tilled fields, of grain harvests, or of pastures dotted with cattle, but he finally admitted that ginseng, and even foxes, might some day bring success.

His capitulation did not go so far as an active role in the business, but he proved helpful. If he were at home and not too busy, the boys knew they would not have to take time to guard pens from the curiosity of visiting fox men. Their father had a gracious and quite effective method of shielding company secrets. He had always enjoyed guests, was famous as a wine maker, proud of his cask-filled cellar, and disappointed that his sons cared so little for his wine. But visitors were easily beguiled into an inspection of his stock and a comparative study of the merits of different vintages. Sometimes they departed with no very clear impression of whether they had or had not seen foxes.

The controversy between dark and silvered foxes had come nearer home, for in May the National Fox Breeders' Association had been organized in Muskegon, Michigan. It also had a herdbook, registration of foxes with three generations of silver ancestors, and an advanced registry for superior silver foxes. Its scoring system differed little from that of the American Breeders' Association. Extra-dark silvers were given nine to sixteen points, silvers six to three, and pale silvers three to one. Its first fox show would be held in Muskegon in December. The Fromms had not tried to register their foxes or to join the association. They never had had a joining instinct, and in the face of such general condemnation of silvered foxes the Company made a virtue of remaining aloof from all breeders' associations. Either the Company or the associations were mistaken about the desirable color of a silver fox, and the brothers were sure it was not the Company.

In November came a lull in ranch affairs and Walter, John, and Henry departed for Prince Edward Island. Walter carried fifteen thousand dollars in a money belt, and credit for seven thousand more. The trip was to obtain information as well as foxes, and the three stopped first at Muskegon to visit ranches of National Association breeders. Here for the first time they saw foxes housed on wire netting, an attempt to control the lungworm, which was becoming a menace. None of the boys liked the idea of wire flooring; they thought the animals were being raised more like rabbits than foxes, and had weak legs from lack of exercise. That this experiment was valuable pioneering work in the health of foxes did not occur in them. A defensive isolation in behalf of their crusade for silvered foxes had affected their opinion toward all group findings, and they would continue to learn the hazards of fox raising the hard way, by experience.

They next visited ranchers of the American Association on the eastern seaboard. Here they were entertained by Dr. Samuel F. Wadsworth, but no discussion of the relative merits of black and silvered foxes marred the luncheon. Dr. Wadsworth arranged for them to meet the secretary of the Association and to make a tour of the better-known fox ranches. The Fromms' admiration for the famous fox, Sheffield, a prize-winner and a fine black male, was sincere. His color might in their opinion be unfortunate, but the gloss, sheen, and softness of his fur were revelations. The boys bought six of his descendants, a daughter and five granddaughters. The following day at a nearby ranch they found six more females, not too dark in color, and of the texture they desired.

It was time now to depart on their real mission to Prince Edward Island. Already they had discovered travel to be expensive. They had restricted train journeys to daytime, that they might see the country. They stopped off each night at hotels near the railroad stations, watched the rates with an eagle eye, and ate suppers of fruit and cookies in their room. They could contemplate the purchase of a silver fox for a thousand dollars but still be disturbed, and often incensed, by the high cost of a night's lodging. Personal comfort had no rights over foxes.

They expected to find finer foxes on the famous ranches of Prince Edward Island; perhaps they might even regret not having saved all their funds for the purchase of Canadian stock. But at ranch after ranch they decided against purchases because the foxes were not only dark but small. John and Henry thought the animals were sickly, had no spirit, and showed far too little silver. They had not realized that English markets preferred even darker silvers than did the American fur houses, and had they needed to be further convinced that they could never admire the small dark silver, the visit to Prince Edward Island would have done it. At the end of two weeks' searching they selected their stock. All were light, ranging from one-half to two-thirds silver, and all were large. They had traveled across the country to buy foxes very much like their own. But they had what they went for, stock from a well-established and long line of domesticated breeders, foxes that for years had been bred for softness of texture and gloss of coat.

On Prince Edward Island, still the most important center of the silver fox industry, ranches carried the names of pioneers, and illustrious foxes were still alive. The boys saw Sir Wilfrid, whom some fox men consider the finest fox ever bred, and Walter took his picture.

Henry took their foxes home and John and Walter went to Boston for the fox show. They were delighted to find that Sheffield had again captured the first prize, and they noticed that females from the Sheffield ranch were larger than the others. This promised well for the six females they had bought.

Neither John nor Walter wanted to leave Boston without going to Walden. Thoreau had been a hero to them in school days, and they were delighted and astonished to find that seventy years had left the neighborhood so unchanged. They sat at the edge of the pond, each carried a stone to the heap at the site of Thoreau's cabin, and they visited the graves of Thoreau, Emerson, and Hawthorne. It was very much the sort of literary pilgrimage many American youths have made but they did it more intensively, spending five days in a detailed exploration of the literary shrines. Then they visited Sleepy Hollow cemetery as well as John Burroughs' home on the Hudson and saw "Slabside," his summer retreat. They arrived in New York City at midnight and left before dawn. The Atlantic seaboard held no further interest for them.

At Christmas Edward and Alice spent a belated honeymoon with his brother Arthur in Florida. Arthur, too, had abandoned teaching, and although his rebellion against the white-collar life had not been as stormy as that of his brothers, it was fully as definite. Moreover he had carried the academic career far enough to establish complete proof that it held no appeal for him. After graduation from the University of Wisconsin he taught high school botany for five years, when he decided to use his training in practical horticulture. His escape had not been through ginseng and silver foxes, but through fruit trees on his father's farm in Iowa. Frederick approved of orchards, though not when they meant what he considered the waste of a university degree. But Arthur's wife, Della Plumb, whom he had met when they taught in the same high school, approved of her husband's decision to change his profession, and the two moved to Florida where he could study growing things the year round. For some years Arthur had been the manager of a citrus orchard.

Now by that strange fate which sooner or later involved all Fromms in ginseng and silver foxes, he agreed to become superintendent for his brothers in the new Thiensville unit. The mysteries of ginseng might be even more fascinating than those of oranges.

A short time later Arthur took his wife Della and their young son John to Thiensville, but they did not give up Florida completely. They kept their home there and spent their winters in the south. Unlike the others, Arthur had not been captured by that early dream and could elude its full compulsion now, but the problems of this unusual kind of farming fascinated him. Naturally a student, he examined each job to determine if there were a better method, and although he did not like foxes as he liked ginseng, he evolved a new type of fox house which later was used by practically every rancher in the country and is still known as the Fromm fox house.

The model, worked out after months of study, achieved an economy in material and labor, provided greater safety and comfort for tenants, and eased the life of keepers. A shed roof, hinged so that it could be easily opened for inspection and cleaning, was substituted for the traditional cumbersome peaked affair. But the revolutionary feature of Arthur's model was provision for two entirely separate homes for each fox family. The old type, with two nesting barrels inside one building and floor space for foxes to loll when they should have been outdoors, entailed a serious cleaning problem. In each of Arthur's houses there was room for only nesting barrel and tunnel. The tunnel, leading from the door to the entrance hole in one end of the barrel, had an elbow to shut off light in the nest. The barrel, set on its side in insulating hay, had an opening in the top, the section sawed out serving as a cover, and firmly fastened to prevent foxes from escaping into the hay. This opening permitted keepers to make inspections, keep abreast of fox family affairs, and give the nest a thorough cleaning. The twin houses were connected by a platform which allowed tenants a comfortable nap in the sun and also served as a lookout post, for foxes take a lively interest in neighborhood affairs. Dual houses, each with an identical tunnel and nesting barrel, gave nervous mothers a choice of homes. Litters could be moved, and often were, but no fox matron would be so addlepated as to bury pups in snow and mud if there were a comfortable and vacant home close by. Minor improvements have since been made in these houses; each time a fox discovers a new way to injure itself or its valuable coat, someone has to think up an answer.

Fox farming is a continual struggle between keepers

seeking to make life safe for foxes and fur, and foxes finding fresh ways to make it otherwise for themselves or their companions. Because foxes are wild animals and can never be domesticated as are horses, cows, or other varieties of farm stock, fox farmers must be continually on the alert. Methods that seem sound may at any moment create a hazard. This happened after the first breeding season in the Thiensville unit. In Hamburg a single wall of netting separating adjacent pens had been successful and was an economy in fencing. New pens at Thiensville were built the same way, but the foxes shipped there either developed new personalities in transit or were affected by climatic changes. Of the ninety-two pups born in the spring, sixteen were killed and a large proportion maimed by mothers trying to kidnap a neighbor's young, or mistaking strange pups for their own. A mother would seize a pup on the other side of the netting and try to drag it through. A fox nursery was filled with casualties — pups with broken legs, tails and feet missing, ears and even noses bitten off. The fencing economy was one of the most expensive the company had ever tried.

At Hamburg, too, fox nature was causing trouble. With an increased herd of eight hundred pairs, neglected details were costly. Coat damage was important. Pens had been made safe for fur with lumber planed carefully to avoid rough edges. Tunnels were smooth passages and doorways were sandpapered so that they could not collect valuable hairs from tenants. But foxes still persisted in digging holes, which wore off fur, and in engaging in fights, which tore pelts. Penned foxes became bored, and developed nervous habits. Persistent scratching of an ear, face, or neck made bare spots, and this damage could not be repaired. By August a fox has made its winter coat; in fall and early winter guard hairs grow longer and more lustrous and undercoats thicker, but nature does no patching. Now that the herd was large enough to yield a good crop of pelters, and since these pelters had no other purpose than to grow finer coats, a new way of life was needed for them.

Edward had an idea, and like so many of Edward's it was a good one. Ranched foxes need not be kept in pens when breeding duties are finished. In the wilds a fox took excellent care of the very fine coat he grew, and an open range providing an approximation of a natural existence would give a fox space, a degree of freedom to attend to fox affairs, and relief from the boredom of pen life. To fence in such an area would be costly, but the experiment held tremendous promise. It was also farsighted thinking, as a range would provide the most practical method for handling the enormous crops of fur the company intended to produce in future years. Pelters could be separated from the breeders, and the work of grading, selecting, and sorting could be finished before the ginseng rush. Two or three months of active life in the forest would not only eliminate damages due to pen life, but would add size and value to the pelt. By September a young fox is almost full-grown. From then until late November, when the fur is prime and fully developed, the fox adds weight, some size, and the vigor of maturity. A forest also provides shade for the sensitive color of silver foxes; too much exposure to sunlight will impart a brownish cast to fur.

The Company adopted the idea with enthusiasm. Reproduction of a natural environment had been its only guide in the beginning with both ginseng and silver foxes, and this was a return to early ways of thinking. Almost at once the partners began to discuss the forms of shelter.

"We can't afford to build a house for every fox!" Walter said. "And if we did, how could we make sure the foxes would let each other live in them? They'd be fighting all over the range."

"How about big sheds?" Edward suggested. "They wouldn't cost much, and foxes like to pile up in heaps."

"We could build them in different parts of the range," Walter said, "but what'll we do when all the foxes try to sleep in one shed?"

Henry laughed. "I never thought I'd hear a Fromm boy talk of building sheds for foxes in the woods," he said. "Ever hear of a wild fox that had a house or a shed?"

Edward and Walter looked at each other, shocked to realize how altered their viewpoint had become. Edward's inspired return to boyhood thinking had not quite carried through, and John did not spare him.

"Remember how we used to laugh at those old ginseng growers because they put peaked roofs on arbors?" he asked. "And that wasn't so long ago."

The first furring range embraced forty-five acres of forest and was finished for fall pelters. It was costly in material and labor. Fencing was heavy and high with an overhang, and was extended at an angle eighteen inches into the ground. The Company intended to outsmart the foxes, and then discovered it had overestimated the craftiness of the animal. In later ranges a three-foot carpet of netting laid on the ground proved a sufficient precaution against escape. For some reason known only to foxes, they dig but never tunnel near a range line.

Perhaps they are too busy doing other things; but when the first fox discovers that by starting his digging operations three feet inside the outer barrier he can tunnel to freedom, the lives of rangers will be considerably more harried.

Enclosure of the area was only half the job; the range itself had still to be made safe for fox fur. A furring range is really a compromise. It must combine the advantages of domestication and wild life and at the same time avoid the hazards of both. The wilderness, too, flaws fox coats — one of the arguments in favor of ranched fur. A safe range has to be almost parklike, can contain no berry bushes, hazel brush, logs in which foxes may establish burrows, or even brush piles. All these tear precious fur. Even slanting trees are a menace. A fox loves to climb, and can be injured in a high jump to the ground. All tempting trees have to be equipped with board barriers.

Communal feed pans also presented a problem. These have to be high enough to prevent a fox from soiling the food of others, and they have to be secure. Foxes delight in picking up any loose object and running off to hide it. Large feed pans were set on stakes and firmly fastened. And there were many of them, for range feeding could not be limited. A hungry fox starts trouble, and once a ranged fox has been killed and eaten, foxes are apt to be missing each morning thereafter. No amount of feeding has completely eliminated cannibalism, and it has been accepted as a small but constant drain. It can be kept in check, however, because meals of good ground horse meat require less effort, and foxes are smart enough to know this.

Catching corrals were needed, as it was obvious foxes

could not be chased over the entire range. Wire division fences were so constructed throughout the woods that they could be rolled up on the fence posts during the months of free range and hooked down on the posts when catching crews began work. The Company discovered that a furring range should be oblong, with diagonal driving fences cutting off the driven area and making the triangle smaller as foxes and crew moved toward the catching corral. This should be always in the thickest timber, since it is natural for foxes to run toward cover.

All the problems of a furring range could not be anticipated. Solutions growing out of complications were of great value later when hundred-acre ranges held thousands of foxes. Patrol trails — trees at intervals of seventy-five feet marked by letter and number — must be laid out so that a ranger could report trouble, or a hazard that might lead to trouble. Because foxes killed trees by digging at and exposing roots, more trees died in the furring range than in a forest. Dead trees supplied the farm with fuel, but brush disposal was a problem. If burned, the fire might kill other trees; if piled, no matter how carefully, foxes always managed to contrive a burrow which wore off fur. It could not even be thrown over the high fencing. The only method was to carry it off the range, and entrance gates were far away. Brush became a heavy item in range cost.

Everyone knew there must be an answer — probably a simple one — but no one found it until six years later. One evening Henry limbed a downed tree. It was late. Carrying brush to the entrance gate would take him until dark, and yet he couldn't leave it. He had an axe, and the logical way to destroy brush was by chopping.

This was only a few minutes' work. Then he scattered the pieces over the forest floor in such a manner that the most ambitious fox couldn't contrive a burrow. The forest would absorb the debris, and once again nature had been made to serve the company. Henry's method for brush disposal has been used ever since.

Chapter Fourteen

I N THE FALL OF 1921 THE FIRST FOX PELTERS WERE
turned into the furring range and the first bed of transplanted ginseng was made on the Roehl farm. Both fur
range and the ginseng garden were important symbols;
they were the beginning of the big expansion era.

The Fromms had now outdistanced other growers.
With new land permitting even greater acreage their
problems would be different from those of smaller gardens, and problems of magnitude. Experiences of other
ginseng farmers could not help them. The Company
must find its own ways to overcome the limitations that
had kept ginseng culture a small business.

Spraying must be done differently and Walter, after
considerable work, finally evolved a sprayer to meet
their own peculiar problem. It was horse-drawn, and a
hose unrolled from its reel as a man carried it down the
aisles of the 143-foot beds. Another man rolled it up as
the sprayer returned, treating the opposite bed on his
return trip. To make this convenient manipulation possible, some means had to be found of maintaining a

constant pressure despite the rolling and unrolling of the hose, and this required a flexible revolving union on the pressure pump. No such piece of hardware was on the market, but Walter improvised such a union from sprayer nozzle heads. He was proud of the invention. The gadget was proof that special tools and equipment could carry ginseng culture from a restricted to a large-scale business — how large depended on the Company's ingenuity.

The boys had conquered one big limitation, forest loam, by substituting pre-planted rye for forest vegetation, even in seedbeds. When they discoverd that rye was not ideal because it left disease spores in the soil, they changed to oats.

Walter believed he and Arthur had beaten another limitation, the necessity of a fall covering of dry leaves. Every year for eighteen years autumn had meant anxiety to the Company lest nature would not arrange her affairs for their welfare. The acid from dry forest leaves had been considered essential, since no wild plant ever had any other winter covering, but Arthur had analyzed both leaves and straw and was inclined to doubt it. He and Walter decided to try the innovation of straw to protect the plants from frost, and a year later he was able to report that instead of weeks of worry, with large crews combing the forest for the last odd leaf, a bale of straw would serve each bed. Like so many answers, it was ridiculously simple.

Thus four problems — land, loam, spraying, and finally, dry leaves — were solved. Walter was even confident that he had eliminated another trouble, weeds that sprang from seeds carried from the forest; but he had merely exchanged one source of trouble for another and a bigger one. Field weeds grew even more luxuriantly than those from the forest, and chickweed, which abounded in baled straw, grew most luxuriantly of all.

The silver fox pelters released on the first furring range did not hold the immediate and rich prospects of ginseng culture. Postwar depression had brought a slump in all fur prices, and the ten silver pelts bought back for $3,510 at the 1920 St. Louis auction were sold later for $1,900. The market forecast held no promise of improvement, but the Company still planned to send their few pelters to market. The trade must be kept aware of silvered foxes, especially now that Fromm pelts were becoming known in the East. In November, 1921, the *Black Fox Magazine* acknowledged existence of the Fromm fur farm: "Fromm stock is equal to any other strain in regard to length and density of hair, and hardier and more prolific. The original stock came from the wilds of Wisconsin, Peace River, Yukon territory, and the interior of Alaska. It has been recently crossed with standard. The Fromms are pioneers and have been at it ten or twelve years. Their animals are hard to beat for prolificness. And their stock is found on every fur farm in Wisconsin."

The belief that Wisconsin native stock was part of the original strain of the Fromm herd persists to this day, and the hardiness of Fromm foxes was attributed to this factor. Henry Fromm says this is absolutely untrue, that native stock was never mixed with their silvers, that their special type of extremely hardy and prolific foxes was achieved by persistent breeding for these very qualities. The original strain was from the large and sturdy Peace River foxes, and the eastern standard Prince Edward Island strain was introduced in 1920 to improve texture.

The *Black Fox Magazine* item was received by the Company with mixed emotions. It was gratifying to be mentioned at a time when the two periodicals for fur farmers, this and the *American Fox and Fur Farmer*, both published in the East, usually carried only news of Association members, of fox shows, of awards and points scored by foxes that conformed to accepted standards. But the Company did not miss the challenge in the comment. No reference had been made to color or to pedigree. The Company was sensitive on both matters. When it had tried to register breeding stock sold to other ranchers the request had been refused, not because the foxes lacked the requisite four known generations, but wholly on the grounds that the Fromms "did not have pedigreed foxes." Size and color had ruled them out of the true blue blood aristocracy.

Unqualified approval of the black and dark silver as the only quality fox was now general. Arguments in its behalf were vehement and backers found any amount of evidence. Small dark silvers commanded the highest prices, even winning over the black fox, once considered so rare and glamorous. A dark silver raised on the ranch of the Central New York Fur Company had topped the C. M. Lampson and Company's great winter sale in London; at an auction where 2,375 silver pelts from all over the world were gathered, this skin had brought $662. High scores in the advanced registration and awards of the Boston Fox Show also proved the dark silver's superiority. Even after the point ratings of the American Fox Breeders' Association had been changed because some ranchers had complained that lighter foxes did not have a fair chance in the competition, "the black fox won hands down," as Robert T. Moore, owner of the Borestone Mountain ranch, said in an article in the *Black Fox Magazine.* Mr. Moore had an enviable record as a breeder and a deep conviction on the desirability of dark foxes. A college graduate and a member of Phi Beta Kappa, he had returned from two years' postgraduate work in the University of Munich to be editor of the Ornithological Magazine for the Academy of Natural Sciences of Philadelphia. Becoming interested in silver foxes, he had raised a strain that was beautiful and famous. He had worked zealously to improve the quality of ranched foxes through the use of fine blooded stock.

But the Fromms continued to prefer silvered foxes, and the breeding season of '22 increased their herd to two thousand animals. The paper dreams of early fox ranching were beginning to come true, but rosy calculations of natural increase never take account of what that increase will entail. Where ten new pens had once been an extended venture, now the Company must build pens by the hundreds. Other needs had become insistent — more roads, adequate equipment for the preparation of fox meals, proper refrigeration, and an outer barrier of paddock fencing, which was considered a basic requirement on fur farms in the East. The Company still used the old log stable built by Frederick Fromm in early farm days. Its permanent crew was a mere skeleton of what the farm really required. It had taken on a few workers — and these men had to be able to do anything; ginseng, foxes, building, or general farmwork — and in rush seasons others from the neighborhood joined the organization.

Farm work became a vital part of the company's operations. With ginseng and foxes it was actually necessary to run a large farm, and fields released from ginseng could be turned over to other crops that would serve the enterprise: straw for mulching, milk for crew and foxes, vegetables and meat for the table, hay and oats and corn for stock. All these were merely ordinary operating necessities, and every year there must be permanent improvement. A bunkhouse for the men was built this summer as Emma Thiel's crew of girl weeders had filled the farmhouse. The carpenter, Bill Cole, finished the bunkhouse in time for the big fall crew, and extra rooms and the attic dormitory in the farmhouse could be turned over to the women. But these were only stopgaps. Major improvements such as outer fencing, refrigerator plant, and barn must wait on future ginseng harvests.

Toynette was sold this summer. Breeding stock was bringing good prices, and she was still an excellent fox. But Toynette was eight years old, her litters had become smaller, and she had outlived her usefulness in selective breeding as the Fromm herd became better than its forebears. If ever a fox was entitled to free horse meat for the remainder of her life, it was Toynette; she was a cornerstone of the herd, she had been tame in the years when foxes were even wilder than now, and she was always a dependable and wise mother. Henry hated to see her go, but he made the sale, and had no one to blame for the decision; it was a summer when money was tremendously important. As he put her in a crate he wondered if men who did such things could ever expect to prosper, but he did not weaken. They had denied themselves for so many years that sentiment now would have seemed a folly. He found some comfort in remembering that other ranchers had been forced to make similar decisions. On his trip to Prince Edward Island when he had paid homage to the great fox Sir Wilfrid, a keeper had said that Sir Wilfrid was to be pelted; he was twelve years old and had failed as a sire. The fox that had earned more than most men earn in a lifetime was destined to be a scarf.

In January of 1923 Edward took the Company's first real shipment of pelts to New York. Since the failure of the great St. Louis firm of Funsten Brothers, which had been caught in the depression with large holdings of furs, commitments to fur shippers, and a sudden slump in price, New York had become the acknowledged capital of the trade. Manufacturers, fur dyers, and fur dressers were concentrated in the city and now it had captured the auction field. Its warehouses were filled with raw fur shipped from every part of the world.

The midwinter sale promised excitement. Ninety per cent of the silver pelts were ranch raised, and while the prejudice of the trade had not entirely abated, it was evident at the pre-showing that the buyers liked silvers. At the auction Edward found the bidding the most spirited he had ever known. Prices were 20 per cent above those of the previous fall, but again Fromm foxes failed to win. They were topped by a heartbreaking margin and derisive buyers advised Edward "to take home those western wolves." After the sale the auctioneer, J. Gordon Noakes, a man of long experience in the fur trade, invited Edward to luncheon. Mr. Noakes liked Edward, liked what he knew of the brothers, and liked the quality of their foxes, even though he couldn't admire the color. He wanted to help. If the Fromm boys had not been so obstinate about silvered foxes they might have made a good profit in a market where ranched silvers were selling well.

"Why don't you go home and kill those damned foxes?" he said. "You ought to know by this time that the public will never have any truck with those all-over silvers. All you boys are doing is losing money. What's the sense in being stubborn?"

The advice was based on sound logic. Comparative auction prices are signposts for fur ranchers, and eastern fox men were culling animals that showed a tendency to too much silver.

But the Fromms went on breeding foxes still more silvered.

Fortunately the Chinese agreed with the Fromms on ginseng — even a Fromm did not attempt to change the preferences and tastes of an ancient people. Ginseng had permitted the purchase of the first silvers, and now it must support two thousand foxes and supply capital for improvements. For several years after the first $40,000 harvest, ginseng at from seven to ten dollars a pound brought from $45,000 to $115,000 annually. In '23 and '24 when the Company was digging four- and five-acre gardens, the production from each acre was higher than in any year in the entire history of the enterprise. Never before or since has it achieved such a record. Each acre produced two thousand pounds of first-grade root and there were in addition the by-products of prongs and fiber. All this money went into expansion.

As on any farm, the barn came first; the small log stable could no longer shelter horses, oxen, mules, milch cows, hay, and feed. The new barn that was built in 1923 was not a barn for that year or the next, but for the years ahead, and it was a big investment. It was also material evidence of the accomplishments of ginseng and silver foxes, and a final proof to Frederick Fromm. He had always planned to replace the old stable, and had guarded building timber from the covetous reach of the young ginseng growers. Now ginseng had built the barn.

But being a root of wild and wayward nature, ginseng complicated the summer with a major disaster. For no reason that could be discovered, the entire harvest of seed rotted. The method of stratifying was the same as always, and for years it had been successful. Changes in the procedure could be only fumbling in the dark, but the obvious way to avoid underground rotting was to place the stratifying boxes above ground. Air currents would supply ventilation, and they did, but too much. Air currents froze the granite sand and dried out seeds, and a second harvest was ruined. Hamburg borrowed seeds from Thiensville and the next year tried stratification of seeds in barrels placed in the basement of the drying house. This was so warm the seeds fermented. Seed loss was becoming serious, for if the Thiensville unit should suddenly lose its seed, ginseng culture would be ended.

The following year Walter tried barrel storage in a cooler room, and once again the seeds rotted. The situation was now acute. They had lost four heavy crops, but at least the last experiment had proved that the unsoundness of the barrel scheme lay in the receptacles themselves.

"I'm going back to stratifying boxes," Walter said.

"We lost two crops in boxes," Edward answered, "and the Company can't stand another year's loss."

"I know it can't," said Walter. He was the most worried of them all. "But when we first started to grow ginseng we used forest loam. I'm going to mix that with granite sand."

Arthur thought of other refinements. The loam must be the fine black variety found only in isolated pockets, and below the surface covering of the forest. It required weeks of searching and scraping — an inch here, three inches there—but at last they had enough. They screened it through fine mesh and combined it with granite sand, one part of loam to two of sand.

They didn't know whether it would work, but were counting on a duplication of the most ideal forest conditions. The screened bottom of the stratifying box would permit some ventilation and the mixture of sand and loam would give more. Three inches of the mixture separated each half-inch layer of seed.

"I'm trying still another scheme," Arthur said. "I'll put the boxes half way above the surface and we'll board the sides to allow some ventilation, but no heavy air currents."

"Do you think it will work?" Edward asked.

"It's *got* to work," Arthur said. "But I'm only guessing."

It was a desperate compromise of all previous methods and it worked. The seeds went through the winter in safety.

"We stumbled on the answer," Walter said.

"I wouldn't call that stumbling," Edward answered.

After four years of disastrous losses, the Company had finally saved a seed crop, but by that time ginseng had developed other troubles.

Chapter Fifteen

THE COMPANY HAD NOT EVEN BEGUN TO APPROACH THE
elaborate equipment of long-established and highly
capitalized fur farms in the East. Only gradually did it
build roads, enlarge crews, set up great blocks of fox
pens, add furring ranges, and begin to enclose the farm
itself. Finally it achieved a refrigerator plant and a feedroom which like the barn had to be built, not for present
needs, but for the years ahead.

In the early days meat for a few foxes could be kept
through the summer with natural ice; many fur farms
used this method. As the herd increased Henry Fromm
and his assistant, Czech, had slaughtered horses in winter, cut the meat off the bones, ground it and frozen it
quickly in outside subzero temperature, and placed it in
the storage space of the icehouse. The hollow square,
walled with ice, had been adequate. But stored meat for
a big herd of foxes made heavy demands on the ice-caked
enclosure, and meat spoiled. Each summer as Henry
crawled through the ice tunnel to get tubs of meat he
vowed that in another year this primitive arrangement

must be changed. A warehouse with a refrigerating plant was one of the things the Company could not get along without. But always another need had proved more imperative.

When at last a wing of what was to become a large warehouse was begun, Henry and Czech knew exactly what the refrigeration, slaughtering, and feedrooms required. An overhead track carried horse carcasses from the slaughtering room to the refrigerators and from there to the big grinder. Dollies and hooks made child's play of handling two-hundred-pound tubs of ground meat. A fox chef had only to look at the day's orders, as definite as those of a hospital diet kitchen. So many breeders demanded so many pounds of meat, cereal, water, and cod liver oil, and because fox fathers shared the family pens, they received the same hearty meals as nursing mothers. Pairs that had not produced did not fare so well and drew "blank meals," a term used for feeding a fox and not a nursing family. The food mixer, a double-sized bakery model, tilted to fill the food tubs, and cereal and water were piped to it from the floor above. Every corner of the feedroom could be hosed and even steam-cleaned. In a nearby room feeding pans were sterilized, and two sets of pans made cleaning a task that could be cared for at the crew's convenience. Fox meals, once a full day's work, could now be prepared and sent to foxes in a few hours.

The opening of this long-awaited addition to the fur farm demanded a celebration, and Henry knew what the ceremony should be. He telephoned the rendering plant to come for the tubs of horse meat, opened the door of the icehouse for the last time, then walked back to the new refrigerating room and turned the switch.

As the years passed fox meals were not always quite so simple. Fox dieticians had brainstorms, and carrots, raisins, apples, cabbages, eggs, oranges, and even bananas were tried. The carrot regime came first. The farm raised fields of carrots and bought every available carrot in the vicinity, only to discover that vegetables made the food spoil more quickly and did not improve the foxes' coats. Henry Czech still shudders when he recalls the banana era; "the food was certainly a mess when we tried that out," he said. Eggs delighted the foxes but did not transform fur. The orange experiment, when every fox received his vitamins from fresh citrus fruit, was abandoned because oranges, too, failed to register in either more or better fur.

The 1923 crop of pelters brought a check in the mid-winter sales for more than thirty-five thousand dollars. Once that sum would have seemed large. Now it did not begin to stretch over the pattern the Company had set, and that pattern was only beginning to take form. Things were doubling up. Where once there were a dozen foxes, then a few score, now there were many hundreds. The first tiny bed of 150 ginseng plants had grown to many acres. The problem of spreading many thousands of dollars over a business which needed so many more thousands than the partners could give it was not essentially different from that of the early days when they had juggled a few hundred. First things still came first. Edward gave more time and thought to efficient management, had to be quicker and keener because mistakes were more costly. Walter worked harder adapting ginseng culture to increased acreage. John and Henry spent even longer days in the fur pens dealing with the complexities that constantly arose in the care of bigger herds.

It was still all farming.

In America fox farming had become a robust industry, and represented an investment of about fifteen million dollars. It was still directed by two organizations until June, 1924, when they joined to become The American National Fox Breeders' Association, a union long urged by leaders in both bodies. The absurdity of two herd books and two separate registrations of purebred foxes had been evident; if fox ranchers could not agree on the quality fox they could scarcely expect to convince the fur trade. The time had come to bury old differences and to set out on a constructive program to advance the standing of the ranched silver fox.

The first annual meeting and silver fox show of the united associations was held in Minneapolis in December, 1924. Members turned their attention to speculation, which had again grown up in this second era of prosperity. With the minor boom that had followed the postwar depression, the silver fox had again become an easy answer for the discouraged. Fox farm advertising in fur periodicals held out dazzling hopes. "Do you want to lift that mortgage? Crestview foxes will do it for you," or "Bayfair foxes will pay your bills." Other advertisements, if less practical, were even more arousing. "Make Our Foxes Your Path of Fortune." "The Super-Fox Will Guide You on the Road to Wealth." Foxes with cups and ribbons and high scores were waiting, eager to take charge of the destitute.

The most important decision of the National Association meeting was to abandon the scoring system, an emergency measure in the early days of registration when pedigrees were necessarily vague. The real value of an animal could now be judged best by breeding histories. To continue a wholly fictitious valuation, which could be used for profit in promotion and speculation, was to defeat the purpose of the Association.

Other basic problems were considered. Need of herd improvement, production of fur as fur, and not as foxes with cups and ribbons, and the importance of medical research were emphasized. Dr. W. A. Young of the New York Central Fur Company of Booneville, New York, which had topped the London market in the sale of a dark silver pelt, spoke of the necessity of trained scientists in the study of fox disease. Distemper alone had cost ranchers untold thousands, and whole fur farms had been wiped out in epidemics. Market conditions were discussed. Robert W. Fraser, American representative of C. M. Lampson and Company of London, assured ranchers that their bugaboo, fear of a saturation point in silver fox pelts, was unfounded. The supply of good silver pelts had not begun to meet demand. Also in fur, as in the history of the automobile, a plentiful supply would undoubtedly open up fresh markets. Once few women had ever hoped to possess a silver fox. Now the number that might hope to do so had increased enormously, and the number of future wearers was incalculable.

That the National Association had chosen a city in the Middle West for its annual meeting and fox show indicated the spread of the fox farming industry, and in the same month the *American Fox and Fur Farmer*, previously published in the East, moved to Minnesota. As the new editor, Harry La Due, explained, this "places us in the geographical center of that area of North America best suited to fur ranching." Mr. La Due's interest in fur ranching had grown out of his passionate conviction of the need of conservation of the dwindling fur resources of the country, and the magazine began to reflect his vision of what fur farming might become. Mr. La Due was a crusader both for medical research in fox diseases and for a thorough understanding of genetics for herd improvement.

Preferences in silver foxes had undergone a change. The dark fox with only a faint scattering of silver guard hairs on the hips, was no longer the most popular. There was a definite swing toward more extensive silver, and pelts with 15 and even 35 per cent of a silver were finding a ready sale. This was a hopeful straw in the wind for the Fromms, but it was a very frail one. The Company and the fur trade were still a long way from seeing eye to eye, and the Company and the fox breeding association were even farther apart. Dealers and judges continued to insist that the silver fox must be small, or at most medium, in size, the silver must be confined to the posterior of the body and, most important of all, the silver must be veiled. Veiling was achieved through the pattern of the guard hair. Each individual hair must have a long black tip, the silver band in the middle must be fairly short, and from there to the body it must be slate color, which was the color of the undercoat. The Fromms were already breeding for a much wider bar of silver, and this characteristic was always accompanied by two others, lighter underfur and an over-all silvering. All three were a radical departure from accepted standards and, while the Company believed that it was working toward more beautiful and becoming pelts, it was alone in this opinion. Though the market price of silver fox was steadily strengthening and the fur was gaining in popularity, Fromm pelts were still topped by others at the auctions.

In the fall of 1924 the Company's furring range held not a few hundred pelters but 1,335. Herds at Hamburg had increased. Range life had improved them and the Company figured it would do even more for the southern Thiensville foxes, so the Thiensville foxes traveled north for their coats. Hamburg was in a different weather belt from Thiensville; two hundred miles north it was fifteen to twenty degrees colder, and had fewer light-hours, which was an even greater factor than cold in achieving density of fur. Traveling foxes required new equipment. The foxes were put in crates, one fox to a crate, and loaded on big trucks. Each trip brought four hundred foxes, and truck drivers prayed they might have no traffic accidents with their precious loads.

Range life added dollars to each pelt. Skins became deeper furred, undercoats more dense, holding the guard hairs well away from the body; the guard hairs, which were really the animal's winter overcoat, grew longer and more lustrous. The activity of the range — the foxes had acres to explore — helped to preserve color, for in a pen a fox may spend so much time sitting down that the silver on his rump turns yellow. But, most important, the northern range was enough colder to make the fur prime earlier; that last period of suspense when a crop is almost but not quite ready for the market was shortened by weeks. Fur crops have their own peculiar hazards, for while harvests of grain, fruit, or any other agricultural product may be ruined at the last moment by drought, hail, or searing winds, these are Acts of God and not inherent in the situation. Pelts, however, are in constant jeopardy, since they must be entrusted to the foxes until pelting time and foxes are subject to unpredictable calamities. Each day that goes well on a furring range is just one day nearer to a successful harvest, and brings that much more peace of mind to owners.

Larger herds had already made the Company aware that it was beginning to have real trouble in the increase of Sampson foxes. A few Sampsons had appeared in the Company's herd five years before, but had aroused no real misgivings. Every ranch had its Sampsons; they were skeletons in the closet, for the admission of their existence would affect the price of breeding stock. But now, where once there had been only the odd Sampson in an otherwise good litter, whole families of the horrors were being born. Naturally the Company culled them, but as the pelt of a Sampson brought only a few dollars the culling of these undesirables had begun to mount into a real loss, and this loss must now be added to the low but unavoidable mortality of the furring range. Accidents, fox battles, and even some cannibalism were inevitable.

Suddenly a wholly new disease broke out in the range. Mortalities were heavy. Each morning the rangers picked up more dead foxes. It was not distemper; this scourge of fur farms had never touched the Fromms, and its symptoms were so well known that they would have been recognized at once. This disease took an entirely different form. Foxes, apparently well and in good condition, were stricken suddenly and sometimes died in a few hours. Henry suspected the range food, although the penned foxes ate the same food and remained well. He watched the food from horse carcass to range pans; he went with the feeders, inspected pans and may even have eaten from them, but he could find no evidence to support the explanation of spoiled food.

Edward sent the carcasses of dead foxes to the laboratory of University of Wisconsin for autopsy. Laboratory reports only deepened the mystery. Technicians suspected poisoning and suggested that paint or some other highly poisonous substance had been left within reach of the foxes. The Company knew this was not the case and concluded that science could offer no help. Similar symptoms had been noticed in pen deaths both in their herds and herds of other ranchers, but since on any farm some illness is to be expected, these deaths had been ascribed to gastro-enteritis, a good blanket term for digestive disorders — a diagnosis which was also of no value. The loss in foxes was very bad, but not knowing the cause of the disaster was worse.

Toward the end of the furring season the deaths decreased, and at last pelting time came. The death rate had been 18.7, almost a fifth of the crop, a loss that could be precisely appraised in terms of income. The Hamburg and Thiensville farms sent more than $200,000 worth of pelts to market, and losing 250 foxes when foxes' pelts were bringing $200 was devastating. The Company wondered what defense it could have should the disease return another year. Expansion had added to its vulnerability.

Chapter Sixteen

T̲HE NEXT YEAR'S CROP OF 3700 PELTERS WAS MORE
than double that of 1924, and the foxes were moved to
the furring range in the middle of September. The Company now had four ranges of from thirty-five to fifty
acres each, separated by wire fencing, and the entire
area enclosed by a double fence. Roads led from one
range to another, and feeding stations were set along
the roads. Catching fences were installed, rangers' quarters built, and the entire wooded area made safe for fur
and foxes. It was a large and costly project and had used
a good share of the previous year's fur check. The bene-
ficial effects of range life, however, had been proved in
the winter auctions and warranted the gamble of holding
a large population of foxes in one area.

Yet the Company knew it was daring an epidemic.
For several weeks everything went so well that the partners had begun to relax. When trouble started, it started
fast. Illness was brief and foxes often died before rangers
knew the animals were sick. Sometimes a fox would be
seen staggering or running wildly and then falling in a

convulsion. Dead foxes were picked up each morning, and rangers patrolled continuously through the day to secure the bodies before they could be eaten by range-mates. It was like no other disease known to fox men. The infection did not spring from a single source, since it had broken out on all four ranges. The only difference was that in those ranges which held young foxes mortalities were higher.

As the epidemic spread and deaths mounted, it appeared as though the entire fur crop might be wiped out. It reached its peak, leveled off, and then subsided, except for isolated outbreaks. But a heavy toll of foxes worth two hundred dollars each mounted into big figures. At the end of the range season the loss was 15 per cent.

Pelting was in progress when Dr. Robert G. Green heard of the trouble and came to see the Fromms. Dr. Green was an associate professor of bacteriology in the University of Minnesota, and his entrance into the fox farming field was accidental. He had been intending to establish mouse colonies for a study of virus disease when the Fox Breeders' Association asked him to investigate fox distemper. This had wiped out many ranches, and the Association had raised a fund for research. Dr. Green's interest was aroused; mouse colonies were unnecessary when fox farms, ready-made laboratories, already existed. He had begun his work for the Association and had published reports in a series of articles in the *American Fox and Fur Farmer*. But the Fromm epidemic, with its unusual symptoms, indicated a wholly new infection.

The Fromms and Dr. Green needed each other. The possibilities in a laboratory of almost four thousand foxes fascinated the scientist, and the Company was desperate for original research into its own specific problem. But with range life over for the year, no really constructive work could be done at once. It was evident that the disease was epizootic; it broke out when foxes were thrown together on the range and spread rapidly. Undoubtedly the source of the infection lay in the pens, where it had not been serious because of large yards and wide alleyways. Naturally the first steps must be made in the laboratory, and a few dead foxes were sent to Dr. Green for autopsies.

The meeting of Dr. Green and the Company led to a definite program of medical research. Dr. Green, a university professor, had no wish to become medical adviser to a herd of foxes, but foxes presented a wonderful opportunity in his own field of immunology. The Company set aside seven thousand dollars as a fund to finance laboratory expense and experimental work with red foxes. Dr. Green and his students contributed their time and knowledge, and herds in Hamburg and Thiensville supplied a large and unique field for exploration. Hopes for the next year ran high.

The pelting of an enormous number of foxes was a new experience for the Company. Only five years earlier Edward had taken ten pelts to market, and in 1923 more than two hundred foxes had been pelted. The bodies had reached the warehouse a half hour after the animals were killed, and each man on the pelting crew could skin a fox in regulation trapper style. The 1924 harvest of fifteen hundred had demanded some team work, but the pelting crew had been able to handle each day's kill. But with 3,700 foxes in 1925 the time from the range to the pelting room was longer, piles grew larger, and trouble started. In three or four hours putrefaction can ruin the skins of foxes piled in heaps, because of body heat. Skins can turn green and valuable pelts suffer damage within an hour.

The harvesting technique had to be entirely changed to fit the new dimensions of the crop. Killing crews were instructed to lay each fox on canvas, never permitting one body to touch another. Trucks that brought these in were equipped with shelves. In the pelting room the foxes were hung around the walls on large wooden pegs, and a method was devised by which each man performed only one task in skinning, keeping the animals moving in a continual procession from peg to final pelt. The last station was the table where Walter took the records from the tattooed figures, showing ranch, pen, and number of the fox. Later, when the fur was sold, the price would be entered, and thus the history of the skin would be complete from forebears to market. Actually the bottlenecks in pelting were not ironed out all at once. Ten years of study went into a system that made it possible to pelt two thousand foxes in a single day, day after day, so that the huge harvests could be gathered while fur was prime.

Range methods, too, had to be altered. Larger herds must be driven to the kill, and the arrangement of division fences was important. The final scheme was to divide the range longitudinally and cut these two long strips into smaller sections. Driving started in the largest section, and when this was emptied it was shut off. As more division fences were lowered the territory for driving lessened, and in the final days the depleted herd was concentrated in the section leading to the corral.

This prevented missing stragglers. Each day's drive gathered only enough foxes for that day's pelting, and the first days of driving were light, allowing foxes to double back.

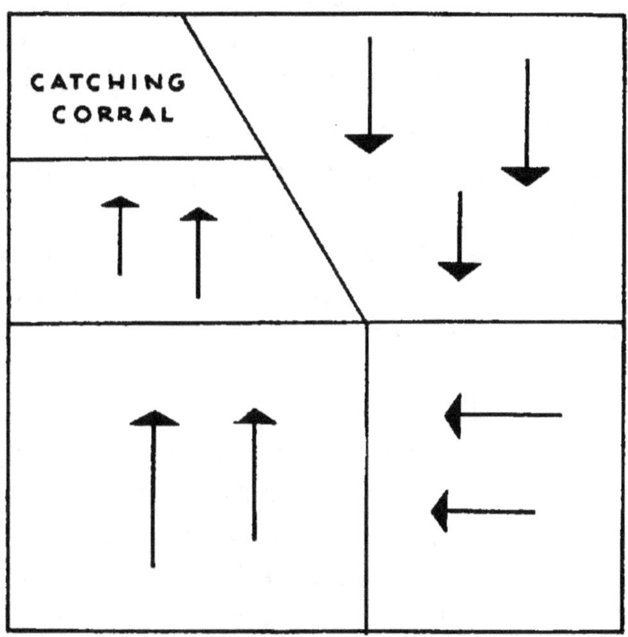

Catching methods were worked out only after several years. At first the driven foxes piled in heaps in the catching corral. Those at the bottom were suffocated and, while a dead fox represented no loss at pelting time, the heaping was hard on fur; the clawing and fighting injured pelts. Either each fox had to be pulled quickly from a heap or must be run down in the open by the crew. Though it is not difficult to catch a fox if a man knows how — with the tail grasped in one hand and the back of the neck in the other, the fox cannot bite — catching a range full of foxes individually took hours.

Edward was sure there must be a better way. The inspiration of the range had come to him through thinking in forest terms, but this approach appeared to hold no solution for the catching problem. Wild foxes are not caught. At this point Edward's subconscious apparently took over, for he awoke one night with the idea of burrows. In the wilds, foxes always run to burrows. A thirty-foot tunnel with a low entrance would appear to the fox as a protective burrow and would hold many animals. A number of these tunnels were built across the end of the catching corral, each one with several top-hatches that could be opened to extract hiding foxes. The scheme worked perfectly. Enough foxes for a day's pelting could be driven to cover in a half hour.

The actual killing was the work of a few moments. For many years the Company used a syringe injection of carbon tetrachloride in the nostrils. Later it changed to electrocution, which was swifter and more merciful. The charge from an automobile battery, stepped up by a transformer, made possible the use of electrodes on needles, and a puncture into the skin at the neck and another over the heart ended life almost instantly.

In January, 1926, fur receipts ran for the first time into six figures, $489,967. The Fromms had not convinced the fur trade that unveiled silver or lighter foxes were desirable, but the permissible line of silver had again moved up. Now the onetime favorite, a quarter or even less of silver, trailed. It began to seem possible that silver might some day be allowed to go unveiled.

Both foxes and ginseng justified the purchase of more land. The ginseng gardens were approaching their limits on the Roehl farm, and the Company bought the eighty-acre Krentz farm across the road. Bigger ginseng acreage, however, demanded greater precautions against root rot, which had begun to threaten the Fromms so seriously that they could not let it creep further. The vast acreage of virgin land in the county had been perfect for growing ginseng, but now that the soil had become contaminated, many growers were in trouble. The Fromms had tried various schemes to check the blight. Machines and equipment were not permitted to go into a fresh planting until every particle of soil which might carry disease spores had been washed away. Roots had been dipped in spray fluid before transplanting. Now the company decided that transplanting itself was one of the chief causes of blight. Not only did handling injure tender roots and allow rot to start, but moving two-year-old nursery stock from the seedbeds to the gardens was spreading the infection. The stratified seed must be planted in the permanent bed.

But it was impossible to broadcast seed in such large acreage. To sow one acre by dropping seed into a trench and covering it with soil required a week's work of ten men, and the entire planting must be done in a two-week period. There was no machinery for the purpose; the Fromms themselves, the only large-scale ginseng growers, had created a unique need. Surveying the planters devised for other crops, Edward decided something might be done with a hand-pushed garden planter. It was an idea. Walter and Herbert Kleinschmidt, ginseng straw boss, went to the blacksmith shop and set to work. They mounted the planters on drawbars, six in one row, seven in the other, and by offsetting achieved a single unit that would plant thirteen rows across a bed. The machine required six men to haul it and two attendants to feed the seed, but with it a crew of eight men could sow three acres in a day. It was the Company's new weapon against root rot, and it removed the limitation which, despite new land, would have kept them small.

As always, the summer of 1926 was spent in building. The boys who had first thought in terms of single dollars and then of hundreds were now dealing with many thousands, but their point of view had not altered, nor had the situation. With the business still suffering growing pains, available funds must first be spread over the most pressing needs. They built pens in numbers that would have staggered them in early years. They purchased timbered land for a fifth furring range and enclosed it. Then, having attended to the requirements of foxes, they built a boarding house for their workers. For years the Company had looked forward to the time when crews could be fed and housed in separate quarters. Now this final divorce between home and industry was regarded, at least by the housekeepers, as the greatest single achievement of ginseng or silver foxes.

In September 6,150 pelters were turned into the furring ranges, again almost double the crop of the previous year. The animals were in good condition. During the summer they had been vaccinated against paratyphoid to clear up secondary complications which Dr. Green's laboratory tests had revealed. There had been the usual pen deaths but not too many, and if any new and mysterious disease had been at work, it was so intermixed with other maladies that the picture was indistinct. Dr. Green felt that only in an epidemic, when the attack was violent and the symptoms recognizable, could data be gathered.

He had his opportunity soon after the foxes entered

the ranges. The disease struck and struck with fury, and again death occurred at the onset of the attack. It seemed impossible that what was apparently an apoplexy could be infectious, and yet no other conclusion was possible. The epidemic occurred only in range life where foxes were in intimate contact, and started about four weeks after they were herded together. There were, of course, many ways in which infection might be spread. Foxes ate from the same dishes at the feeding stations and stole food from one another. In a quarrel two foxes would stand face to face with forefeet braced, their mouths almost touching, threatening each other with deep-throated snarls. They were cannibalistic and ate the dead and dying.

Through the fall of 1926 Dr. Green and his assistants spent every week end at the furring range. They set up a laboratory in the warehouse, performed autopsies, studied carcasses both bacteriologically and pathologically, made slides of diseased tissues, collected blood and specimens of brain, spinal cord, and vital organs from infected foxes. After working almost through a Sunday night they would drive home with a carload of fox carcasses for tests with university laboratory equipment to supplement their field work. One batch of foxes had no sooner passed through the test tubes than the group was out for another week end on the farm. Through the range period Dr. Green and his assistants spent their time with the dead and dying, with stench and pus and diseased tissues. When pelting began they examined the carcasses of healthy animals, comparing findings with those from the victims of the disease.

Before the season ended they had made a detailed study of more than 125 carcasses and collected data concerning the 748 deaths that fall. The mortality rate was an improvement over the previous year. To the Company 12 per cent was still appalling.

But to the doctor the research was beginning to take shape. The onset of the disease was so sudden that an animal's forces could not rally to combat the infection. The outcome seemed to depend on the fox's own immunity; either it died quickly or got well. The rapid cycle of the disease carried through symptoms of hyperexcitability into convulsive seizures, spasmodic twitchings, and finally a lethargic state almost like sleepwalking. Since the epidemic set in with violence soon after the foxes were turned into the ranges, apparently the disease was endemic in the breeding pens. On the range it ran a course of about four weeks, during which the death toll was between 15 and 20 per cent, and then subsided to a lower rate, which suggested that some foxes had developed an immunity. Because the different ranges separated the animals by ages, the doctor was able to discover that young foxes were the most vulnerable.

When field work on the range was finished, Dr. Green continued to experiment with red foxes in the laboratory. He explored every possibility. It seemed incredible that an infection with such power to kill could be so elusive. Red foxes infected with the blood of the diseased range foxes went through the same cycle, from symptoms to death, but he did not know why it killed them. Sometimes he sat up all night to watch the infection at work. Once he recorded a fatal termination seventy-two hours after he had heard the faint scratching of the fox's toenails in the first spasmodic contraction. Finally, after months of following one false clue after another, he became convinced that the infection was a filterable virus that attacked the higher centers of the nervous system. At last he had found a pathway to follow.

The Fromms, however, could not be expected to share in this faint hope. For the third successive season they had suffered a heavy loss in foxes almost ready for the market. It began to appear that their only chance for survival lay in growing so big even disease could not touch them.

Already they were thinking, not of a herd of a few thousand foxes, but of one of forty thousand — even fifty. Fur trade favor had begun to swing in their direction. At the midwinter auctions of 1927, while the over-all silvers still failed to win approval, full half-silvers had topped the sale. Fromm pelts had not established record prices, but the entire crop had brought the gratifying check of $785,153. Such sums would carry the Company a long way in its fight for brighter foxes. At the auction Edward had seen the products of others. Ranchers who took awards at fox shows were important in the stud books and were still playing the speculative game of producing breeding stock. They had sent pelts to market which had no size and no uniform standard of excellence and were not thinking of fox farming in terms of fur. To the Company, however, it was the fur that counted, not one record pelt, but a crop in which each pelt was a skin of quality. To achieve this meant a longer gamble, but the winnings might be great. In another year the Fromms would return to the market with more pelts — bigger, brighter, better.

The robust check from the fur crop compensated somewhat for ginseng troubles. In spite of all precautions, root rot was increasing. The blight that had forced so many growers out of the industry was now a real threat to the Fromms. Of the many growers in the country who had once carried on a large and profitable business the Fromms were almost the only survivors, and they must continue to survive. Extensive land holdings, a big inventory in shade arbors, machinery, trained crews, equipment — the whole plant investment, representing years of work, could be liquidated now only at tremendous loss. But they did not intend to be defeated, and backed this determination by buying a third farm, eighty acres across the road. It was good land for ginseng, and a companion piece to the Krentz farm; it rounded out the Company holdings.

The family in the old homestead had increased. Edward and Alice had two daughters, Henry and Mamie had a son and a daughter, and in January Walter married Mabel Woller, a girl of the neighborhood. They had known each other for years and had met when, as a youngster, Mabel had weeded ginseng. They both loved flowers and growing things, and it promised to be a happy and companionable marriage. But young families, and three generations, overflowed the old farmhouse.

The Company needed homes as badly as it had once needed roads, fences, pens, arbors, barns, drying rooms for fur and ginseng, crews' quarters, and all the equipment of a fur farm. Henry and Mamie saw possibilities in an old log cabin in the center of the homestead furring range. Built of birch logs, it had been the Company's first office and later was used for maple sugar boiling parties. When these woods were converted into a furring range the foxes had spent their days trying to tear the cabin apart, but Henry, who enjoyed creating something out of nothing, chose it for his home.

"I always liked that old cabin," he said, "and we want to live in the woods."

Walter too desired trees around their home, but he and Mabel wished to have a great open space for a flower garden. He found a site in the furring range that provided both. Fromms like to live near their foxes.

John's wants were slight but unalterable; he insisted on privacy. A corner in the upper floor of the warehouse was ideal, because it could be barricaded against intrusion. Footsteps on the stairway could warn him in time to escape to the roof, and the telephone, which the Company insisted was a necessity, could be silenced by taking the receiver off the hook. John's energies were never wasted by the irritations of a telephone, for he made sure it could be used only for outgoing service. When he planned his upper-story citadel the Company feared he had forgotten how necessary the forest had always been to him. "There's miles of woods around me," he said, and the others knew that John's old habit of solitary wandering was not broken.

The Company built and furnished these three homes according to the requirements of the dwellers. That it should do so seemed no different from the procedure of the early days, when a boy had needed new shoes or Henry had had to go to the Battle Creek Sanitarium. A farm was expected to take care of its people, and the Company was still essentially a farm. Corporation status had not changed the boys' thinking, nor had it altered the old association of "The Wolves" when the four had given everything to a Company and its cash crops. Now the Company, become a creature of substance, repaid those first years with as little accounting as had gone into its building. Any earnings above its needs or those of its builders it retained, and because its welfare was always the primary concern there was no danger that its treasury would be raided.

This attitude has carried through the years. The Company has never paid a dividend. The four brothers have always drawn equal salaries and in a corporation of like size, these would be considered less than nominal. Its top staff members receive as much. A Fromm never says "I" and seldom "we." It is always "the Company," and the words still mean what they meant to the boys who used them first as a symbol of a structure in which four sharply-defined individuals could find a common denominator of achievement. Then hardships were not personal, and now possessions, too, are the Company's.

As the Company's cattle provided butter, cheese, milk, and cream, its forests supplied fuel and its gardens produced vegetables for all its people, now with homes needed, Bill Cole, construction boss, and his crew began to build them. There was no talk of estimates any more than a farmer counts eggs used for his table. To Henry, as inveterate a builder as any beaver, each year's improvements opened new vistas. A great glassed-in room would permit sunlight for growing shrubs in winter; an elaborate system of screens and shades would make it a cool retreat in summer. A fountain, fed from the near-by spring, would add the charm of tinkling water, and since a fountain was so easily achieved, an indoor swimming pool was possible for all the Fromm children to enjoy in the dog days of August. Before Henry ran out of building ideas the big house in the forest did not contain one stick of the original log cabin.

Walter's approach was more methodical. He knew

before the plans were drawn that his conservatory must be high enough to shelter full-grown orange and grapefruit trees. In the winter he had an exotic setting. In summer he could enjoy the forest, and the making of his garden proved to be as long a process as Henry's building. Year after year it continued to expand, down the slope, into the woods, across the road, and over the fields.

While all this building was in progress, range foxes participated in and added to the excitement of construction. Foxes pick up any object — hats, coats, handbags, cameras, lunchboxes, and tools — carry them away and usually manage to conceal their loot so well that it is never found again. For months foxes were seen carrying tools, and they seemed to prefer hammers. Workmen learned never to put down an implement or to hang coats on tree branches. Habits had to be adjusted to fox neighbors. Henry's children guarded playthings. Mamie and Mabel watched the laundry on the line. Cars were never parked outside or garage doors left open. Henry enjoyed all these proofs of fox sagacity and cunning until the day he laid down a hammer and a moment later saw a fox loping with it into the forest. Henry chased the fox for an hour. When the fox decided it had put a safe distance between itself and Henry it would drop the hammer and pause to rest, but always, just before Henry was within arm's length, it would pick up its loot and start off again. It was a grand game for the fox, and Henry never retrieved the hammer.

Foxes always managed to make life diverting for their owners. Occasionally they timed their deviltry. In the period when the price of silver fox was high and scarfs were most popular, foxes suddenly took to biting off the tips of tails. No one knew whether they bit off their own or the tips of others, but how it happened was not nearly as important as the fact that the habit spoiled the value of the pelt as a scarf. The Company decided to stop it by dipping the tails of all pups into a solution of pine oil. This could best be done when the tattooing crew removed the young from the mothers and put them in pens. Already the crew consisted of a half-dozen agile boys to catch the pups, a man to tattoo, another to read the record to the tattooer, and a third to rub vaseline on the tattooing and treat the ears to prevent ear-mites. Now they added a tail dipper, a specialist who wore rubber gloves and a rubber apron. This was the first job on the fur farm of Arthur's young son, Johnnie. He liked foxes almost as well as did his uncles.

In the fall of 1927 almost seven thousand foxes were on the range in the last days of September. In October the epidemic was well under way again. This was the fourth year of the attack, and its violence at the onset threatened an increase in the mortality rate. Deaths were occurring early and the pelts of the dead animals were far from prime. To make this even more discouraging, the price of silver fox was advancing, and each dead animal picked up by rangers represented a bigger loss in dollars. Dr. Green had not yet discovered the identity of the disease, nor had he been able to make a successful transmission with the virus to experimental red foxes. Until this was done, he was still working in the dark.

In the previous year, Dr. J. A. Allen, veterinary surgeon and pathologist in charge of the fox research station of the Canadian Department of Agriculture, had published a book on fox diseases and reported the same symptoms on other farms. Foxes ran blindly in circles, suffered seizures, and died soon after in convulsions. Practical ranchers guessed it to be some form of rabies. In an examination of carcasses, Dr. Allen failed to find any changes in vital organs, and the only evidence he discovered was a catarrhal inflammation of the ear in which mites and bacteria had been found. Dr. Allen had concluded: "At this stage it is difficult to say definitely just how these convulsive seizures are produced, but it is probable that the mites act as a constant and irritating stimulus to the nerves in the inner canal of the ear."

Dr. Green and his assistants again spent week ends on the furring range, and continued the work of the previous year. Male fox #998 was picked up on the first day of October. The carcass was still limp and warm and in good flesh, and the autopsy showed no evidence of other complications. A virus was made from the brain and spinal cord.

Ten days later in the university laboratory Dr. Green got his first clear-cut transmission with this virus. It contained a pathogenic agent capable of producing a fatal attack. He had isolated the infection. Almost two years had been spent in the search, but now the course was straight before him.

He named the disease fox encephalitis, and in the flush of what was only a hopeful beginning he planned the work. It might take years, but when he finally succeeded in immunizing foxes against encephalitis he would have made a real contribution. It was a thrilling thought. He was eager to go on, and confident that he could not fail now. He had not yet written the Fromms about what he had accomplished when he received a letter from Edward. The Company had held a meeting, and in posting up the losses it had decided to discontinue medical research. The results thus far of the expenditure of seven thousand dollars, did not seem to warrant continuation of the arrangement.

It was a critical time for fox research, for the Company, and for Dr. Green. The Company had to know how to battle the epidemic, and Dr. Green had to have a laboratory of thousands of foxes. The doctor's reply to Edward was the basis for understanding and for future faith. He reminded the Fromm brothers that the seven thousand dollar fund had been established, that only two thousand had been spent, and if his work were to stop, the Company, not he, was entitled to what remained. Then, without waiting for an answer, he departed for Hamburg and his usual week-end study of dead and dying foxes.

The Fromms said nothing more about discontinuing research, and when the seven thousand dollars was gone, thousands more were poured into the work. In the next ten years more than a million dollars was spent by the company on research in fox encephalitis and distemper.

Results of the 1927 study were immensely valuable to a scientist. As hundreds of dead foxes went through his laboratory Dr. Green followed his slender clue of one clear-cut transmission of infection. Thousands of slides were made. Scores of live red foxes died in the scientific mill. The man was as determined and unswerving as the Fromms themselves.

At the end of the season, the range loss was 17 per cent. As long as endemic encephalitis existed in the breeding pens the Company must expect this. A firm must grow big to absorb such drains. But if grief from epidemics and root rot was mounting, as was the need of gearing the assembly line to care for more foxes and ginseng, so was the income.

The January 1928 sale of the New York Auction Company was a triumph for the Fromms. The market news reported that the sale offered 8,841 silver fox pelts, and of this number 6,600 came from Fromm Brothers of Hamburg and Fromm Brothers-Nieman Company of Thiensville, and that "taken as a whole the collection of Fromm pelts was the best ever sent to New York markets. From the moment the sale opened it was apparent that records would be made."

It had been a long time since that first dream, but at last Edward sat at an auction that made fox history and watched company pelts bid to $500, $550, $565, $600, even $685. This brought as great a sense of triumph as the check. It read $1,021,000, the largest check ever written for the fur of a single shipper. The fur trade had approved bright silver.

Again foxes had to pay the way for ginseng. The last ginseng garden had not been worth the digging; at least 90 per cent of the roots had been destroyed by rot. The Company hesitated. Should it go on? Was the market for this exotic root as precarious as the growing of it? To learn at first hand whether ginseng had a real future as an article of trade, Edward went to China. He became convinced that the Chinese were a people of enduring customs, that ginseng was firmly imbedded in common usage, and he reported on his return that there would always be a market. The real threat to a ginseng future lay in blight. Known methods of dealing with it had proved useless, and now the Fromms believed that disease spores were carried by the seed itself, spores that must be killed without destroying the fertility of the seed. It would be a delicate operation, but unless the secret of how it might be done were discovered, gingseng culture was ended for the Fromms. Arthur, a trained horticulturist with a college degree in botany and science, was the only member of the family equipped for the experimental work. And even Arthur was not sure whether it could be done or how many years it would require, but he began.

When more than eight thousand foxes were turned into the furring range in the fall of 1928 there was some hope that an epidemic of encephalitis could be avoided. Dr. Green's work had gone far enough to make an attempt at immunization. Before the pelters left the pens, every fox was vaccinated with virus attenuated with sodium ricinoleate. Later, on the range, the disease appeared in the vaccinated foxes, but with a lowered mortality rate. Dr. Green posted the results as findings in the ineffectiveness of an attenuated virus, and these findings were conclusive, since they were based on an experiment with eight thousand foxes. The Company added up the season's loss of 785 foxes in dollars and found even 9 per cent disheartening. Keepers were suggesting that perhaps the epidemic wouldn't have been bad this year anyway, and that it might have been the hypodermic needle and not encephalitis which had killed the foxes. Also, John reported that more than the usual number of foxes had failed to fur out properly and had been culled as Sampsons.

No one, scientist, ranger, or member of the Company, could overlook the fact that the herd of pelters had suffered a dreadful last-moment loss, and in a year when Company foxes brought record prices. Nevertheless the January 1929 fur auction was again a triumph, even greater than the previous season. This year the New York Auction Company's check was for $1,331,679. Now Fromm foxes had a new name in the East; the fur trade, which had called them western wolves in 1923, referred to them as the "million-dollar foxes."

But Edward and the others knew that this sudden turn in favor was only a halfway victory. The fur trade had accepted a brighter pelt, shimmering silver unveiled by black, but the ultimate wearers were not even aware of its existence. Until the public knew how glorious the silver fox might be and demanded it, the Company's future product could not be sure of a market. In the years ahead the Company would raise thousands of foxes, and each fox must find a wearer. Nothing less than a national advertising campaign would accomplish this result.

Foxes without a public, ginseng threatened with blight, herds menaced by encephalitis, and foxes themselves not as bright and beautiful as they might become — it would be years before the Company could achieve a silver fox as lovely as they'd dreamed of. There was still so much to do.

Chapter Seventeen

ONLY DR. GREEN WAS SURE THAT HE WAS MAKING progress in his laboratory investigations. It was slow, exacting work, and too often results were disheartening. The adventure of small triumphs and greater defeats could not be shared by others, for only a scientist could understand what was being accomplished.

Almost nothing was known about the virus. Even the specific manner of the infection's attack was a mystery, and was to remain so for a long time. Undoubtedly it lay within the higher centers of the nervous system, and Dr. Green believed it might be found in the nerve cells of the brain. A long series of experiments failed, however, to support the theory. He tried different methods of inoculation, both intramuscularly and directly into the brain, and examined foxes killed in various stages of the disease. He studied tissues in special fixatives and made sections of the central nervous system, livers, spleens and other vital organs. All led to nothing.

The virus of the famous fox #998 was used in a

series of infections; sixty-six foxes were inoculated, and of these forty-four died. It was presumed that the twenty-two survivors developed an immunity. Following this lead, Dr. Green made a pooled virus of dead foxes, combined it with serum from recovered animals, and tried with this mixture to find a method of immunization. Groups of red foxes injected with it survived; control groups, given only virus, showed a high mortality rate. These results held out hope. Apparently serum from recovered animals contained protective antibodies capable of neutralizing virus. But serum alone, from which Dr. Green had hoped to get a passive immunity, gave such temporary protection that it was abandoned.

Meanwhile the Company, reading laboratory reports that the encephalitis virus capable of killing foxes had been prepared and a hyperimmune serum capable of neutralizing it had been developed, had to seem more philosophical than it felt about the slowness of research and the possibility of another year of heavy loss. Red foxes saved in the laboratory held hope, but to save silver foxes on the range was the goal.

The financial aspect of research work was clarified by the dissolution of the Fromms' partnership in the Fromm Brothers-Nieman Company. This occurred in early April 1929. The partners differed on two major issues, the cost of medical research and the wisdom of a large appropriation for national advertising. Edwin Nieman, who had married Erna Fromm, remained with the Fromm boys. He believed that a firm raising thousands of silver foxes must fight disease losses, and that so large a crop of fur warranted an initial promotion expenditure of a hundred thousand dollars. This was not out of line with a crop of ten thousand foxes averaging two hundred dollars each. John F. Nieman, his father, and his uncle Charles did not agree. Holdings in the Thiensville ranch were divided; the Herbert A. Nieman Company became a wholly separate organization owned by the elder Niemans, and the Fromm Brothers-Nieman Company of Thiensville was made a corporation owned by Edwin Nieman and the four Fromm brothers. What had promised to become a kingdom of silver foxes was split into two separate states, each determined to grow big in its own right. The division of the original Fromm-Nieman Company resulted in fewer pelters for the Fromms in the fall of 1929, but by reserving all possible breeding stock, they hoped to rebuild the herd next year into one larger than ever.

More foxes than anyone else was what the Company was determined to have, and it added pens, not by a few hundreds, but by many hundreds. The market in silver foxes warranted large expansion. America was having a buying boom. The stock market was creating new millionaires, and women who had never before dreamed of owning a silver fox were potential customers. In the past ginseng had financed expansion for the Company, but now with blight in the gardens and a rapidly declining price in root the Company turned to banks, and for the first time in its history became a heavy borrower. Banks now regarded fox ranching differently from fifteen years earlier when Alwina's farm had been mortgaged to buy three silver foxes.

Alwina lived to see those three silvers grow into a mighty herd, but death finally released her from invalidism. Though for years illness had shut her off from friends she was a woman not easily forgotten, and everyone who had known her came to the little Lutheran church from which she was buried. Families drove in ancient sleighs from small hamlets, automobiles arrived from the cities, and the little churchyard with blanketed horses and shining modern vehicles was somehow right for Alwina's funeral. A pioneer whose wifehood had begun in a log cabin, she had had the vision to see new ways coming and the courage to salute them with spirit. The Fromm farm with its ranks of fox pens and ginseng arbors was not the farm she and Frederick had imagined when he felled trees in a virgin wilderness for their first log cabin, but hers was the valor to smooth the pathway of a daring dream.

In June research in fox encephalitis was still wholly a laboratory project but, pushing ahead for practical results on the furring range, Dr. Green decided his work with virus and hyperimmune serum had gone far enough to warrant an experiment with silver foxes. Tests had shown silver foxes more susceptible to the virus than reds. A group of twenty-five young foxes on the Thiensville ranch was selected for the initial test; a week later, when this appeared to be successful, fifty were injected; and another week later, one hundred were vaccinated. Apparently all three experiments were successful. Even keepers, who had looked on research with misgiving, became optimistic that the more susceptible silver foxes could be protected even while the nature and behavior of the deadly virus was being explored. Practical results to fox owners could go hand in hand with research. At the end of the third week, when no injected fox had encephalitis, a large part of the fur crop, between two and three thousand, was injected.

But encephalitis, the scourge of foxes, had a card up its sleeve which no one had suspected. A few days after the major part of the herd was vaccinated the first foxes of the first injected group developed encephalitis. It was obviously a delayed infection. The import of this was instantly recognized: every fox given the deadly virus was in danger. As the deaths came, the pattern of mortalities could be charted. These would occur between twenty-eight and thirty-five days after injection, and the crucial period, when reached by the final large group of foxes, promised to be a catastrophe. Even the prompt use of serum could not prevent a heavy loss. In the first group, which did not receive serum until after the disease appeared, deaths ran 15 per cent. In succeeding groups, the mortality was lower, but it was impossible to save all the foxes. The loss in silvers was estimated by the Company at fifty thousand dollars.

It was a magnificently large experiment, and although its extent was unintentional, results were definitely conclusive and were later confirmed in an experiment on laboratory reds. These findings, however, would cheer only a scientist. The occurrence of deaths after four weeks from the delayed infection which had been so costly, indicated that in a certain percentage of cases a protective immunity had not developed, and that the serum in the combination dosage had been eliminated to such an extent that defense against the virus was no longer afforded.

Although all the facts were useful later, it was an expensive step ahead, and medical research fell even lower in the estimation of the keepers. To them Dr. Green and his needle became a menace. The Company was more understanding about the disaster and Edward even achieved a bit of humor. "Doc, we've never quite believed what you had in that bottle was really the stuff that killed foxes, but now you've convinced us."

The Thiensville experiment in June proved that the hope of immunizing the fall pelters was futile. Again the fur crop was vaccinated against encephalitis with attenuated virus in sodium ricinoleate, a brain solution of 4 per cent virus in 2 per cent castor oil soap. While this did not give immunity it meant some protection, and this turned out so well that Dr. Green began to believe he was on the verge of a solution. The 3,786 pelters suffered only a 3.2 per cent mortality, the lowest the range had shown in years, the lowest it would show in many years to come, and in a season when silver fox was bringing good prices.

In spite of the 1929 market crash, the price of fur had not declined. The Fromm shipment was not so large as it had been in the two previous million-dollar years, but the quality of the pelts was better. This consistent improvement of Fromm foxes aroused Eastern comment, and one fur journal carried a leading article comparing Fromm products with those of others.

"The insistence of Fromm Brothers that their continued success in the production of high quality silver fox pelts was due mainly to skill in handling of animals during the so-called furring season, was met with some skepticism by the fur trade prior to the offering of the latest crop of Fromm pelts. . . . Comparison of the Fromm Brothers' collection with the rest of the world crop has brought a marked change in the attitude. . . . Skepticism gave way to surprise, and many were the skin handlers who sought explanation. The Fromm answer was the Fromm claim advanced before the marketing of the crop; that the handling during the furring season is the determining factor, and that to this handling too little attention has been paid by the breeding trade as a whole."

This confirmation of the Company's belief that the quality of the fur crop held the real answer to success, stiffened its determination to make fur ranges safe for foxes. Soon after the midwinter sale the scope of research was enlarged by the establishment of the Fromm-Green Research Foundation, which was to make a study of both encephalitis and distemper. Range losses from encephalitis had deepened the Company's fear of the possible advent of distemper, for while encephalitis preyed on furring ranges, distemper stalked through pens and whole farms. The time to prepare against disaster was before it was upon them.

Dr. Green proposed the foundation to Edward. This took confidence, for the doctor had not yet conquered encephalitis, and the fiasco of serum-virus injection was still chalked up against him, at least in the minds of the keepers. Edward liked the idea and the others in the Company agreed. Even Edwin Nieman, who might have been expected to have misgivings, said that they must find out how to fight fox diseases if they were to raise a larger herd of foxes. Dr. Green, being as aggressive and single-minded as the Fromms, was a natural ally in the difficult business. The ambitious program of the foundation was a justifiable gamble on the future, and if the Fromms were long-term gamblers, so was Dr. Green. Foxes, money, years of work, and the reputation of a scientist were wagered on the none-too-sure chance of ultimate success. Funds for the work were raised by assessing each unit three dollars a fox. Not only were Fromm herds to be laboratories, but each fox must do its share to make the world safe for foxes to come.

Attenuated virus was continued as a temporary defense, at least, against encephalitis. The big test was in 1930 when the Company, having accomplished its purpose of rebuilding the herd, put 10,998 pelters on the range, the largest fur crop thus far. The mortality jumped to 7.5 per cent and eight hundred foxes were lost through encephalitis. But more dismaying was a sudden and mysterious increase in Sampsons. John suspected that chemicals were giving a brownish cast to pelts, making fox coats dry and harsh and preventing them from furring out as they should. It appeared that foxes were being protected from encephalitis only to be transformed into Sampsons. Many fox men believed Sampsons were made, not born. Chemicals, hormone secretions, and even malnutrition, have an effect on fur. The government, however, had made a study of Sampson foxes and reported that established facts "tend to prove" Sampsonism an inherited trait. Since then it has been suggested that this characteristic may even be a recessive, following Mendel's law of recessives. Thus any carrier of Sampson blood would be a menace in a herd. Like other fox ranchers, the Fromms had culled recognized Sampsons, but had permitted others with no visible trace of the characteristic to go on breeding. The Sampson strain had been spread through the herd like spatters from a mud puddle, and inevitably half blood Sampsons had passed on the taint.

The Company made two decisions. John was to begin a rigorous extermination. The father, mother, brother, or sister of any Sampson was to be culled from the herd no matter how beautiful the color or how fine the fur. Also the sodium ricinoleate vaccine was to be discontinued. John was adamant on this. He did not intend to cull handsome silver foxes only to make more Sampsons with a chemical preparation. Dr. Green was convinced nothing in attenuated virus or pure castor oil soap was capable of transforming foxes into Sampsons, but a Company confronted with a loss of more than 10 per cent in Sampsons might be forgiven for taking an emotional rather than a coldly intellectual view of the situation.

Meanwhile some other method must be found to protect foxes from encephalitis. The passive immunity obtained from serum lasted from twenty to thirty days. If pelters were given serum before they left the pens, and the fur were pelted early, the crop could be harvested before an epidemic took many victims. This meant a shortened furring season. Foxes must have the forest shade of range life by the middle of September. Adults' coats deteriorated even more quickly in pen life than those of pups, as the guard hair is apt to lose its clearness and impart a rusty cast to the entire pelt. Early pelting was also disadvantageous because two full months are required to make the undercoat dense and strong and to grow the guard hairs. It was, however, the lesser of two evils.

The serum was administered to a herd of more than ten thousand pelters, the epidemic held off for almost a month, the foxes were pelted as soon as possible thereafter, and losses were held to 7.7 per cent. It was still a big loss, and the Company regretted the lack of those last fur-making weeks. The Fromms were seeking perfection, and this could be achieved only by turning foxes on the range in August and holding them until the fur was at its best in the middle of November. Not until science had eliminated epidemics would the most glamorous foxes be possible.

The work of the research foundation had been curtailed now that the industrial depression had set in. The need of drastic economy compelled abandonment of the research on distemper. The price of silver fox slumped like everything else, and the price of ginseng root did not pay growing costs. For the first time in its history the Company had bank trouble. The large expansion, seemingly so justified in the summer of 1929, had now put them in debt. Foxes which might have sold at good prices in the January auctions of 1930 had been held over as breeders for the augmented herd, and they were bringing only eighty dollars. Even lower prices were indicated in the future. Only the strictest economy could prevent the banks from becoming the real owners of a herd of silver foxes. Distemper might be a potential menace, but financial difficulties were the immediate danger.

Work in encephalitis, however, could not be halted. Now Dr. Green believed he had made a significant discovery which might clear up the mystery of the infection's attack. In laboratory work he had come upon intranuclear bodies in the endothelial cells of the brain cavity. If these bodies were what he hoped and suspected, he might prove that the specific inclusion body of fox encephalitis attacked, not the nerve cells of the brain as he had first surmised, but cells of the capillary bed. It was as yet only a guess. The trail would be long, and at the time he had no conception of how long it would be.

In the meantime foxes must be protected against the enemy of the fur range, and the procedure for 1932 was even more ambitious than that of the previous year. Since serum gave an immunity for only twenty to thirty days, and at any time after three weeks encephalitis trouble could be expected, the pelters should be given successive injections to be sure of protection. Then the herd might be carried through an entire furring season in safety. As a scientist, the doctor was certain these succeeding shots would maintain immunity, but he had no idea of the practical difficulties involved. The Company was well aware of these, but was still undeterred.

"We should experiment on one range this year," Edward said. "Two range shots would carry the crop through a full furring season."

"It'll be the first time anyone ever caught up fifteen hundred foxes in the thick woods," Henry said. "We can't drive them into the tunnels. They would be sure to suffocate."

It was an entirely new problem. Foxes must be caught, treated, and returned safely to the range. Some mortality was inevitable, since every time foxes are caught and handled losses occur. Accidents, rough treatment, or overexcitement might kill them, and there were bound to be a few broken legs. Considerable thought was given to the catching cages. These were made of netting, and sixty of them were built in a row across the end of the catching corral. The doors were operated by trip wires stretched to men hidden in the woods, who would drop the doors when cages held not more than twenty foxes. The foxes were to be driven in a body past the doors. When the leaders reached the last cage and found themselves cornered in the corral they would run into the open door of the cage, and when this was closed others would fall back to the next, and continue thus until all the cages were filled. The plan seemed perfect. If foxes behaved normally and door attendants acted promptly, the pelters would be confined and ready for an injection with a minimum of loss.

The driving crew ate its usual six o'clock breakfast and was on the range at seven for a day that will never be forgotten by owners, rangers, or keepers. The foxes of the range were started toward the catching corral, and as driving fences were closed to shut off retreat, the herd massed in smaller areas. It was a warm October day. The temperature reached seventy by midmorning and even in the early hours foxes fell exhausted from running in the heat. Others ran so fast that they broke their necks in collision. What was to be a flowing stream of animals turning into open cages became a mass of milling, terrified creatures. Door attendants did not always act promptly, and a moment's hesitation meant forty or fifty foxes piled in a heap so that ten to twenty foxes were apt to be suffocated. Men worked desperately to separate mounds of clawing, snarling animals. Others tried to drive stragglers into the empty cages.

The morning became a nightmare to keepers and owners. The injection dosage of horse serum was heavy and given in the abdominal cavity, which made it necessary to hold the fox upside down for the injection. Some foxes, released after treatment, ran a few steps and toppled over dead. Others ran a hundred yards into the woods where John and Walter found their bodies, and returned to report that dead foxes were lying everywhere. This was the final straw for Henry.

"Better let encephalitis kill them!" he stormed. "It's a sin to do this to healthy animals."

Henry was for stopping the experiment at once, and the majority opinion was with him. Those who had lost all faith in science bitterly protested such wanton destruction. Even those who believed in the injections argued that the loss from encephalitis could be no greater, and that loss was only a probability. These foxes were dying or being crippled before their eyes. Keepers angrily demanded why they should run foxes to death or kill them with a hypodermic needle. Suffocated foxes, foxes with broken legs, foxes which had died from the injection, were a terrible indictment of science and of doctors. If the treatments continued no one could guess how many would die. Yet if all the foxes on the range were not treated there would be no way of determining the value of the experiment. Everyone had ideas, arguments, protests, or suggestions.

At such a time Edward, clearinghouse for the ideas of all and the most farsighted gambler of the Company, usually made decisions. The role had been both thrust upon him and was of his choosing.

"What'll we do, Ed?" the boss of the treatment crew asked.

"Finish the injections," Edward said. "These dead foxes have been wasted unless we can judge results."

Research in silver foxes requires stalwart men.

The work went on. When the job was finished, 346 silver foxes lay dead in the corral, but every fox still alive had been given an injection. Eighteen days later they received another, and encephalitis did not take its annual toll from that range. The following year almost twelve thousand fur range foxes received two injections of the serum. In later years this procedure was followed with as many, and even more, range foxes, but never again was another day as bad as the first. Methods improved with experience. A better serum was used and the dosage was cut so that foxes need not die of shock. The driving crew began at earliest daylight so as to finish in the cool morning hours. The Company learned to wait if possible for a cold day, but the timing had to meet that inexorable deadline of three weeks between injections. Driving technique changed. A crew of a hundred men was used, and the door operators became more vigilant to avoid crowded cages. Experienced men handled the needles, assistants filled syringes, and the injection was subcutaneous in the loose skin of the flank.

With this better technique and luck in weather and fox behavior, two thousand foxes were treated in two hours and losses were only about 2 per cent in each treatment. With worse luck seventy-five foxes would be lost in every fifteen hundred. Only one range could be treated in a day, and a crew of one hundred men treating foxes on twelve ranges robbed the fall ginseng rush of needed labor; but the injections held range losses to approximately 8 per cent and at the same time enabled foxes to reach full perfection in winter coats. But whether the Company had good or bad luck in the range shot of serum, the method was quite as hard on owners and keepers as on foxes, and everyone looked forward to the time when permanent immunity could be achieved with one shot given in the pens.

Dr. Green believed this would be possible eventually, but only after a long and tedious exploration of the behavior of the virus. Research had gone far enough to establish proof of his surmise about the attack of the infection — a long step forward. The inclusion body of fox encephalitis did not attack the nerve cells of the brain as might have been expected, but instead invaded only the endothelial cells. The endothelium, a single layer of flattened cells lining the cavities of the body, had been the hidden pocket for the infection, and to make the search even more baffling, only the endothelial cells of the cerebral capillary bed were attacked by the virus. Having traced the infection to its lair, Dr. Green was in a better position to attack the problem of immunity, but in this, too, the disease faced him with peculiar factors. The costly Thiensville experiment had shown the danger of delayed infection, and it had also left in the minds of many a real fear of the danger of live virus. Many experimental foxes would die before the procedure and the amounts of serum and live virus could be accurately determined, but gradually the secrets of this strange and deadly virus were being uncovered with microscope and test tube, and a herd of hyperimmune foxes was being developed to supply serum. Despite delay and disappointments, the Company knew that the eventual achievement of a permanent immunity would more than justify all the years and money spent on the project, and each season the Company grew more eager for results.

Then suddenly success in fighting encephalitis became relatively unimportant. For the first time distemper struck the farm. In the summer of 1934, when Fromm silver foxes were being shown at the Century of Progress Exposition in Chicago, when the campaign of national advertising had begun to show results, when the women of America had become more aware of Fromm silver foxes, and the first faint show of prosperity promised to relieve the dark years of the depression, distemper broke out simultaneously in two units at Hamburg. Mortalities were 75 per cent in the infected areas, and if the disease spread with the same severity, the farm would be wiped out as had been the farms of other breeders. Almost at the same time a distemper outbreak occurred at Thiensville, and both farms knew they were engaged in a battle against a new epidemic.

Nothing had been done in distemper research since the need of economy had halted the work three years before. The obvious first measure was to find some antidistemper serum vaccine or serum already manufactured, which would aid in holding down losses. The original intention had been to develop a killed virus or a modification of a distemper virus, and now laboratory work was started.

Meanwhile every precaution known to fur farmers was enforced to prevent spread of the infection. The variety of the disease was virulent. Each morning fox carcasses were buried. Commercial antidistemper vaccine was administered. Sanitary precautions were observed. Crews washed their hands between tasks, walked through disinfecting solution as they left each yard. The Company went through the horror of its first distemper epidemic with farm stock dead and dying, whole fox families cleaned out by the infection, and even whole blocks doomed. Only the enormous extent of the project saved them.

In spite of distemper, the Company was able to put twelve thousand pelters on the range, but even here distemper continued the attack. The fur range mortality was 17.9. This was as bad as in the early days of encephalitis, and until a sure method to immunize against distemper was discovered there was little hope that losses would be lessened. Compared to this new disaster, and the threat it held to the future, encephalitis paled as a killer.

Chapter Eighteen

R ESEARCH IN DISTEMPER CONTROL REQUIRED AN
experimental unit, and the Company bought a bankrupt
fox farm a few miles from the Thiensville ranches and
opened the Fromm Laboratories. The administration
building was converted into a laboratory, and the pens
provided housing for experimental foxes. A small permanent staff was installed and the Company prepared
for an aggressive campaign.

More than ten years earlier several research projects
had been carried on in distemper. Dr. Green's investigation of fox distemper for the breeders' association
had been contemporary with the study of canine distemper by Laidlaw and Dunkin. Several other men,
among them Puntoni and Lebailly, had worked on
canine distemper, and out of these various studies
several immunizing agents had been developed and
were being manufactured by biological companies. The
Fromms must depend on one of these vaccines or serums
until the Fromm Laboratories succeeded in the modification of a distemper virus with which young foxes

could safely be inoculated. The idea of the modification of a virus in an animal host had its origin in the discovery of the smallpox vaccination by Jenner and was used by Pasteur in his work on rabies.

Such a modification of the distemper virus would be a long and costly process. In the changes induced by serial animal passage, the virus becomes extremely virulent for the animal host, and at the same time loses virulence for some other species. This is accomplished by the adaptation of the virus to the animal host, and is in the nature of induced mutations. Three families are susceptible to distemper; the weasel, which includes the mink and ferret, the raccoon, and the dog family, which includes the fox. Laidlaw and Dunkin had utilized the ferret in their experimental work. It was highly susceptible to distemper regardless of whether the virus originated from a related species, such as mink, or an unrelated species, such as dog or fox. In choosing the ferret for his work, Dr. Green was influenced by the fact that the serial passage of a virus through a species might bring about a modification which would have a lowered virulence for an unrelated species, and he hoped to find an immunizing agent effective and safe for young foxes. The doctor had no idea how many passages of virus generations (the term used to describe the fatal termination of an infection in the host) would be necessary, but he warned the Company that he would not undertake the project unless assured of support through a hundred generations. This was an extensive undertaking; it might, and eventually did, cost more than a million dollars. It was a singlehanded battle against a scourge which had already cost the fox industry many millions, but it was the kind of battle that appealed both to the Company and to Dr. Green.

The Company considered itself fortunate in having an animal host that might make possible the modification of the distemper virus. Had such a host existed for the encephalitis virus, the problem would not have been so baffling. In his search the doctor had run the gamut from mice to monkeys, and found no species which could be used to attenuate the deadly encephalitis virus to a low virulence for foxes; he was now trying to accomplish immunization by some other method.

In distemper the route was clear, but preliminary work had to be done before the actual modification could begin. The attack of the virus was verified. It was different from that of encephalitis, for it attacked the nerve cells of the brain and never the capillary system. Also the particular strain of distemper that would be chosen for modification must be determined. This was done only after many strains from the herd of infected foxes had been isolated, tested, and found to be immunologically identical with the standard strain used in biological products. Eventually this standard strain was selected, since it was highly pathogenic for foxes, dogs, and ferrets.

The experimental unit required careful planning because of the highly contagious nature of distemper among all susceptible animals, and especially ferrets. Every precaution must be taken to avoid contamination of a natural distemper virus. Ranches from which ferrets were purchased were inspected; laboratory ferrets were kept in quarantine, and inoculations were performed in small pens built in the center of a large fenced area. The individual cages were covered with fine copper wire sunk into the ground to prevent the entrance of flies, and the ferrets themselves were protected from contact with this screen by an interior wall of fine-mesh wire. Cages were opened only in a heavy mist of fly spray. When a virus generation was completed by the death of a ferret, the carcass was immersed in lysol, taken to a special room where the spleen was removed aseptically and placed in a vial for culture, storage, and use in further transmission. Despite these measures, early in the experiment the modified virus suddenly developed increased virulence. If this were the behavior of the virus, some other method of approach must be devised. If it were the result of outside contamination the work must be redone with greater vigilance. When finally contamination was detected, a special quarantine ranch for ferrets was constructed, and thereafter only ferrets from this ranch were used for the transmissions, and were brought from the ranch to the experimental farm in sterilized cages.

From time to time, as the number of virus generations increased, tests were made on red foxes. These test animals must be completely free from any natural distemper infection, and to make certain of this only wild foxes, dug from dens, were used. Later, as the progress of the work warranted experiments on silver foxes, it became difficult to make sure that the animals were not already infected with distemper, as the disease had now spread all through the ranches. Twice experiments went wrong for this reason. Another time the virus again developed increased virulence from contamination, despite precautions. And once, when the virus had been carried through a sufficient number of generations to promise some effectiveness, all the material from the experiments was destroyed because of a misunderstanding on the part of an employee. The serial passage had to be started over again.

In addition to the ferret passage, work was carried on to produce a killed virus vaccine and a hyperimmune serum from foxes. It was hoped that these would hold down losses but, while they proved of some value, they were not effective in fighting epidemic outbreaks. Also work on permanent immunization against encephalitis had to be continued, although losses from encephalitis were now far less than those from distemper.

To further complicate the work of the Fromm Laboratories, Chastek paralysis broke out among Fromm foxes. This disease was given the name of the fox rancher on whose farm the symptoms had been first encountered. Because of the nature of the symptoms, the disease was first suspected to be a new virus infection. An initial spastic paralysis became progressive. A fox ran with short stiff jumps instead of the usual easy fox gait, then exhibited more bizarre movements as groups of muscles became spastic while other groups remained usable. This strange behavior was followed by complete paralysis in which the animal became rigid with head drawn back, then coma, and finally death in from one to four days. Experimental transmissions proved the disease could not be communicated, which thoroughly discredited the virus theory. Autopsies showed degeneration of internal organs, and the microscope revealed heavy hemorrhages in the brain. In every instance Dr. Green encountered the disease appeared a month after the extensive feeding of fish had begun. Yet food poisoning was not the cause, because in every case the fish had been of good quality.

On the Fromm farms the disease began with a few

deaths on all the ranches, and then fatalities climbed to an average of twenty-eight a day. Because of the doctor's close association with this large herd of foxes, he was able to verify his early deductions that the disease was caused by fish. When more than 10 per cent of fresh fish was given, a Vitamin B_1 deficiency resulted. The reason for this baffled Dr. Green, but the administration of Vitamin B_1 corrected the condition. This was a definite and immediate scientific contribution to fox farming. It was only some years later that Dr. Green was able to carry through his research in this disease and prove that a constituent in the fish diet, especially when heads, tails, skins and intestines of fresh fish were used, chemically inactivated thiamin in the fox's stomach. This was similar to the disease of alcoholic encephalopathy in man, in which alcohol raises the Vitamin B_1 requirements of the tissues, thereby causing the extreme depletion of Vitamin B_1. This discovery satisfied Dr. Green's scientific curiosity, although ranchers had long ceased to kill foxes with an unbalanced diet of raw fish.

If fox diseases were driving laboratory work forward with feverish anxiety, the troubles of the scientists were not comparable to those of the fox owners. Hamburg had a second severe outbreak of distemper in which daily pen losses ran from 50 to 150 foxes, while Thiensville went through continual tribulation with the disease. No one understood why the southern unit suffered more, but Thiensville had little respite. The intensity of the disease varied. It died down in winter, only to flare in spring and summer, when the young would die in great numbers. If June were passed in safety, distemper attacked in July. Foxes that had received a dozen treatments of canine serums and vaccines might live through the summer only to die before the pelting season. The dose was increased, new remedies were tried, but nothing held down deaths. The annual loss in pups went as high as 40 per cent, and four thousand and even five thousand annual mortalities occurred in a herd of from twelve to fifteen thousand foxes. Distemper became a nightmare. Every scheme man could devise to control infection was useless, even the most ingenious elaboration of sanitary precautions. The feeding crews wore special coveralls, rubber aprons, and gloves, walked through disinfecting fluid at the door of each yard, changed gloves and had aprons sprayed with disinfectant between pens, and never touched a sick or dead fox during feeding routine. Such measures doubled the time needed for feeding, and each evening huge vats of the gloves required for the day's feeding went to the sterilizer. Fox carcasses were picked up by a separate collection crew, and each carcass put in a special airproof bag.

Yet morning after morning foxes sickened, carcasses were carried from the pens, and a pit large enough in which to burn from 150 to 200 animals was dug. Crews were doubled to perform all these extra tasks of a farm which staggered under an epidemic. The horror and hopelessness of it weighed down men's spirits. Even the months of reprieve were months of dread waiting for the inevitable revisitation. The research which was to save them was only a vague report, a mysterious process being carried on in a laboratory. Keepers lost faith in hypodermic shots, microscopes, test tubes, viruses, and serums.

On top of these big summer losses, the fur range mortality in the herd of twelve thousand pelters was 20.8.

Pelters reached the range so weakened by disease that in giving the second immunizing shot against encephalitis, as many as 250 foxes might be killed on each drive. Only the magnitude of the herd enabled the project to survive, and it was a question of how long even such mighty herds could do so.

In the following summer, 1936, distemper broke out again at Thiensville, and now the infection had crawled into every unit. Crews and owners were tensed for another season of futile precaution, useless injections of canine distemper serum, and inevitable deaths. Medical research reached a new low in the keepers' estimation. Despite the Fromm laboratories, experiments, and scientists, their weapons against distemper were not different from those used by other ranchers, and the outcome of their battle might be fully as disastrous.

Dr. Green's announcement that he had at last, in 1936, perfected a method to immunize permanently against encephalitis did little to reinstate science in ranch opinion. While the new method of permanent immunity put an end to the need of catching foxes on the range, it transferred an even bigger task of fox treatment to the pens. Three injections were required. A first shot of killed virus raised the threshold of immunity, a second of virulent virus and serum gave foxes a mild attack of encephalitis, and a third of serum alone caught these foxes still low in immunity and carried them safely through the critical period until they developed sufficient antibodies to provide immunity. The shots were given at three-week intervals, beginning in late May, and now in addition to all the extra tasks caused by distemper a herd of twenty-five thousand foxes must be put through nine weeks of treatments.

The triumph, once so eagerly awaited, of furring ranges freed from encephalitis went almost uncelebrated. Loss through distemper of 18.3 per cent of more than sixteen thousand pelters was so disastrous that owners and keepers could think of little else. Nor did the Fromm Laboratories' report in October raise high hopes. Dr. Green summarized the distemper situation. Canine immunizing agents had proved thoroughly unsatisfactory. The twenty-seventh generation of ferret origin virus had been tested on fifty-six silver fox pups with a low mortality of 9 per cent. A still more effective fortieth generation would be available in the spring. "It would seem," he concluded, "that a safe method for the use of virus is at hand."

At Hamburg the Fromms prepared still another bulwark against distemper, that of segregation. The Bohl farm three miles from the Home Farm was purchased, and pens were built to house fifteen hundred foxes. These were for breeders and the choicer foxes. In case of an outbreak of distemper on the main ranch, this breeding stock would be protected. Three miles should give safety and yet permit food and supplies to be brought from headquarters.

In the spring of 1937 the fiftieth generation of virus was tested as soon as young red foxes, dug from dens, were available. The virus showed increased virulence. Further tests proved the ferret passage virus had been contaminated by a more virulent virus in the previous fall, while the thirty-sixth generation was being passed through ferrets in the outdoor screened cages. The work of a whole winter had been lost. The serial passage was resumed at the thirty-fifth generation, and the ferrets were moved to a special quarantine room inside the building. The room was sealed and ventilated with filtered air, and doors were opened only after a heavy mist of fly spray had been turned on for fifteen minutes.

Fifteen generations must be redone when time was so precious, and it was work that could not be rushed. Ferrets were killed two weeks following inoculations, the spleens tested for ten days to make sure these were sterile, then ground and tested again. Haste could be made only with infinite precaution, but the work of rebuilding generations was advanced as fast as possible to be ready for a large-scale experiment with ranched foxes in the summer.

In July, distemper flared in two blocks of pens at Thiensville. Each block consisted, as usual, of four hundred pens and was cared for by two keepers. The initial mortalities were heavy. Dr. Green suggested to Edwin Nieman that these blocks be chosen for the experiment with live virus. Faith in research was at a low ebb in the southern unit. Keepers, straw bosses, the office force, and even the auditor were opposed to experimental injections; maintaining distemper was bad enough without adding to the losses. In the face of this general distrust, Edwin Nieman hesitated. As part owner of a fox farm, Edwin had gone through eight hard years — reorganization, expansion, depression, bank trouble, encephalitis, distemper, enormous bills for useless remedies, and heavy cost in research. Now the doctor proposed that he embark upon a major experiment with live virus, attenuated and modified to be sure; but the very words "live virus" and carried a threat since the encephalitis disaster in 1929.

To make the decision even more difficult, Dr. Green could not assure Edwin that the injections would end his distemper troubles. "The infection has bored in so long at Thiensville that it can't be choked off suddenly," the doctor said. "Distemper is bad now, but it could be worse. You could have a wipe out in those two blocks, and such an epidemic would spread to others. But if we go in this summer and clean up the worst of the infection, you can have a farm free from distemper in another year."

A scientist was talking to a man who needed a miracle. An ultimate wipe out would mean complete defeat, and Edwin Nieman agreed to try the modified virus. But his decision demanded courage.

When word of it reached the keepers, indignation boiled over. They recalled the fiasco when the live encephalitis virus had killed foxes. Keepers have long memories, and no man becomes a keeper unless he really likes foxes. Now even the owner of the herd had betrayed them and their charges to the ruthlessness of science.

The morning when the injections were to be given Dr. Green reached the farm at daybreak. He was prepared for trouble. Edwin, universally liked by his men, and whose opinion had never been questioned, did not expect a demonstration. He was startled when the group of angry keepers confronted Dr. Green.

"You've killed enough of our foxes," the spokesman said. "This time we're stopping that crazy needle business."

"You'll do nothing of the sort," the doctor said. "Edwin and I know this is the only way to save these foxes."

"The way you saved that lot of foxes from encephalitis!" Another man stepped forward and shook his fist in the doctor's face. "I was a keeper then and I remember how foxes dropped dead all around us. We've had enough of this science. Go back to your college and let us take care of raising foxes."

Others joined in angry protests. This was a matter between the keepers and science, and if Edwin said anything, no one heard him while Dr. Green and the keepers shouted threats and recriminations. It was not a scientific argument. The doctor won, not because he convinced his opponents, but because he could shout louder and show even more passion than the others. The injections were given, although no Thiensville man except Edwin Nieman had any faith in the procedure.

As the doctor had warned, the injections did not stop the epidemic. In both blocks foxes died through the summer, and keepers charged every death to the needle. Not so many died as Dr. Green believed would have done had there been no effort at immunization, but the mortality — 40 per cent — was higher than anyone cared to think about. In the fall the furring range deaths were equally shocking. Of the 19,821 pelters, 11.9 per cent died of distemper.

The time had come for appraisal. The Company posted up the books and decided it "was spending a lot of money to kill foxes." Canine antidistemper remedies had cost $100,000 to $150,000 each year, and once had mounted to $165,000. Each furring season had brought a heavy loss in pelters, and this year two thousand silver foxes almost ready for the market had died of distemper. Added to this were the high mortalities in the two blocks of pens where the injections had been given. This was the most discouraging figure in the entire appraisal. Edward called the doctor's attention to it as the two men looked over the year's report.

"Did Edwin Nieman tell you how many foxes we lost in those two blocks?" he asked.

"Distemper had gotten a real foothold," the doctor said. "I think a loss of only 40 per cent is good."

Edward stared at him. "I don't see how it could be worse," he said.

There appeared to be no common ground for argument. The Fromms were not convinced that a modified virus would save foxes. Their doubts made them unwilling to depend on it as their only weapon, and since research was being carried on abroad, the Company suggested the doctor go to London and find out what was being done in other countries. The doctor's faith in the modified virus was unshaken, and before he left for the east he arranged for the laboratory to continue to build up generations. He intended to be prepared for the next bout with distemper.

In February, while in New York and about to sail for London, he was recalled to Hamburg by long-distance telephone. The Bohl farm was in trouble. Soon after pelting season a few deaths had been noticed, one fox gone here, another there. Then empty pens appeared. At first keepers had accepted the few losses as the inevitable mortality of any fur farm, but now distemper was suspected. Dr. Green hurried to Wisconsin, made autopsies and knew the suspicion was correct. For the first time he had an opportunity to use the virus at the onset of the infection, and he had already telephoned the laboratory to prepare fifteen hundred units, now in the fifty-third generation.

But the Company had no intention of using the fifteen hundred units of modified virus. It could not afford to take a 40 per cent loss on the breeding stock of the Bohl farm. Even more important, wholesale injections would endanger the puppy crop. John and Henry were adamant on this point. In the early days of fox farming a female handled even in December would be too nervous to breed in late winter. Now foxes were less wild, but injections at the end of the breeding season would end all hope of increase. Females were heavy and must have quiet. The noise of the treatment crew, the barking of foxes, and the excitement of being caught and injected would so stir up mothers they would never settle down for the whelping season. Abortions and litters of dead puppies could be the only result of injections which were not even of proved value.

The Company reached its decision even before Dr. Green confirmed the suspicion that distemper had attacked the Bohl farm. Other methods must be found. Sulfa drugs, recently discovered, had been used in the treatment of canine distemper with some success and might be the miracle remedy the company needed. At least it was worth trying. The sulfa product was not yet available in the market. "But we hoped you might be able to buy it for us," Edward said.

It was an effective announcement that Dr. Green was to be denied his opportunity, but firm as was his faith in the virus, he accepted the decision without argument and with understanding. The foxes to be saved or lost belonged to the Fromms. The fifteen hundred units of fifty-third generation virus lay unused in the laboratory and the ferret passage was carried no further. Dr. Green arranged for the purchase of the sulfa product when he went east to sail for London, and the Fromm future was, as always, in their own hands.

By March distemper had invaded every corner of the

Bohl farm. The sulfa drug proved useless, and canine distemper serum was no more effective than in previous epidemics. The virulence of the strain of distemper was greater than any yet encountered. The precious puppy crop was almost ruined. Almost invariably all the pups in an infected pen died, as well as one or both of the parents. The Company suffered an 80 per cent loss of pups and a 45 per cent loss of breeders. Nor did extraordinary precautions arrest the spread of the infection. Crews were not allowed to enter infected pens even to pick up dead foxes, and these lay rotting in the sun to add to the horror of the plague. The earlier concern for the puppy crop was forgotten, as anxiety now centered on the parent foxes. These deaths were far more serious. For years the herd had been so ravaged by distemper that the company was in no position to absorb such losses in breeding stock.

Finally efforts were bent only on restricting the infection to the one farm. Nothing from the Bohl farm was taken to the main ranch. Platforms were built at the roadside and feed carts from the home ranch stopped only long enough to drop the load. Workers were not permitted to visit headquarters. They, and even the farm itself, were shunned by everyone who had the care of healthy foxes.

The three miles that were to have safeguarded Bohl farm foxes were now the sole protection of the main herd itself. Then in early May distemper suddenly appeared in two areas of the Home Farm. Apparently the disease was of the same virulent strain, and if it ran through the pens taking pups and breeding stock, the Company was finished as far as fur breeding was concerned. A herd which had taken more than twenty-five years in building would be gone. The Company's faith in modified virus was no greater than it had been three months before, but it was the only weapon left. The Company decided that Fromm foxes would have "either their first shot of the virus or their last." Come what might, a fur farm lost or saved, it must take the chance. Edward sent for Dr. Green.

When the two men met in the ranch office, the doctor knew this was Edward's lowest moment. For the first time he did not look at the doctor as he talked.

"Distemper has appeared in two spots on the Home Ranch," Edward said. "You say you never had a chance at an epidemic until it was a runaway. This one has barely started. You're in charge."

The doctor nodded. He didn't speak because he couldn't. This was the opportunity he had awaited so long, and it caught him unprepared. The fifteen hundred units of modified virus were all he had. And he needed scores of thousands to fight distemper in so large a herd. He did not admit this to Edward. It seemed unfair to add to Edward's heavy burden, and another man's panic would increase his own. It was his job to get the virus.

He telephoned the laboratory staff to put the fifty-third generation of virus into fifty ferrets without losing a moment, and to bring him the fifteen hundred units. Before they arrived Dr. Green had decided on his campaign. The amount of virus was too small to be used in offensive tactics. Defense alone was open to him. Certain pens had the disease and he must keep it there. With his meager supply of virus he formed rings of inoculated foxes around the infected areas. The Fromms must have wondered why a man who had always thought in terms of vast experiments on hundreds and thousands of foxes began his work so cautiously, but they did not ask, and he did not tell them.

In the laboratory Dr. Green cut every corner to produce more virus with the utmost speed. Where ferrets had been allowed to live two weeks after inoculation, he killed them in a week. Spleens which always had been tested for ten days to make sure of sterile material were ground at once. But despite the need of haste he took every precaution time allowed, mixing only three spleens in a batch. Thus if one spleen happened not to be sterile he would avoid a large batch of spoiled virus.

The first lot of modified virus was mixed, tested, and rushed to Hamburg in eleven days. With this Dr. Green deepened the ring around the infected areas. Each week end thereafter he drove to Hamburg with more virus to widen the protected area. As each batch of virus was used, other batches had more time to be tested and were becoming safer. Fromms and keepers undoubtedly attributed the small batches to a new sense of caution. The Company never learned until much later that the doctor had brought all the virus that existed at each time.

Three weeks after the first inoculations the epidemic had not spread. The rings had held. At the end of four weeks, there was no doubt that the epidemic was declining. At the end of the fifth week, Edward stopped into the doctor's little room in the warehouse.

"We have no epidemic," he said.

Medical research, which at this point had cost the Company almost a million dollars, had saved the fur farm. One result of the vaccinations astonished the doctor as well as the Company. The modified virus, expected to be only an immunizing preventive, worked a cure in some cases. Where one pup had died in a pen, others which must have been already ill with distemper when they were vaccinated, got well. Apparently modified virus had the capacity to provide a quick and vigorous attack, and yet permit the animal to live. In pen after pen pups survived an exposure to the virulent distemper. Keepers began to speak to Dr. Green again.

It had been a long haul, but the menace of distemper was ended. In 1938, a crop of 22,500 fox pups were vaccinated against distemper. In 1939 all the foxes on all the ranches were immunized and the 32,883 foxes in the furring range had a mortality of 3.5 per cent. For the first time in years a crop was sent to market after a season in which there had been no disaster.

Success in the distemper battle did not end medical research, but rather opened up its possibilities. The virus was put through further generations. Distemper and encephalitis vaccines were produced for other fur farms, and for this manufacture a large laboratory staffed with workers and equipped with the most modern facilities was built on the experimental unit.

Dr. Green proposed to make this laboratory serve the fur farms of the Middle West, and he envisioned an ambulance service which could dash out and bring in sick foxes and new diseases for scientific study. A special truck was built, with a separate double garage to serve as a receiving room for patients. The fox which had produced so distinctive and unusual a disease as encephalitis might have others. The same idea occurred to the Company.

"Suppose Doc brings in some troubles we've never had," John protested to Edward, "and then our herd gets them before he knows how to control them."

"The sick foxes will be kept in a special isolation ward," Edward said.

"And how about the flies and bugs that will come in on this ambulance truck from the infected farms?" Henry asked. "Let them loose and we're in for trouble. He can't isolate a fly."

This Dr. Green did not propose to do. A sprayer installed in the ceiling of the garage would destroy all insect life in the returning truck. The ambulance truck, the receiving garage with sprayer equipment, and the isolation ward were prepared. And stood idle. No other farm developed a new and fascinating disease. Edward found the elaborate and unused service an amusing topic.

"Doc," he said, "apparently other farmers don't have the troubles of the Fromms. I hear the isolation ward still hasn't had a patient."

"That garage won't be wasted," the doctor said. "There's plenty of work to be done yet in distemper. Dogs have distemper."

"And perhaps those canine antidistemper remedies don't help dogs any more than they helped our foxes," Edward said. "Would your modified virus work on dogs?"

"Why not? They are a related species. And if we can produce a permanent immunity for dogs, we've done something."

So hundreds of dogs lived in the laboratory while it was being demonstrated that ferret-passage virus had an extremely low virulence for canines. Lost dogs, unclaimed dogs from city pounds, black dogs, white dogs, big dogs, small dogs — all were added to the experimental groups. They rendered life unbearable for neighbors with their constant barking, but they served in the discovery of a permanent immunizing agent for canine distemper. The ferret-passage virus was carried to the sixty-third and even seventy-ninth generations. Field tests were made with the assistance of a number of veterinarians, and finally the Fromm Laboratories could announce that no dog need have distemper. The research was a logical outcome of all the years when antidistemper serums were poured with such futility into the vast herds of Fromm foxes. The Fromm Laboratory's vaccine is now used by veterinarians throughout the country, two hundred thousand units were sold in 1946, and plans were made to increase production. Safety for dogs was a by-product of fox farming. Unlike the fox vaccine, its value cannot be computed in dollars and cents, as those who have known the heartache of losing a dog understand so well. Medical research for silver foxes has profited from earlier discoveries in canine research, but the silver foxes have repaid their debt.

Foxes also have repaid their debt to the ferret family, although research in a modified virus for permanent immunization against mink distemper is as yet uncompleted. To accentuate the virus and achieve a low virulence for minks the host must be of an unrelated species, and in this foxes could serve members of the ferret family. Foxes, however, had one disadvantage. Ferrets produce three litters in a year and foxes breed only once; while to avoid possible contamination in the fox host, only wild pups dug from dens can be used. A limited number of hosts, and these available only in the spring, retarded the work of building up generations. In 1941 the fox-passage virus, attenuated in twenty-five generations, was produced and used on a large group of ranched mink with encouraging results. Mortalities were less than 5 per cent. However, the same experiment repeated the following year on an even larger group of mink was so unsuccessful that the work was temporarily abandoned, and the laboratory centered its efforts on the development of a killed-tissue vaccine. This did not provide permanent immunity and had no curative effect, but gave immunity against distemper if the animal had not already contracted the infection. But distemper was too serious a problem to wait for perfection in mink farms, where close housing makes it possible for an epidemic to flash through a block. The killed-tissue vaccine was available to mink ranchers in 1942, and has proved its value in arresting epidemics. In 1945 the experiment to produce a permanent immunizing agent was resumed, and the fox-passage was begun again at the first generation. In 1947 the fox-passage virus was not yet ready for a major test, but the laboratory is convinced that it will succeed in accomplishing for mink what it has for dogs and foxes.

Perhaps the strangest twist in the fight against distemper was when the fox vaccine of the Fromm Laboratories stopped an epidemic that threatened to wipe out the silver fox industry of Prince Edward Island. The boys who had made a visit to the island long ago and looked with envy on the long established ranches could not have dreamed that some day Fromm foxes would save the herds in the birthplace of the silver fox industry.

When distemper vaccines for foxes and canines had been perfected, the Fromm Laboratories again turned to work on encephalitis. The Company was happy to have any permanent immunization against the disease, but three injections and nine weeks of treatment were a heavy burden, and too, Dr. Green considered encephalitis an unfinished task. No animal host for the modification of this virus has ever been found. Search for a successful procedure to combine serum and virus in one shot for permanent immunization goes on today, and is only a part of the general purpose of finding the best and most economical way to raise foxes.

In 1946 three units of silver foxes were given a one-shot of serum and encephalitis virus. The first unit of three hundred experimental foxes developed encephalitis in ten days. In the second unit of five hundred foxes, the method was changed and results were satisfactory, but five hundred foxes were not enough to prove that a procedure had been perfected. A second group of five hundred foxes received the same injection, and of this group fifty foxes had encephalitis. A high percentage of the sick foxes was saved by the use of serum. In the fall all three units of foxes were turned into four experimental ranges for further test in close contact with one another. Of the four experimental ranges, two had no trouble. A third range, holding 500 foxes, lost 100 foxes from encephalitis. The fourth range of 150 showed 40 deaths, and to make results even more baffling, animals on a range with no deaths came from the same pen block as those of the range showing a 20 per cent mortality. Research for the desired one-shot must start all over again. But had the Fromm Laboratories accepted the findings of one unit of five hundred foxes and of one furring range as conclusive proof that the serum-virus mixture gave permanent immunity, and had the Company used this method with the main herd of foxes, the mortality in the present-day herd of thirty-five thousand pelters would have been enormous. Volume has been valuable, even in research.

Chapter Nineteen

THE DEPRESSION CAUGHT THE FROMMS IN 1931.
Expansion and national advertising, both necessary if
the Company were to take advantage of the hard-won
fur trade favor, had been heavy drains, in addition to
losses from disease. As if these were not enough, the
price of silver fox went lower than at any time in its
history. The average fell to $120, then $80, and continued to drop. No one dared guess how low it might go.

Again the industry faced extinction. Breeding stock
went begging. Raising a fur capable of such price de-
clines held no hope of profit. The boom which had
started in the twenties ended, and this was the last
speculative era in silver fox farming.

The Fromms' primary interest was in the sale of pelts;
but the glamor of a silver fox scarf, even for a woman
who might afford it, was not in line with economies that
the depression had made fashionable. Yet the fur crop
had to pull the Company out of difficulty if the Company
and not the banks were to be future owners of the fox
herds. Ginseng could not help. The price of the root did

not pay the cost of growing. Fluctuations in the two crops were caused by different factors, but in 1931 both fox and ginseng markets dipped simultaneously. Ginseng production had reached a peak in America, and floods, revolutions, and political unrest in China had caused hard times. The Chinese still wanted ginseng but could not afford former prices. American growers were forced to sell for two dollars, and even one dollar per pound. Rather than do this, the Company stored its ginseng in the warehouse.

The situation in China was beyond even Fromm intervention, but the silver fox problem was on home ground. Depression prices could not be altered, therefore markets had to be widened. Instead of a single pelt around a woman's neck, why not a two-skin scarf, four or five skins in a garment, or even fur as trimming?

Multiple-pelt manufacture in silver fox would be an innovation. Fur garments had usually been limited to the short-haired variety. In 1926 a silver fox jacket was made on order by Max Koch for Marshall Field and Company. It had presented a new problem in fur manufacture, since silver fox had never been manipulated by the fur process which the fur trade calls "letting out." This is accomplished by slitting the skin in narrow strips and sewing them together to obtain the length required; the piecing gives greater pliability to pelts for draping, and permits perfect matching. "Letting out" was used in working mink, seal or other short-haired furs, and long-haired furs which were not too bulky or in which the color was more or less uniform. A coat made of an unworked skin, even in so small an animal as a mink, would resemble a patchwork quilt.

Fur workers had never used this technique for the

precious silver fox. Always sold as a scarf, its beauty was never desecrated by razor or sewing machine. Now it must be, if the fur were to be used for garments or for trimming. In 1932, when the price of silver fox went to forty dollars, a fur once so costly that a single skin was a prized possession could be used in profusion. It appealed to Edward Fromm as an inspired treatment for silver fox.

"What an evening wrap the silver fox would make!" he said. "Think of that richness wrapped around a woman!" He meant it. To Edward the silver fox has always been the most glamorous fur in the world. Naturally he thought of evening wraps, and of wide collars, lavishly trimmed coats, and borders of silver fox around sleeves and skirts.

Edward went to Paris. The Wisconsin farmer visited every famous couturier. He talked to designers and argued with fur workers that the silver fox could be manipulated as a lavish trimming or as a luxurious garment. Edward was very sure and intensely earnest, but the originators of the world's fashions did not catch fire. They took the matter under consideration. Edward left silver fox pelts in his wake with a prodigality which departed from the frugal precepts of his early training, but no new fur styles apeared to be forthcoming. Having failed in his missionary effort, he turned to the second purpose of his European trip, the sale of Fromm foxes. He trudged from one leading furrier to another just as years before he had made the rounds in New York. French and Italian women saw the large bright silvers, and liked them.

On his return Edward continued proselytizing for multiple-pelt manufacture of silver foxes. Not only would this enlargement of the fur's purpose help to absorb Fromm harvests, but Edward was sure it would reveal the entrancing beauty of the pelt. A few American designers showed interest. The silver fox was a becoming fur and could replace the luxurious sable, which was rapidly disappearing. Almost overnight, as so often happens in fashion history, that trend became a definite style, and the current started in the direction of Edward's thinking.

Silver fox gained countless new wearers, and even at depression prices the Company ceased to worry about banks. Volume, the Fromms' old bulwark against disaster, again served them, but another long-sought Fromm goal fitted into the new picture. The uniformity of their pelts simplified the matching of fur, so necessary in multiple-pelt manufacture.

As markets widened and herds grew larger, new problems in merchandising confronted the Company. Thousands of nondescript silver fox pelts had been going to market from competing breeders, skins that resembled nothing so much as a strange breed of cat in bad condition, and yet because they were silver foxes they had brought good prices. American women had to be informed of the proper qualities of a silver fox pelt. Many had never seen a good one and, oddly enough, while women are the wearers of fur, few have an instinctive feeling for its beauty and enchantment. The Fromms proposed to tell the public about silver foxes, and especially Fromm foxes, but a large appropriation for advertising necessitated some means of identifying the Company's product. This was difficult. A label must not harm the pelt or be lost in manufacture, must be readily seen by the customer, and easily removed before wearing. An ear marker would spoil the appearance. Tatooing would become illegible in dressing. A stamp on the skin side of the pelt would be hidden when the fur was made up. Yet it was essential to the Company that a woman be assured the fur she bought had been raised and pelted on the Fromm ranch.

The ultimate solution was a metal medallion. Several methods of attaching this had to be successively abandoned when the Company discovered how easily it was transferred to other pelts to give aid and comfort to competitors. A Company which had guarded property and secrets as zealously as the Fromms was quick to recognize this practice. Finally the medallion was sealed in the nose of every pelt with a wire ring which permitted it to hang loosely. At the time the Company considered this the perfect answer. No other pelts could masquerade in Fromm medallions.

The medallioned foxes were advertised as pedigreed. The Company, once refused registration in the silver fox stud book, was now the only breeder who could use this term. Not only could the Company supply the pedigree of every medallioned fox, but it did so. Each medallion carried the number of the fox, and when it was returned to the Company the buyer received a certified pedigree giving name, date of birth, and breeding history through four generations.

The fox breeders' association did not challenge the use of the term "pedigreed." The famous studbook, once so important, had been forgotten in the collapse of speculation in the depression, and now breeding stock was important only in terms of the fur it produced. Fur as fur had become the objective of fur farming. In this the Fromms had led the way and had made a definite contribution to the fox industry as a whole. Nor was this their only service. They had proved the fallacy of the old-style breeding procedure of a dark to a silver, had shown that foxes could be bred for a predominance of silver and yet retain purity of color. They had altered a public's preference. Fromm foxes had never won a cup, a gold ribbon, or a high score in points, yet not only the fur trade but even wearers were beginning to prefer them. The four farm boys who had never seen a fur around the neck of a woman when they decided silvered foxes would be more becoming, had justified the fantastic notion. Now they were engaged in making foxes still brighter.

A definite decision had to be reached on the advisability of continuing ginseng culture. When the price of dry root fell to one and two dollars, many growers sold all roots large enough to harvest and allowed gardens to deteriorate. Even the spraying of plants was too expensive at such a price. Others decided to ride out the storm, and sold roots for whatever they could get. The Fromms had stored their ginseng since 1931, but in 1933 trouble in China threatened even a worse situation.

The Company's problem was complicated, because ginseng culture was threaded through the fur project. Rush seasons in the two industries dovetailed and made it possible to employ key men throughout the year. Fur alone would not permit this, as men of high caliber would not be attracted by seasonal employment. Nursery stock, too, required years to develop and, if abandoned, might never be rebuilt. Vast holdings in land and an enormous inventory in ginseng arbors and special equipment represented a staggering capital investment.

The gardens still suffered from blight, but Arthur was convinced he could eventually defeat root rot with a seed treatment. Experiments in ginseng were necessarily protracted. Not only did seeds require a year to germinate and another half year to develop green shoots, but root rot often did not appear until the second or third year of growing. Arthur's scientific attitude demanded certainty, and this could not be possible for several years. But the Company had learned to wait on science. Encephalitis was giving them practice in patience, and they were as certain that Arthur would eventually solve root rot as they now were that Dr. Green would defeat encephalitis.

Storage of harvests and the costs of production were different matters. Ginseng culture, which had to be large because of the investment, would cost forty to fifty thousand dollars each year. Nor was it known how long ginseng could be stored with safety. A weevil had destroyed small crops of other growers, and no one knew its origin or what it fed on when it had no ginseng. Farmers reported that boxes and closed barrels of the root were chewed into powder by the pest. The Fromms had stored two harvests in warm rooms above the power plant and, though frequent inspections had not uncovered weevils, they did not know whether such luck would continue.

The Fromms held a company meeting, one of the few in their history. Usually a matter was decided by a chance encounter when two partners involved in a question talked it over and relayed their decision to the others. But continuance of ginseng culture was too important for such informal methods. The four partners met in the office. Walter, as head of ginseng, spoke first.

"We've worked too hard on ginseng to give it up lightly," he said.

"We could put the money in silver foxes," Henry said. "Most fur farms don't have a second business."

John said nothing. He talked only on policies affecting the blood strain or the quality of the herd.

"In ten years or less there will be no overproduction of ginseng," Edward said. Growers will dig root already planted, sell it, and give up the business."

He went on to speak of conditions in the Orient. Since his visit there he had not believed Japan would be content with a small section of China, and the "incident" might start a war which would last many years. But a market in ginseng would exist so long as there were Chinese people. Of this he was convinced.

The meeting went on for an hour. If they continued ginseng culture the Company would have the product to sell when the market was re-established, while other growers would have neither nursery stock nor seed. The Company might become not only the largest grower of ginseng in the world, but perhaps the only grower. Meanwhile they could be building a stock pile for the Chinese nation, and ten years was not too long for a Fromm gamble. They had spent almost thirty years in carrying 150 plants into big acreage.

Walter looked relieved.

"I'll tell the boys we'll seed that eighteen-acre garden," he said. "It's ready for fall planting. And we needn't worry about where we'll store the root this year. The crop won't run over ten thousand pounds."

Save for root rot, they would have had a harvest ten times as large, but no one reopened the question of ginseng culture, nor did anyone suggest Walter make the fall seeding smaller. The Company need not have held an official meeting. Walter and Edward could have talked the matter over and relayed their decision to the others, for no member of the firm had the slightest notion of turning his back on an unfinished project. Ginseng and silver foxes had started out together, and they must continue until the end.

In 1934 the Century of Progress Exposition in Chicago offered the Company space in the General Exhibits building. This would be its first public appearance in the consumer world. Edward thought forty thousand dollars could be well spent in telling the women of America about silver foxes, and obviously Henry was the one to tell them. He took charge of the exhibit, and because creative drive was tied to fervor, he completely ignored the appropriation. The project cost one hundred thousand dollars, but Henry achieved one of the most unusual and talked-of exhibits of the Fair.

Henry's way of telling the story of the silver fox had the drama of contrast. The central feature was a floor show. A large circular revolving platform was divided in two sections; mounted foxes in a winter scene occupied one side, and models wore beautiful fox furs in the other. The platform made a complete revolution every two-and-a-half minutes and the models maintained a constant parade. They appeared from one door of a dressing room, walked across the stage to disappear through another door, and came out wearing a new fur. A dozen models, with scarfs, muffs, capes, and evening wraps were in a constant procession, and the platform revolved from ten in the morning until ten at night.

Since Henry, the perfectionist, was determined that

the foxes must appear to be in a real forest, the outdoor scene required continuous redressing. A truck made weekly trips with balsam, moss, and shrubbery from Hamburg. The use of artificial snow could not be avoided, but Henry made certain it was heaped and sculptured to look drifted, and the lighting had to give the feeling of the woods on a cold winter morning. Henry badgered workmen, changed installations and light bulbs, and sometimes remained all night to experiment with a new and inspired scheme. In the first weeks of the exhibit he slept as often on the trunk holding the fur garments in the dressing room as in his hotel, but a night's sleep was well lost if he could more nearly capture the illusion of foxes on the range. When Henry was finally satisfied, if he ever was completely satisfied, the scene probably appeared the coldest ever achieved outside of the north woods.

The rest of the exhibit completed the story of the silver fox. Photomurals seven feet high showed the life on the range. A continuous moving picture followed the work of raising and feeding a herd of foxes and grading pelts. It also showed the color development of the silver fox from nature's first experiment in a cross fox to the full silver of man's selective breeding. Mounted foxes were of varying degrees of silver, as were the furs worn by models.

The exhibit caught the public. Henry accomplished what he set out to do, for men liked it as well as women. He dramatized the history of the silver fox, and people without previous interest in, or knowledge of, what man had done with a mutation, learned the difference between the old black silver, three-quarter, half, one-quarter, and full silver. It was showmanship but not conscious showmanship, and therefore more effective. The luxurious garments and the sophisticated black and chrome fittings of the hundred thousand dollar exhibit were only superficial evidences of the compelling passion that had made the presentation possible. It was more than a story of silver foxes that Henry told. It was a sort of folktale of America; a strange mixture of small beginnings, mistakes, and fortitude; a homely story of hardships and great courage — the age-old story of many boys who have dreamed of accomplishment, and who have followed the narrow pathway of that dream.

It was not even a success story. The herd of silver foxes was not yet the herd they had envisioned. Nor was it a story of security won, nor of an impregnable citadel. Early in the exhibit Henry learned that distemper had struck the farm. Even while he talked about silver foxes he knew that in another year there might be no silver herd to be bred into brighter silvers.

Chapter Twenty

IN 1936 THE COMPANY BELIEVED IT WAS BIG ENOUGH TO make a bold departure from tradition and ask the market to come to it on its farm in Hamburg, 1,200 miles from New York's Seventh Avenue. Since the beginning of the fur trade in America, fur auctions had been held only in the great centers of the industry, Leipzig, London, St. Louis, and New York. Pelts went to the market always, never the market to the producer.

A farm auction was a daring gamble. If successful, it would make fur trade history and add immeasurably to company prestige. If it were a failure it would jeopardize that prestige, built in costly national advertising; and not even Edward, whose idea it was, had any proof to offer that eastern buyers would make the long journey to Hamburg. The other three, none of whom had ever attended an auction, were in grave doubt, but even more eager.

"I'd like it," Henry said, "if the first time I ever saw a Fromm pelt auctioned it could be on our own farm. But will the buyers come?"

"There's one way to find out," John said, "and that's to ask them. And where else are they going to get a crop like ours of full silvers."

It was a strong argument in the Company's favor. Not only was theirs the largest single offering of silver foxes in the country but it was the only real collection of bright silvers, and in a year when the public wanted brighter foxes. Popular demand for the rare coloration of full silvers had outrun supply. Style trends had changed in a season, but only generations of breeding could add silver hairs to fox pelts. The dark fox males, formerly prized as breeders, had left on the other herds of the country an imprint which could not be eradicated for many years. Fromm herds had never harbored these darker males and now Fromm pelts, instead of begging for fur trade favor, were competed for by buyers.

Henry's story of the silver fox, told to countless visitors at the Chicago Exposition, had aroused an awareness of bright silvers and of the company that had pioneered them. That exhibit had completely ended Fromm isolation. The boys who had once carried guns and regarded all visitors with defensive resentment were now accustomed to a flood of tourists, eager to see the silver fox at home. No one had enjoyed this new era more than Frederick Fromm. He became the official guide, and spent his days showing his sons' farm to a curious public. He never failed to point out the first fox house built by John and Henry.

"That's how all this started," he would say. "And what you see around here now, they did in spite of me. I didn't want them to be fox farmers, and they never got any help from me."

Frederick Fromm died in the winter of 1934 at seventy years of age, and while he had watched the tremendous expansion in the enterprise, he did not live to see the real triumph of the silver fox. In 1936 it had become one of the most talked-of furs in America. It was being used lavishly in trimmings. The two-skin scarf was customary. The silver fox jacket, requiring five skins, had swept the country as a glamour garment, and evening wraps were the height of luxury, utilizing quantities of pelts. The old fear that the silver fox would lose desirability when no longer a rare and precious fur had been proved groundless. The saturation point appeared to be as far away as ever.

Stores throughout the country featured Fromm bright silvers, and the drama of a first farm auction would not only carry on the story of the silver fox, but would enable stores to assure customers that pelts had been personally selected at the source. Edward counted on this argument to induce the buyers of the country to come to Hamburg.

"If we are ever to market our own fur on the farm, this is the year to try it," he said.

Emotionally the farm auction meant a great deal to the Company. For years the Fromms had talked of the time when they could complete the circuit on home grounds. To Edward, who for twenty years had carried pelts to market and knew the bitterness of defeat and the intoxication of fur trade favor, the farm auction would be a milestone. The only fear was a refusal from the buyers.

In early winter the Company issued invitations for February. As the Fromms awaited the reaction of the fur trade they were more worried than they admitted, even to each other. If the audacity of the scheme met with a rebuff there was nothing the Company could do about it. Success or failure lay in a wholly unpredictable decision and even John, who usually considered mail, telephone, and telegraph an invasion of his privacy, formed the habit of dropping into the office of a morning.

The suspense was ended by news that a New York group had arranged to come by special railroad car direct to Wausaw. The novelty of a fur farm auction had appealed to the trade, and a majority of the buyers was enthusiastic. Those who were not could not afford to miss a sale where competitors intended to buy silver foxes. Furriers throughout the country announced that they would be represented, and Pacific coast men planned to arrive by plane. Now the success of the auction was up to the Company. The Fromms, swinging into preparations, engaged a wing of a Wausau hotel, arranged for transportation to take visitors between hotel and farm, set up a display room in the warehouse, converted the boardinghouse dormitory of the girl ginseng weeders into an auction room, and provided food, drink, and comfort for nearly a hundred guests.

Two days before the buyers would get there the worst storm of the winter set in. Snow fell for a day and a half and, as always after a storm, the temperature went down. The Fromms helplessly watched the snow fall and read the thermometer, and the visitors arrived to find fifteen-foot snowdrifts and a temperature of thirty-eight below zero. To the Fromms' astonishment, their guests liked it. The north woods were exactly what they had imagined, and even the few who had come in a spirit of skepticism were caught by the challenge of environment. Each became a stalwart man who dared rigors and hardships to wrest pelts from the northern wilderness. It was a magnificent beginning.

After the party had been installed in hotel quarters, and stores had been raided for overshoes and women's woolen hose for stocking caps, busses followed the snowplows twenty-two miles to the farm. The guests arrived chilled, and hungry for the big noon dinner in the farm boardinghouse. Long tables, flanked by benches, were set with enamelware plates and cups, and steel knives and forks. Kitchen and dining room were one, and odors from kettles and ovens of the big ranges met them at the door.

Farm atmosphere captivated. The Fromms remained themselves, and had made no changes in farm routine. Their only concession to metropolitan life was a bar which could serve any drink called for. A meal or a lunch was available at any hour, and Mamie Fromm, aided by a staff of girls from the neighborhood, acted as hostess.

The traditional pattern of a fur auction was not changed. A period for preliminary inspection is always provided for buyers to examine pelts and estimate values in order to bid by lot number. This inspection is made with care. A blemish, a faint off-tinge, or a worn spot can make the difference between an unusual pelt and a merely average one. The finest pelts are sold singly or in matched pairs, and the evaluation is a matter of the most painstaking judgment. Before the auction each buyer examines the pelts he intends to bid on and knows those pelts in detail.

Three days were allowed for inspection. Henry was in charge of the display room. A staff of 150 men carried in lots, or bundles, of pelts for the buyers' scrutiny. The long table for inspection was under a row of windows, and the company provided white coats for the visitors, a practical and thoughtful attention, since fox hairs cling to wool. The buyers examined pelts, made cryptic marks in notebooks, and watched fellow buyers to see who might be bidding in competition. The display room was a paradise for fur lovers. Seventy-five hundred pelts were heaped on tables, hung from racks, or slung from shoulders of hurrying men. New York had held larger sales of silver fox, but never had so many bright silver foxes been collected in a single room.

When visitors wandered about the grounds their identification cards were inspected by uniformed guards wearing stars, cartridge belts, and revolvers. The side-arms were a Fromm touch, an idea borrowed from the policy of insurance companies, which had never considered the north Wisconsin woods, a favorite retreat for Chicago gangsters, a safe district. Although no raid had ever been made on ranched furs, an armed escort had always accompanied the fur crop to the railroad. The boys who had built Fort Moreland had seen nothing fantastic in two armed guards accompanying each loaded sleigh to the railroad, or in extreme vigilance now. And metropolitan visitors enjoyed the aura of suggested danger.

The auction began at noon on the fourth day. This was the real test of a market on home grounds. If the sale dragged or buyers were conscious of pressure methods or seller reluctance the farm auction would be declared a failure, and one more disastrous because the Fromms had been given their chance to prove the soundness of the scheme. No amount of local color and stage setting would make buyers overlook the fact they had traveled a long way to buy silver fox and then had been denied a fair opportunity to do so.

Fur values fluctuate tremendously, and an auction provides a bargaining ground on which producers' hopes and buyers' valuations may reach a compromise. The auctioneer is a selling agent for the producer, but he is also an intermediary. Edward had assumed a dual role, and it was the first time he had ever held a hammer. His two callers, one an auditor of the company and the other its New York representative, had never stood behind an auction table. The buyers were veterans in the traditional secretive bidding of the fur trade. Each had his unique method of attracting the attention of the auctioneer without revealing his bid to a competitor. Signals were furtive, a twiddled pencil, a raised eyebrow, a momentary glance, a finger to the ear, a slight movement of a thumb, while no other muscle of the body betrayed alertness or even interest. But if Edward had stage fright as he began to cry his first auction, he did not show it. A quick wit, a quicker intuition, and an instinctive sensing of the temper of the crowd, reassured buyers that they had not made the journey in vain. He kept the auction moving and lots sold quickly. If a sale was concluded and none of the three amateurs behind the auction table knew the identity of the buyer, Edward fell back to farm methods and asked the man to introduce himself. This informality and the makeshift auction room in the girls' dormitory were unique in fur history. The Fromms did not pose as anything but farmers, and the hardened buyers liked them the better for their lack of pretensions. And this friendliness helped the sale.

Silver fox sold 15 per cent higher than it had in the previous month in New York. When one pelt was bid to $450, the highest price paid since the depression, the buyers stood and cheered. The first private fur auction established a second record; it was the first 100 per cent sale in silver fox history. Not one of the 7,500 pelts remained when the auction ended, and the average price was seventy-five dollars. Silver fox had made a recovery, and the Fromms had carried their pelts one step nearer to the consumer. Important buyers gave interviews to the press commending the quality of Fromm pelts, and the soundness of a scheme which permitted stores to select furs on the farm where the fur was actually produced. Stores were delighted to give customers this guarantee of quality. New York trade journals carried accounts of the unique sale. Buyers promised to return next year.

Almost at once the Company began preparations for a second and more ambitious auction. Since the sale had proved that buyers would travel to the source of the supply, the Fromms saw an opportunity to make Hamburg the silver fox market center of the country. The Company proposed to auction, not only its own pelts, but those of other ranchers. An organization, Federal Furs, was established, under which name the fur of other producers would be offered, and Dr. W. A. Young was engaged as marketing specialist. Dr. Young, a pioneer in the industry, had been head of the famous Booneville ranch in New York State, one of those wiped out by distemper. He was admired and respected for his progressive ideas in fox ranching.

The bigger venture of Federal Furs required larger quarters, since auctions of a silver fox center could hardly be conducted in a boardinghouse dormitory. The Company built a seventy-five thousand dollar addition to the warehouse, a two hundred-foot wing of three stories. The upper floor was devoted to display and auction rooms, and lighting was especially designed for inspection. Harry La Due, one of the three men who judge leading fur shows in America, has said this room has the finest light for appraising fur of any in the world. If light contains either red or yellow rays, even from the reflections of buildings across the street, a cast is thrown on the fur; this is a difficulty in appraising the color of fur in a city. At Hamburg the display room has a northern exposure and faces the forest. Above the wall of windows is a skylight the length of the room. A shield of louvered slats on the roof prevents the direct rays of the sun from reaching the glass and insures shadowless light beneath. To avoid shadows and smudges caused by passing clouds there are shades which can be easily manipulated with ropes. Furs can be examined without an unreal tint confusing the valuation.

The enlargement of the warehouse made other changes possible. Rooms were built for storage of the ginseng stock pile, now the harvest of six years and promising to be that of many more. Slaughtering room and feedroom were rebuilt to meet the demands of larger herds, and refrigerating rooms and added trackage were provided to handle greater quantities of frozen meat. A grinder was installed with a seventy-five horsepower motor. It was the hog used in sawmills to tear slabs into sawdust, and it could grind frozen quarters of meat without preliminary sawing, handling fifty horses in two hours and crushing bones with no danger of splinters. (Only horses' molars defied the machine.) With these alterations the feedroom reached its final state of adaptation to the peculiar needs of a farm which feeds more fur-bearing animals than any in the world.

Including the Thiensville unit, the Fromm farms use 113,000 pounds of food each day.

Other improvements were made. A gatehouse was built, at which auction visitors presented identification cards. The boardinghouse was enlarged, because three hundred employees had now outgrown the quarters built more than ten years before. New York buyers at the next winter auction would find more room, but steel knives and forks, enamelware dishes, and oilcloth would still be on the tables. In the kitchen, however, every electrical contrivance in the form of bread mixers, cake mixers and whipping gadgets would facilitate the work of cooks.

Construction work was finished before the fall ginseng rush when the company would dig its first big harvest in several years. Root rot had almost closed in on the Fromms. It had been as constant as distemper, and for no reason anyone could discover the intensity of its attack was variable. Losses might run anywhere from 40 to 90 per cent. In the previous year loss had been so great that the harvest had been scarcely worth digging. Arthur had been experimenting with a formaldehyde solution to kill disease spores. This was not a new method in horticulture, but the strength of the solution was tricky. It must be strong enough to kill disease spores in the outer coating of ginseng seed but not strong enough to destroy fertility, and Arthur was not certain that he had perfected the solution. He believed he had the problem solved, but until his experimental garden had safely passed the third year of growing he could not be sure, and he wanted to be so before a large acreage was planted with treated seeds. The Company, however, considered the formula the lesser gamble. If it worked, it meant success. If it did not, they were no worse off than they had been with root rot. So treated seeds were used in the 1935 planting, and the seedlings had gone through the first of the three summers necessary for proof.

Two years of suspense seemed minor compared to other ginseng problems. The Company's assumption that ten years might elapse before a ginseng market would be re-established in China now seemed the wildest optimism. For four years the Japanese had been seizing territory in North China, and open conflict appeared certain. No one dared to guess how long it would be before the price recovered. But neither blight nor a war in China could induce the Company "to abandon ginseng lightly."

Costs, however, must be cut down. Production of a root for which there was, and might be for years, no market, was costing fifty thousand dollars annually, and every year brought new ginseng grief. If blight caught the garden the harvest was scanty. This year's crop, which had miraculously escaped blight, presented a washing problem. Washing root had always been the greatest handicap; it slowed digging, for digging teams must wait on washing. Different ideas had been tried, and finally the splash method was used, since this did not remove all the soil, and the Chinese preferred a light brown root. The root was splashed in a large metal basket which two men lifted and dropped in the stream. It was backbreaking work, and slow. A dozen men could wash only five thousand pounds a day, and washing the coming harvest of more than a hundred thousand pounds might slow digging dangerously close to frost. Also the root must be out of the drying room before this was needed for the crop of sixteen thousand silver fox pelts; ginseng and foxes were dovetailing in an uncomfortably close schedule. Edward said some way must be found to speed washing.

Herbert Kleinschmidt, ginseng straw boss, and Walter Fromm, arrived at the blacksmith shop the next morning with the same idea. A large wire-mesh cylinder, belt driven, should wash root as clothes are washed. The splash method could be achieved by building in shelves the full length of the cylinder and, as the cylinder revolved, the root would fall from a shelf to the water below and eventually be carried up on another shelf for another splash. The number of splashes would be determined by the length of time required for root to travel from the entry hopper to the exit of the cylinder. The forward movement of the root could be effected by the screw method. Cleats, fastened to the shelves and set at an angle, would thrust the root forward, and the pitch could be altered to hasten or delay the process should the preference in color change.

Walter and Herbert worked two weeks to build the washer, and were so sure it would work that they held up digging until the machine was completed. After that the machine *had* to work; if it didn't, there would be no time to dig root and splash-wash in the stream. Suspense and excitement were high the morning the washer was taken from the blacksmith shop. In the trial run the builders found they had succeeded better than they hoped. Three men could wash six thousand pounds of green root in an hour, thus ending the greatest bottleneck in ginseng culture.

In early January preparations were complete for the 1937 winter auction, to be held February 15 after a preliminary week for examination of almost twenty thousand silver fox pelts. Practically every buyer of importance in the country had announced his intention of attending, and one hundred and fifty thousand dollars worth of skins had made Hamburg the leading silver fox market of the country. The offering was made up of Fromm pelts and those of three hundred other ranchers.

The idea of a selling organization already had proved successful. Other breeders had been quick to see its advantages. Federal Furs' sales commission was 2½ per cent, while the cooperative auction held annually in New York by the fox breeders' associations charged 6 per cent. At Hamburg furs would be handled, graded, and valued by experts in silver fox. All commission money would be spent in national advertising to promote the silver fox, and this would benefit other ranchers as well as the Fromms. But the greatest advantage lay in the fact that leading buyers of the country would come to Hamburg prepared to buy their year's requirements. Federal Furs had unified silver fox interests.

The American National Fur Breeders' Association did not approve, for it, too, had become a selling agent. The deflection of three hundred members would reduce the Association's offerings in the New York sale, and other members were threatening to make the change. Now the Fromms' controversy with the Association was no longer on pedigree or color, but on methods of merchandising. And the Company, with a program for national advertising, spectacular auction and display quarters, large refrigerating rooms, an expert staff for grading and appraising, their first farm auction a proved success, a group of eager and important buyers, and an auctioneer who had already won his spurs, appeared to have the best of the argument.

The Fromms' own crop of fur was the largest as yet in their history. Ranges had held sixteen thousand pelters, and Fromm foxes were brighter than ever with a larger percentage of full silvers, though this percentage was not as large as had been anticipated because of a big loss from distemper. The 1936 epidemic had preyed on the full silvers.

In the pelting season the Company had achieved its ambition of pelting two thousand foxes each day. The assembly line system had finally been perfected, and bottlenecks which piled carcasses had been eliminated. Pelting was done in a series of small operations, each man performing only one task. One slit the skin on front legs from foot to elbow, a second slit the hind legs to vent and around. The foxes were then carried to a table four feet wide, and twenty feet long, covered with gunny sacks to absorb blood and moisture and protect the fur. Here hind legs were skinned out to flanks, toes cut out either with pruning shears or knives, and the tail skinned out almost to the end. At the second table noses were cut as far as the eyes, and the fox was hung on a swiveled chain from the ceiling. Next the head and neck were skinned to the shoulders and the fox went to the wrapping crew, because the pelt must not be blood-stained. A cloth was wrapped around the head and fastened with a rubber band and the fox went on to the back skinners, who ripped out the rest of the tail, stripped bodies and front legs, and cut out the front toes. The pelt was then ready for inspection. If there was damage it was easy to know in which operation it had occurred. Then records were taken from tattoo marks in the ears, the medallion carrying the number of the fox attached to the nose and the pelt went to the final dressing. This was done with a hardwood or bone scraper. The pelt was then fitted on a stretcher board and placed on a rack for drying. After drying, pelts are examined, graded, appraised, and put in lots, or bundles. Each lot contains pelts of as nearly the same quality in fur and color as possible. At this time comes the excitement of selecting the best pelt in the collection.

Every auction had a best pelt, first selected by graders and talked of by buyers; its purchase was an honor. The Fromms studied all their finer furs and agreed that fox Number 2989 was the most perfect pelt they had ever produced. In life its name had been Silver Celebrator I, and it had twenty-eight generations of known ancestors, but 2989 became its title as fur experts grew lyrical over its beauty. It was a large pelt without a blemish, silky and deep in fur, a bright silver with a distinctive black cross on the shoulder. Word of it traveled to New York. This was the perfect silver fox, one of those miracles of nature and of breeding. Fox 2989 became the highlight of the coming auction. Men talked of it as people had once talked of the Hope diamond. No one knew what its price would be, but fur men determined to possess it.

Less than a month before the sale the Company's lawyer, Charles F. Smith of Wausaw, discovered an 1858 state law that imposed a tax on the gross sales of any auction held outside a city, which sold other than a farmer's own property and products. The measure had been justified at the time. The business of early merchants had been hurt by itinerant auctioneers who disposed of distress goods in rural communities. After the law stopped the practice it was forgotten, but it was still applicable to the Company if the Fromms auctioned the fur of others. Since the act would, in effect, kill a project of benefit to fur ranchers, it ought to be changed. The greatest obstacle was lack of time. The inspection of pelts would begin February 8, only two weeks away, and buyers would be on their way to Hamburg before that.

State legislators agreed that the matter was important. It had not been the purpose of the law to interfere with the sale of home-grown products, but the Fromms could not proceed with a hundred and fifty thousand dollar auction in the face of this tax threat. A statute was introduced in the legislature, and a hearing set for January 28. By speedy enactment and immediate signature of the governor, the law could be repealed in time. The question appeared to be so simple a matter the Company did not consider it necessary even to warn buyers that the big auction of 1937 was threatened. Edward would go to Madison with counsel for the Company. The difficulty was as good as settled.

Then the American National Fur Breeders' Association heard of the law and the proposed legislation. It, too, engaged counsel and prepared to oppose the new measure. Suddenly the correction of an out-dated law had become a fight. The 1937 auction, the establishment of a world center in silver foxes, and company prestige hung in the balance.

Chapter Twenty-one

A FIGHT WOULD MEAN DELAY, AND DELAY WOULD BE
as crippling as defeat. Time was the opposition's strong-
est weapon, but the Company won an initial victory
when the senate and assembly agreed to sit as a committee of the whole to hear the arguments for and
against a bill to rescind the out-dated law. Edward
Fromm, Harry La Due, Dr. Green, the Chairman of
Hamburg township, fur ranchers, and lawyers hurried
to Madison and appeared before the legislature to present their case. Charles F. Smith, the first speaker,
explained the miscarriage of the true intent of the old
act, and Edward arose to make the main plea.

With his deep conviction that the new bill was just
he did not expect stage fright, but as he looked over
the assemblage in the cold and formal setting of a legislative hall, his voice failed him. This had never happened before. He tried a second time and when no
words came he was truly frightened. The whole legislative body of the state was gathered to hear him, he bore
the major responsibility — and he could not speak. Slowly
he poured a glass of water, took a sip, and visibly pulled

himself together. Then the dam broke. Words flowed more and more smoothly as he explained how the Company had found New York auction methods unsatisfactory and how it wished to promote both fur ranching and marketing. Disposal of fur on a Wisconsin farm in the center of their important industry would permit small producers to be present, sense the market trend, and protect their offerings. A rancher unable to attend a sale in New York often found himself "sold out." Market trends and prices could be determined only in an auction, and men who had spent a year producing pelts had a right to dispose of them under the most favorable circumstances. When Edward finished it was evident he had impressed the lawmakers.

Harry La Due, whose life has been devoted to the promotion of better fur and fur ranching, imparted the lyrical touch. "Fur farming, to me, is the most satisfying, interesting, thrilling occupation of man," he said. "I've seen it develop from a secretive, backwoods, private enterprise to a world-wide, very definite part of animal husbandry. I remember the early pioneers, the fabulous prices for breeding stock, the groping for knowledge, the bitter disappointments, the splendid achievements, the trials and tribulations of those pioneers. I've seen the fur trade turn up its nose and then beg for their offerings. A law should not put further obstacles in the way of such men."

Dr. Green argued for the rights of man, contending that a farmer, whether of wheat, corn, or fur, should be permitted to sell his products within his own state if he desired. A fur auction was the traditional method of marketing pelts, and it should not be denied to citizens of the state.

The Association presented claims that the farm auction was aimed at the interests of the Association and would have a disruptive effect on the entire industry; that the bill was being railroaded for the benefit of a large, wealthy producer. They carried the fight from the joint hearing to an assembly committee room. This delay threatened defeat, and the Fromm wired buyers to postpone departure. They did so with reluctance, but a fruitless journey to a non-existent sale was more than mere cancellation.

The opposition was strong in the committee room but the bill was reported favorably and passed the house by sixty-nine to twelve. It went at once to the senate, which suspended its rules and passed it twenty-two to six. As a legislative correspondent reported to his paper, neither branch "saw much danger in a bill which would bring business to Wisconsin." Governor Philip La Follette signed it, and the ancient act imposing a 20 per cent tax was dead three days before the opening of inspection week in the Fromm display room.

Word was telegraphed to waiting buyers and they flocked to Hamburg, almost as jubilant over the victory as the Fromms. But when they arrived they did not talk of legal complications. They talked only of fox 2989. Everyone wanted to see the pelt, and it was brought many times to the table beneath the long skylight in the new display room. Seasoned buyers would stand in silence, finding no words with which to appreciate a color, so clear and so unbelievably lovely, revealed in its true beauty. The pure light disclosed the illusive shading, the luster, the sparkle, the pure magic, of the bright silver. "That display room was worth building just to show such a skin," Henry said.

Men talked of nothing else in the week of pre-showing. Who would buy it? What price would it bring? Not until midafternoon of the second day of the auction did "2989" appear on the board above the auctioneer. Buyers looked at the number. Not a man moved a muscle but tension filled the air, tension that had weight and bulk. "I could feel it from the stand," Edward said later.

The bidding started at three hundred dollars and went quickly to a thousand. Now only the serious contenders were in competition and as bids went up by hundred-dollar steps the field thinned. At fifteen hundred only two remained, and the real rivals were in the open. Trencher Furs of New York and Marshall Field and Company of Chicago had prepared special promotion with fox 2989 as a spearhead, and neither firm had known of the plans of the other. Neither could afford to show signs of weakness, and yet eventually one must concede victory. The "ups" came fast. Edward and the callers turned from one bidder to the other. Trencher Furs offered $2,000, as much as anyone had believed the pelt would bring, but George Metheral of Marshall Field and Company signalled $2,100. Now no one knew where the price might go, but the New York bidder did not raise his head. Edward waited a moment, then brought down the hammer. Fox 2989 had been sold.

Only once before had a higher price been paid for any fox. In the early years of the industry a black fox had brought $2,627 in London, but no one had expected to see such a sum approached again. The thrilling climax to the long suspense of 2989 brought spectators to their feet with cheers. In the excitement the auction was adjourned until evening. Buyers made speeches. Men discussed the bidding as a race is rerun.

No other highlight could approach that of 2989, not even the million-dollar mark in sales that was reached at noon of the third day. When the auction ended, more than a million and a half dollars' worth of silver fox had been sold. Fromm Furs brought 10 per cent more than New York prices. Federal Furs, the consigned pelts, more ordinary in quality, sold 5 per cent above New York prices.

Pelt 2989 went on to triumph. Its picture stretched from top to bottom in full-page advertising in Chicago newspapers. The drama of its purchase made this arresting advertising copy: "'Have you seen 2989?' they asked each other, up in the north woods of Wisconsin where Fromm Brothers hold their famous sales. Word sped that this number marked a pelt like nothing ever seen before. A skin so large, so deep and bright with silver that experienced buyers grew lyrical as a debutante at sight of it. . . . Last week, in the tense silence of Fromm's auction, Marshall Field and Company bought the miracle pelt — and made fur history. The price, $2,100, was the highest that a full silver was ever known to bring. Bidding adjourned. Excited speeches were made by buyers not easily excited." Elsewhere the advertisement considered the possible purchaser of the pelt: "We don't know who is going to wear 2989, but we know some things about her. We know she is quick to beauty. She'll see at once that this glorious fur with its thick, soft mane, its deeply marked black cross, its brave bright silver, is a king among foxes. She'll know that the quiet joy of its possession will be hyacinths to her soul. She may be blonde against its blue black, or dark in harmony with it, but she'll carry her head like a princess."

2989, most talked of pelt in America, was displayed

in a glass case in the same fur salon where, twenty-four years earlier, Henry Fromm had asked a puzzled saleswoman to show him a silver fox, because he had never seen one. Henry, when confronted with this as a coincidence, did not find it startling. "We've always known we were going to raise good silver foxes," he said.

Auction successes of the next two years, when the Company held three sales annually, autumn, midwinter, and spring, provided some defense against the tremendous losses from distemper. So long as the Fromms had foxes to sell and prices were good, they could survive, even though sale figures made the mortality rate the more deplorable. Federal Furs, too, was successful. At each auction more ranchers consigned their products to the organization.

Visiting buyers enjoyed the Wisconsin auction and spoke of the farm at Hamburg as "Fromm's Resort." In spring and autumn sun tanning was the noon hour occupation, and when the day's inspection work was done, swimming parties went to Rib River. Baseball was played in the horse pasture, buyers teaming up against breeders. Buyers protested the umpires' rulings on fly balls and grounders, claiming unfair discrimination. Being on the heavy side and short-breathed, they were in no condition to compete with men who grew ginseng and raised silver foxes.

Jokes were carried over from one auction to another. At the sales, where Henry always acted as one of the "callers," everyone wanted to sit in his section. Henry's head was bald and in fly season he went armed with a swatter. Every time a fly approached him he raised the swatter, and he also raised the swatter when he caught a bid. Even Henry wasn't always sure whether it was a bid or a fly. Buyers said flies were costing them $2.50, but no one would have been willing to miss watching Henry's intensive warfare against flies.

The Company also had its joke with the trade, one of serious intent, but carried off with good humor. The medallion sealed to the nose of a Fromm pelt had not proved a completely successful identification of a Fromm fox; the nose, with its medallion, could be cut off and sewed on another skin, and this was frequently done. When Fromm pelts were used in garments the medallion was a by-product, and could be attached to scarfs of the sick cat variety, thus injuring the Fromm reputation. The Company purchased a number of these scarfs from stores, selected the poorest, and made a surprise offering at an auction. The rack was brought in with ceremony. Edward's extravagant praise of the quality and his description of the years of painstaking breeding necessary to produce such magnificent specimens was almost drowned in laughter, but it was a warning that if this practice did not cease the Company would take other measures.

Mutations in silver foxes had appeared in herds in the middle twenties. Breeders did not call them mutations but "freaks," forgetting that less than twenty years earlier the silver fox had been called a freak. Even as late as 1912 leading geneticists had not fully determined that the silver coat color was a recessive trait which followed the Mendelian law of the recessive. In the meantime a few practical breeders who had no knowledge of genetics but a remarkable memory for pedigrees, had developed an uncanny ability to select animals that would "nick," as fur men call it, to produce superior offspring. Judgments were instinctive; but somehow such men — and John Fromm was one of them — could recognize animals with blood lines that could be carried to a high state of perfection. A good breeder cannot always state his reasons, but he knows intuitively the difference between those animals capable of heading an exceptional strain and those with definite limitations.

The silver fox, however, had become so standard that men forgot it was originally a rare color phase, and new colors or variations appearing in herds were regarded with suspicion. Breeders' associations, in an effort to establish the quality fox, ruled that members must destroy these freak foxes. A litter of pearl foxes, which appeared on a ranch in Minnesota in the middle twenties, was destroyed. The Canadian National Association did not permit a freak fox to be kept on the same ranch with the standard, and obviously no fur farmer could afford to maintain a special ranch for a few foxes of a strange new color.

After the depression, registration in the studbook formerly so important in both Canada and the United States, was forgotten, and line breeding was not so general. Offcolor silver foxes began to appear, and in 1937 a rancher sent a number of strange pelts to a Fromm auction. The skins were not black and silver, but a blue shade resembling platinum. No one knew how to list or grade them. They were offered in one lot and sold. Afterward the buyer asked for more; customers had liked them. None existed. The rancher had culled every fox of this color, parents and offspring, from his herd.

In the thirties this was frequently the fate of mutations. Breeders, unaware of their value, pelted themselves out of good fortune, but it became known that silvers were capable of producing strange new variations. White-faced foxes appeared in the heard of A. K. McNeill, a rancher in Canada. Some had white patches on the paws, and even a median line on the chest. At the time no one realized there were many varieties of the white-marked fox. Mr. McNeill liked the white faces, thought their silver guard hairs were brighter than those of the standard, and he bred them. When the Association ordered these freak foxes culled, he resigned rather than do so. Insistence on his right to raise variations founded the white-marked mutation.

The controversy between Mr. McNeill and the Association reminded Henry of a female the Fromms owned in 1917. She had a white patch on a paw and her pups had white patches, but Henry had noticed that her pups were brighter than those of others, and the black hairs had a greater luster. He was interested in the phenomenon, but the female and her pups were culled. The rigorous selective breeding practiced by the Fromms was hard on oddities. They were as stern with whims of nature as they were with veteran breeders who had carried the strain as far as possible. Although other ranches considered a 10 per cent replacement adequate for improvement, the Fromms replaced 35 per cent, and have replaced as high as 55 per cent in their determination to produce brighter, larger foxes of uniform quality. A company following so costly a procedure would not temporize with any fox family with a tendency to depart from the type which it was seeking. This is undoubtedly one of the reasons the country's largest herd of silvers has never produced mutations.

The platinum, the first mutation in silver foxes to be marketed, appeared in Norway, and its possibilities were recognized early. The color variation was a dominant trait, since a mating between platinum and silver produced litters in which half the pups were platinum. Olmar Brager-Larsen, a Norwegian fox breeder, espoused the cause of platinums. His work in promotion undoubtedly smoothed the way for the mutations in both foxes and mink which appeared later, just as the Fromms' crusade for the lighter scintillating silvers had smoothed the way for platinums. The Fromms were the first to depart from the accepted and traditional darker furs, made the public conscious of the attractiveness of lighter fur, and pioneered color, which is so important in the furs of today.

America was ready to receive the platinum with approval when in 1939 Brager-Larsen brought 116 skins of this rare fur. Custom litigation arising from this importation was not settled until February, 1947, when a federal court ruled that duty had been illegally collected by the United States. The decision held "imported platinum skins are from foxes which are mutations of the silver fox" and were not in existence at the time of the passage of the Tariff Act of 1930 but came into being in a litter of silver foxes "by a fortuitous biological change known as a mutation."

In the late thirties fur farming took on new and absorbing aspects. Mink ranching was not only firmly established but was going forward rapidly. The platinum and white-faced mutations of silver foxes were being talked about. Blue fox ranching had also become an important branch of the industry. Naturally the Fromms were aware of, and interested in, all these possibilities, but at the time they were engrossed by other problems. Distemper mortalities were 40 per cent in 1937. The February, 1938, auction offered thirty-three thousand pelts. Members of Federal Furs had increased. The price of silver fox, while not as high as in 1937, was still good. Hamburg was an established and important market, and the many details of a merchandising operation were now added to those of raising foxes, fighting distemper, and growing ginseng. The epidemic on the Bohl farm followed almost on the heels of the February auction, but the spring fur sale was held as usual.

In May, when the main herd was threatened with a wipe out by distemper, the Fromms determined to use the modified virus of ferret origin. By midsummer the Company found itself delivered of its greatest tribulation. Not only was the menace of distemper ended for that year but for all the years to come. Fromm foxes had proved this beyond doubt, and other fur ranchers could be safe. At the September banquet given for ranchers who sold through Federal Furs, Dr. Green told the exciting news that their most feared enemy had been defeated. "At a date not far in the future, ranchers can laugh at distemper," he said. Vaccines for encephalitis and distemper in both mink and foxes would be available to fur farms as soon as laboratory facilities made this possible.

For the Fromms even the threat of blight was gone from the ginseng gardens. A sufficient time had elapsed to prove that Arthur's formula for seed treatment had saved ginseng culture. The Company could continue to grow root so long as it had space in the warehouse to store it. Each year one more room had been filled with boxes of fibered root, and now a great pile was yet to be sorted and fibered. It was heaped from floor to ceiling and from wall to wall.

In jewelry shops in China a single perfect root, wrapped in folds of silk, is shown a wealthy customer. Here in Hamburg was a mountain of ginseng.

Chapter Twenty-two

THIS PEACE WHICH HAD COME AT LAST TO FOX PENS
and ginseng gardens was an unusual experience for the
Company. After thirty years of driving and being driven,
it now knew that peace should not be confused with
security. In any year foxes might fall from their high
place in public estimation, and at any moment a new
killer might prey on herds.

The Company began to look around. Already Henry
and John had talked of raising mink, as so many years
before they had talked of raising foxes. Not only would
this diversify their farming, but mink had certain merits.
A short-haired fur, it could fill a different purpose from
that of the silver fox, and was so durable that even a
mink could not wear it out. It was becoming increasingly
popular, was rising in value, and production of a mink
pelt cost about seventeen dollars as against thirty dollars for a fox. Also mink ranching presented a fascinating
new problem to men who would never lose their enthusiasm for fur bearers.

There could be no thought of duplicating a wild

existence for mink. They are warriors. For weight and size, the weasel family excels in ferocity. Even battles that do not end in death ruin pelts, for teeth are sharp as needles and will perforate the skin of an adversary. So ranched mink must be housed individually. Pens are small, made entirely of wire mesh and set on posts. Apparently mink enjoy this peaceful and separate existence. A unit of mink pens gives an instantaneous impression of a contented and strangely busy little community.

John, too, had been curious about mink and in 1936 had bought a few trios. Mink, unlike foxes, are not monogamous, and matings in the wild are wholly the result of chance encounters. They are sold singly, or in trios of two females and a male. John's early purchase had not been with an idea of fur production. He merely found them a new and interesting animal.

"You can get close to a mink," he said. "He isn't timid like the fox and a keeper has a chance to watch what's going on."

In the summer of 1938 Henry said that if the Company were to have mink it should have good ones. He went on a buying trip and bought twenty dark mink of good quality, paying seventy dollars each. In the next few years the Company bought more, added hundreds, then a thousand, until in 1941, by increase and purchase it owned a herd of fifteen hundred. In 1946 the Company pelted 24,000 mink and owned 11,500 breeders; the next largest grower pelted 16,000. In seven years the Company had built the largest mink farm in the world.

In planning large-scale production, pen details were important. Henry, as housing expert for fur-bearing animals, experimented to achieve economy in keeper's time. John attended to the details of the mink's domestic life. Everything the Company had learned in years of fox ranching was valuable now in building a mink farm on an assembly line basis. Buying visits to other mink farms were object lessons for Henry. Impractical construction lost many minutes at each pen. A nest box in the center made inspection difficult, as the mink had to be driven into the box and the box lifted from the pen. Or, if the young were to be examined, the mother had to be driven from the box. The Company could not afford a fifteen-minute struggle with a determined mink, or spend hours chasing agile animals that escaped when the top gate of the pen was open.

Pens which had nest boxes outside at one end opening into pens, not in the center of the pen itself, would permit inspection, handling, and the proper care of a mink family with no necessity of lifting the top gate. The first Fromm pens were built to this design, and from time to time Henry added improvements. A metal sheet, fitted in grooves, could be dropped to shut off the nest and keep the mother in or out. The nest box had two hinged covers, the inner of netting for easy inspection of the litter, the outer of wood to serve as roof. The bottom of the box was hinged to drop down for ease in cleaning. The floor of the pen was made of netting for sanitation, and an extra layer of finer mesh prevented small kits from falling through. A metal tab on the outside of the pen indicated whether the mink was a light or heavy feeder. A rack held a card giving the breeding history of the inmate, and this record went with the mink to any pen it occupied.

Improvements have gone on through the years as John or a keeper discovered a detail that hindered assembly line methods or was a hazard to fur. When mink chewed the circular openings to wooden nest boxes these were capped with metal, for restless mink's countless trips from pen to box would wear even mink fur. Equipment was constantly discarded and remodeled. Whole batteries of pens were built to test one innovation against another. In the long room of the warehouse where pens and nest boxes are built, not by dozens and scores but by hundreds, is a great heap of inspirations which went wrong—feeding boards and pans, drinking fountains, special safety catches, top gates, and catching boxes. Henry looked at it.

"In this game, equipment must be scrapped almost before it is finished," he said. "There is always a better or more economical way to do things."

Tens of thousands of mink pens for a proving ground, endless vigilance, ingenuity, and attention to the smallest detail, have resulted in a system of housing which provides the maximum welfare for fur bearers with the minimum of labor. A feeder can care for five hundred pens. A watering cart makes the rounds twice daily, and drinking fountains are filled with a hose and so built that the mink has water at all times, yet cannot soil the supply or get wet. Water injures fur. In breeding season when extra help is needed, one keeper can manage 100 females. Each is bred two or three times during a season. Misses are costly. Four kits should be the average production for mink, although mutation mink sometimes average less since color, as well as fertility, is so important.

Pens which provided for ease and speed in catching

proved invaluable when at last a vaccine was available to build immunity against distemper. This disease travels quickly in the dense population of a mink block and has caused enormous losses, even in the early days when ranches raised only standard mink; now it holds an even greater threat to herds of mutations built up at tremendous cost. The Fromms had been lucky in mink distemper. This scourge did not strike while Fromm Laboratories were working to develop a mink vaccine, and as soon as the killed-tissue vaccine was available, it was used throughout the farm. This provides only passive immunity, and each mink must be given at least two injections annually. The enormity of such a task might justify some hesitation, but the Fromms will never lose a healthy respect for epidemics, and until the laboratory has perfected a permanent immunizing agent, the treatment crew must make its semiannual rounds. Men on this crew, unlike those working with foxes, expect to be bitten, and usually are. A mink is small, slippery, exceedingly agile, and can double back and bite the handler. Even heavy gloves do not provide complete protection, but this has not slowed up the assembly line system which makes it possible to vaccinate twenty thousand mink in three days. The crew consists of twenty-four men and two doctors, and the mink are carried to the doctors as fast as syringes can be used. More than nine thousand breeders and a twenty-four thousand kit crop are vaccinated twice a year. This means almost sixty-seven thousand injections annually.

Mink, unlike foxes, are polygamous, and this presented a new problem to the Fromms at Hamburg, although the Thiensville unit had already experimented with polygamous foxes, not a new idea in fox farming. In the early days of the industry ranchers discovered that the fox, known for its devotion to one mate, could in some instances be persuaded to be less faithful. Such a change in fox ways had obvious advantages. The blood strain of a superior male could be spread more quickly through a herd, and a valuable sire need not devote an entire year to paternal interest in one family. But the fox was not a natural roamer, and schemes had to be evolved to break down his fidelity. Some ranchers kept pairs together until the actual time of ovulation and then quickly changed the males. Describing this method in a fur trade magazine, the writer warned: "Care must be observed to remove the mate not only out of sight, but as far away as possible, so that the female will not be distressed by any awareness of him, and the polygamous male must be removed immediately after mating for fear the two animals will become accustomed to each other and the male thereafter refuse to be polygamous."

Later it was discovered that certain males accepted a polygamous existence without protest. Some fox men have argued that the fox might not have been originally monogamous, since male survivors of pairs in which the female had died or been pelted often becomes a dependable polygamous breeder. But other males, accustomed to a regular home life, insist on one mate, and the large number that do so makes the proven polygamous fox a definite asset in a herd.

Polygamous fox mating is costly in labor. The period of ovulation is short, only three days, and a female must be examined daily as this period approaches. Then mating plans may miscarry at the last minute. A male may kill a female. Or even worse, an intractable female may so intimidate a valuable polygamous male as to make him useless as a sire. The silver fox is sensitive and, if repulsed or hurt in a fight with a belligerent female, especially if he is young and inexperienced, he loses all interest in that female or any other for the remainder of the breeding season. The males, too, are seasonal breeders, and their season is short. There is always the possibility that they will be unavailable before all the females have reached the period of ovulation, thus rendering potential fox mothers non-producers for a year. Polygamous fox mating has its peculiar problems, but the Thiensville unit believed the advantages were worth the extra labor.

In either system infertile matings are a constant and unavoidable loss. In young foxes, "misses" run anywhere from 15 to 35 per cent, and in older foxes at the peak of productiveness they are 6 per cent. Any number of factors will increase this. Excitement during the breeding or whelping seasons registers in census figures. Diet is of great importance. Overfed foxes will not breed, nor will the undernourished. Vitamin deficiency lowers productiveness, as the Fromms discovered in the early thirties when it accounted for 40 per cent infertile matings among young foxes. This field is not yet fully explored.

Nor is the effect of hormones fully understood. At Thiensville Johnnie Fromm, the son of Arthur, and Loyal Wells, head breeder, with the aid of a professor from the University of Wisconsin carried on an experiment to induce two breeding seasons each year. They had imagined the females would present the greatest difficulty, and when they not only induced a second breeding season with hormones, but were able after considerable research to adjust the hormone dosage to bring about a normal ovulation, they were jubiliant. Herd production could be doubled, or at least so they believed until they attacked the problem of the male breeding season. They expected some trouble in making this simultaneous with that of the female but, having conquered one problem, were convinced they could solve the second. Instead they discovered hormones had no effect on the male, and the experiment was temporarily abandoned.

"But I'm sure we'll be able to do something with hormones yet," Johnnie said. "Science is making new discoveries every day, and our next experiment may be successful."

The unpredictable nature of the male silver fox defeated Thiensville in another instance. A superior and polygamous male was purchased, and to encourage his tractability and self-assurance, keepers made a pet of him. He was given raw eggs and oranges when other foxes ate only cereal and horse meat, and his house was in the center of a private estate. Because he was a beautiful fox and a valuable animal he received a great deal of attention, learned to take eggs from the hands of keepers and to expect each visitor to arrive bearing gifts. He began to like people better than he liked foxes, and, perhaps, by some queer fox reasoning, decided to be the only fox in the world. For no matter how glamorous or how eager was the female, he disdained all advances, and this complete lack of interest continued through the years. Not only did he give up his polygamous habits, but he refused to be even monogamous. A thousand dollars' worth of fox lives in comfort, eats eggs, and carries on his neurotic ambition. He is happy, and so beautiful that no one can bear to pelt him.

At Hamburg foxes had always lived in pairs. Henry and John have never changed their opinion that foxes are more contented in family life. And a year's food and shelter costs less than the extra labor involved in polygamous mating. When grading is completed and pelters have been selected, the new pairs are placed in breeding pens. Occasionally foxes do not instantly approve of John's choice of their mate, and pairs bicker, but the keepers' reasoning is pragmatic.

"The only way those foxes can get a divorce is to get out of the pen," one said. "They may not care about each other now. But one good fight will clear the air."

Although at Hamburg the Fromms had never been interested in the experiment of polygamous fox mating, they could not change the established habits of the mink, and keepers had to learn to handle polygamous breeders. This is not so difficult with mink as with foxes, however, for the mink's period of heat is longer. Its duration is not definitely known, but both males and females announce its arrival with clucking sounds. The warlike nature of the mink presents a hazard. The pair must be watched constantly, cannot be housed together, and must be separated immediately after mating. Vicious fights occur between the sexes. A successful mating is not always possible, and pairs must be introduced with caution. A hostile female can destroy all mating instinct in a young male for the remainder of his life, and this is a real disaster in mutation breeding when blood strains have been scientifically crossed and recrossed in a long experiment to produce a certain type of animal. A young mink so ruined might be the precious one in sixteen, product of years of breeding and alone possessing the traits essential for a new mutation.

Even in strains which are established, infertile matings cut the totals of fine stock, and keepers are jealous of their records of increase. No one likes to see too many zeros on the charts when the first rough census is taken a week after whelping. The exact census is recorded when the kits are about a month old and can be handled and accurately counted. If the increase averages more than four kits, the keeper is a happy man.

Mink are good mothers. And busy mothers. One wonders how the wild mink manages to care for a family. The ranch mother, with food delivered twice daily, is completely occupied with nursing the litter, carrying supplementary meals to youngsters in the nest box, dragging babies to the pen for naps in the sun or, on a warm day, moving them to the shade under the ramp, whisking them to the safety of the nest box at first sight of a stranger, and bringing them forth again when the danger is over. Transportation is by the nape-of-the-neck method, and nature grew a patch of heavier skin to stand this wear and tear. A kit even half-grown and almost as large as the mother will go limp and let itself be dragged. The speed with which a mother can remove three to ten babies from sight is startling. When the youngsters are safely hidden she comes out to scold the intruder, and a long aisle of pens will be filled with indignant females chattering about the thoughtlessness and ill-manners of anyone who thus disturbs a community nursery.

Mink meals must be served promptly. Breakfast is

never later than six-thirty, for fear hungry kits will begin to eat each other. When litters are too large for one mother to nurse properly, keepers distribute the excess among mothers with smaller families. The question of adoption must be left to the mink.

"We lay the kit on the ramp at her door," a keeper said. "If she comes out and drags it in, that kit has found a home. If she leaves it outside, it's no soap, and we hunt another home. Mink have minds of their own."

Kits are weaned when eight weeks old, and pelters are sent to the furring pens. This is the final grading time although checking for pelters and for breeders goes on constantly. Long before this, John Fromm has decided whether a series of matings has served its purpose in the general breeding program, and what new matings will further establish the color and quality the Company is seeking. Now the suitability of a mink as a breeder must be finally determined. Its genetic history is significant, but the animal must be carefully examined in a wire catching cage to make sure it has possibilities. The grading of live animals is different from the grading of a pelt, when the grader sees the finished job. In live animals the grader must be able to recognize potentialities, and one who can do so is an instinctive fur breeder. This final appraisal is the purpose of John's last round when he moves from pen to pen, studies the card histories, examines mink, and then, his decision made, pencils a blue cross on the cards of the fall pelters. While this examination is going on mink families romp happily inside the pens, quite unconscious of the momentousness of the occasion. Someone said there was a certain Jehovah-like omnipotence in John's role.

"I never thought of it that way," John said. "It's a good thing no one has the right to decide in this fashion about us humans."

Feeding many thousands of mink and foxes is a huge daily task. Each block of mink and fox pens has its own horse-drawn food cart. The horses, like the old milk wagon steeds, know their routes and stop and start without orders. The mink and foxes know their horses, and become upset and nervous if a new horse takes the route. Some of the fox men believe that foxes do not like to be served by gray horses and that this may be a matter of racial memories. Other feeders point out that Fromm horses are usually bay and the foxes are accustomed to this color. No one has gone into the question of the possible color blindness of the fox, although the Fromms believe that even bright colors disturb the animals, and the feeders wear only gray and tan. The fox food cart is more elaborate than one for mink for it must carry two sets of scales, two men and a huge pile of sterilized food pans. Fox food is weighed and the pans of the previous day are picked up for sterilizing. Two feeders can care for four hundred pens. The mink food cart is smaller and has a jaunty air. It has only to carry the food and the one keeper who cares for five hundred pens. Mink feeding pans are fixed equipment, and the feeder has to be agile when he opens the top gate to ladle in the daily ration. A mink is quick and doesn't hesitate to bite the hand that feeds him.

"If mink had rubber teeth they'd be great little pets," a keeper said. "But you can't help liking 'em."

The feeding hour gives the man an opportunity to check on the health and general welfare of each of his charges. This is especially important in the fox units where pens, forty by fifty feet, spread over a greater area, and the supper hour may be the keeper's only visit that day. Keepers note foxes' appetites and demeanor. If uneaten food remains, the fox may be sick, or the diet should be changed. The fox's address, his pen number, is recorded for an early morning visit. Many addresses in the same neighborhood are alarming.

The appetite of each charge is of deep concern to a keeper. Nursing mink mothers, especially, must be watched. It seems incredible such small creatures can supply proper nourishment for such rapacious broods, but they make up in quality for quantity. Mink milk is highly concentrated. At the first sign of a lagging appetite keepers order special meals, such as liver. No one on a fur farm can comfortably conclude that animals which are hungry will eat anything. They must eat to grow and to make fur, and fussy eaters must be placated. The fur bearers are the real producers.

Housekeeping details at Hamburg are handled by Henry Czech, straw boss of the feed room, and like most of the other straw bosses, he has been with the Company for a quarter of a century. In that time these men have met all the crises which could arise. Henry Czech conducts his department on an assembly line basis, but with the flexibility of a diet kitchen. Reports from keepers list nursing mothers requiring augmented meals, litters weaned, mothers returned to a standard diet, "blank meals" for non-producers, and special foods for fussy or sick animals, for in so large a population there inevitably is some illness. Henry and his crew have the tubs of food ready when the carts form in a long line, drive up to the platform, take their loads, and start through the forest to the pens. Twice a day this enormous quantity of food goes through Henry's kitchen. When the last cart has started forth, the clangor of the huge hog and big mixer is stilled and the feed room is sterilized and polished. The same routine goes on at Thiensville.

A food strike on the part of even a small number of fur bearers can involve all departments which handle their rations. Once when keepers noticed mink were not finishing meals their complaint was fully as indignant as that of the mink. Unthrifty animals would reflect on them.

"The mink don't like their meals and the keepers don't like them either," the spokesman said.

Slaughterers, refrigerator crew, feedroom staff, John, and Edward held a conference. All knew the food was not spoiled or contaminated, but no one can argue with a mink. Their conclusion was that somehow the meals had changed, and for the worse. Henry Czech suggested a different formula. More water would insure a thorough mixing and greater uniformity. Slaughterers thought that if the shoulders and hindquarters were slit the horse meat would chill more quickly. The refrigerator crew reported that meat should be hurried to the freezing room, but too many trips to zero temperatures in the summer when the crew was hot and perspiring caused colds, and an extra man must be added for this service. All of these things were done, the mink sent in a favorable report, and both mink and keepers were happy.

In the lull following the defeat of distemper the Company began another experiment with fur-bearing animals. Blue fox fur ranching had been carried on for years. This fox, a color phase of the white arctic fox, offered both advantages and problems. Very prolific, with even eighteen pups in a litter, it cost less to feed than the silver, could be housed in smaller quarters, and was the only long-haired fur except the platinum that was blue. But it was small and coarse-furred and had a woolly undercoat which matted and looked shabby with wear. It was not a fine aristocratic animal, as is the silver. The Alaskan blue fox had always been in disrepute. At auctions Sampsons had sometimes been sold as Alaskan blues because a lack of guard hair was a similar characteristic. The Greenland strain, however, was a better fox, a true blue, and had some silver. The Company believed that by selective breeding this Greenland strain could be given size and a silver sheen, the blue tone could be deepened, and the undercoat improved. Blue foxes respond to selective breeding more quickly than silvers, and a change in color can be effected in a few generations. Also the blood strain very quickly becomes either better or worse and replacements must be heavy.

The Company bought fifty foxes of the Greenland strain, paying $7,500 for them. They chose animals with silver well down on the legs. The morning the foxes were uncrated each man in the inspection group was bitten. No one escaped — Edward, John, Walter, Henry, Arthur's son Johnnie, or the keepers. All had picked up countless foxes, but the two-hand hold effective with silvers was no defense against the cattiness of blues, which were such contortionists they could double back and bite the handler.

Keepers did not like them. Men accustomed to the reserve of silvers found these newcomers brazen. Blues will stand close to the netting and stare back, even at strangers. They yap at keepers, their summer coats are particularly untidy, they are addicted to worms, mothers insist on dragging their young about the pen, and treatment crews dread their days in the blue fox unit. No one gets through without at least one bite.

Furthermore blue foxes are polygamous. This was a problem at Hamburg, where foxes had always lived in pairs. Thiensville, experienced in polygamous breeding, did not consider it too great a defect. Hamburg tried to adjust itself to blue fox habits, had only a three-pup average increase, and then decided the blue fox would have to adapt itself to the Fromms. No one had ever attempted to raise blue foxes monogamously but the Fromms did, and succeeded. They increased the pup average to five and a half, and had contented foxes. Thienville's increase with polygamous breeding was six, but Hamburg refused to struggle for that last half-pup. Blue fox mothers became accustomed to the continuous presence of the sire and appeared to enjoy his company. Eventually there was no more bickering in the blue fox pens than among the silvers.

Wholly from an academic interest, the Company proved silver and blue foxes could be crossed, although the two have an entirely different chromosome make-up. The blue has fifty-two chromosomes, the silver thirty-four, and the genetic pattern of the mating is similar to that which produces the mule. It had been believed that the two would not produce, but silvers and blues kept together from puppyhood paired successfully. Offspring of the crossing have forty-three chromosomes and are as brazen as blues and as sensitive to disease as silvers.

The Company is now the largest producer of blue foxes in this country, but its significant accomplishment is the startling change it has achieved in less than eight years. Vitamins and proper feeding have doubled the size of the blue fox. Formerly six skins were required for a jacket and now four skins are ample. Silver, color, and texture were improved by selective breeding. Instead of scanty silver hairs on the legs, the entire pelt carries a silvery sheen. The fur is thicker and softer. The undercoat is less woolly. The color is now a lovely shade which can only be described as tawny blue, because there is no term for a hue that has such life and interest. The results of the Company's fifteen years of work astonished Harry La Due.

"What you fellows have done to improve blue foxes is a contribution to fox farming," he said to Henry. "You've proved what ranching can do for fur."

Henry smiled with pleasure, thought a moment and then said, "Our blue fox is a lot different from the one we started with. Now it's beautiful fur, but we're going to make it even better."

The 1938 furring range held more than thirty thousand silver foxes. This was approaching the magnitude of early dreams, and no epidemic would stalk the ranges. In one year the crop had increased by ten thousand pelters. These were brighter than ever, and must be harvested in the short period when the fur is prime. Pelts left too long on the backs of foxes will go off in color, or the fur becomes overgrown. Weather also affects coats. Rain at the last moment will discolor fur and make it rough, or even curly. Even the range had not settled the menace of sunlight to the fragile color for, after leaves fall, foxes like to loll in the sunshine of the last warm days. Priming fox coats is a tricky problem in itself and must be a simultaneous process for both fur and leather. Blue, or unprime, leather does not tan well, and only when the leather is gray or almost white is the undercoat at its best. This synchronous conditioning of both guard hairs and leather is achieved by proper feeding, which must be adjusted to various ages. These are kept on separate ranges, the classifications being youngest pups, older pups, and adult foxes. Older foxes cannot be given too much meat early in the range season. They have body size, and heavy meals go into fur production. Their guard hairs would reach the peak in color and sheen before the leather was gray and the undercoat fully developed, and this fine overcoat would deteriorate in color and quality while the leather was reaching condition. To bring out all the necessary qualities at one time, adult foxes are held back. Pups can be rushed with heavy meals, as they are still building body, and the meat goes into bone structure and muscle. They will reach the peak of fur and leather at the same time if fed a highly nutritious diet. The younger pups are separated and pelted last, after two or three weeks more growing time.

These problems in nutrition and separation by ages are factors which demand that feeding and ranging shall always be flexible. Perfection in fox coats will never adapt itself completely to the assembly line technique.

The Hamburg midwinter auction offered forty thousand silver fox pelts. Not only was the Company's herd larger, but membership in Federal Furs had increased, and in a year when both producers and buyers were disturbed and unsure. The price of silvers was not stable. Despite the tariff, Norway had flooded the market with silver foxes, and no one knew whether the price would be further weakened by so large an importation. Uncertainty had determined fur houses, which formerly had purchased a stock pile for a year's manufacturing, to buy only for temporary needs.

Buyers' resistance was further complicated by an inherent defect in the idea of a farm auction so distant from the center of the fur world. Buyers had begun to act as a unit. One could purchase for many, and share costs of the long journey. At Hamburg, too, there was no possibility of the surprise bidder who might change the whole trend of an auction. In New York he is the silent man whom no one knows, who has inspected offerings, attends the auction, sits in a corner, and suddenly gives competition to buyers who had expected to purchase for much less. His presence has the same potentiality for drama as the man who has filled a straight flush in a poker game and laid low. But at Hamburg in the ten days of pre-showing, buyers knew which lots competitors would bid on. Treaties were made over evening card games at the hotel. Had silver fox been in keen demand competition would have been sharpened in a group of purchasers, but with the falling market the Fromms could easily suffer.

Tension was high as the auction opened. Federal Furs were offered first and brought prices as high as could be expected. No rancher felt the need to protect his furs with a buy-back. Producers and purchasers had found a middle ground for trading. But with the first offering of Fromm pelts, which always had sold at a premium, prices dropped. After a few lots had been disposed of, Edward began "to take bids off the chandelier," as fur men say when an auctioneer looks over the heads of buyers and accepts a mythical offer. It was an announcement that the Fromms did not propose to sacrifice their pelts. This procedure continued through several pages of the catalogue, which listed a dozen lots on each page. At the end of the sixth page Edward stopped.

"The situation in silver fox is not good," he said, "but is not as bad as your bids indicate."

He explained that while there might be some justification for doubts as to the future of the market, the over-all picture did not bear this out. Good silver fox was in demand and would continue to be; the price must strengthen soon. "If you have not come here to buy," he said, "we will have to discontinue the sale." His conclusion had the force of the wholly unexpected.

Auctions had been canceled but never in fur history had one been stopped after it began. Buyers arose and protested that the sale must go on. They had come to buy silver pelts and had the right to expect this opportunity. Edward agreed to offer the listings of six more pages. The auction was resumed but prices were no higher. Edward continued to buy back Fromm furs. The bidders waited. Sooner or later the Fromm faith in the value of their silver foxes would be shaken. At the end of the sixth page Edward closed the book. "Gentlemen," he said, "the sale is ended."

Even after the warning this announcement took the buyers by surprise, for no one had thought Edward would actually take so unprecedented an action. The Fromms stood behind the auctioneer's table. The buyers gathered in angry groups below and then asked for a place in which to discuss the matter. Henry led them to a large room used for cereal storage. The staff carried in chairs and the buyers retired behind closed doors.

Meanwhile the Fromms held a conference. They were determined, even though they knew the situation might mean disaster. Then they heard men stomping down the stairs of the warehouse. The Fromms looked out the window. The buyers were crowding into busses, bound for town.

Chapter Twenty-three

A SECOND COMPANY AUCTION HAD MADE HISTORY, BUT
not the kind of history the Company wished. Buyers
returned to New York vowing they would never again
go to Hamburg. Ten days later, when the price of silvers stiffened in the Montreal auction, they were not
so vehement.

Edward wrote a letter to the trade, pointing out that
the low bids at Hamburg were not justified by market
conditions and that already facts had proved him right.
The letter was followed by an announcement of an
early spring Fromm auction. The same pelts were
offered, the same buyers arrived. The bids were accept-
able, the auction was a success, the trade wanted
Fromm silvers, and afterwards Edward said, "The decision to stop the midwinter auction, which might have
resulted in a major disaster for us, proved to have
been wise."

Although the early spring auction had provided a
successful market for silver foxes, the Company had
discovered the vulnerability of farm sales. Four years
earlier they had served a purpose, had stimulated an

interest in silver fox and carried the Company one step further along the way of pelt to wearer. Now this one step was not enough. With the price of silver fox declining and the use of the fur decreasing, the downward trend, if it continued, would make an isolated farm auction perilous. Even the scheme for the identification of Fromm pelts had misfired. The Company had invested a million dollars in advertising, with the device of the Fromm medallion as an integral part of the campaign, but what had been intended as a guarantee of Fromm production was now appearing on skins easily recognized as inferior. In the previous season more medallioned pelts had been sold throughout the country than the Company raised. If this continued the medallion eventually would be worthless, and the Company's reputation jeopardized. To John and Henry, in charge of the herds, this was almost more distressing than the decline in price, but both these were Edward's problems. He proposed a solution one evening when the four brothers and their families met for supper at Walter's. No one thought of it as a company meeting, but the affairs of the Company were a natural topic when the Fromms ate potato pancakes and syrup. It was like the early days when the boys had made them over a campfire while they talked silver foxes.

"We've come to the time when the Company must complete the circuit from pen to wearer," Edward said.

He meant manufacture. It was a new idea to the others, but they had learned to take new ideas in their stride. Since four farm boys had decided they preferred silver foxes, they had been embarking upon uncharted courses. All these had been logical assaults on barriers across their paths, and now Edward felt they faced a new one. Silver fox must be kept alive in the market. As fur farmers they would have to look to others to push the product, develop new styles and new uses, and show the possibilities of the fur. As manufacturers they could do this, and at the same time protect the medallion, even profiting from its former misuse. The public was very conscious of the identification, and this could now be turned to their account.

As a fur producer the Company was peculiarly well situated to become a manufacturer. An enormous crop was a subsidy, for a large inventory permitting mass production, specialization, and year-round operation. Fur workers could handle one type of fur instead of having to work on many. Silver fox garments could not only be better, but could be produced more economically. Control of the product from raw fur to finished garment would enable the Company to intermesh all the processes of carrying a crop to the consumer, and make one process serve another. It was assembly-line thinking carried to its ultimate conclusion.

"The Company will have to open an eastern office," Edward said. "We can begin with an auction and open the factory later."

A headquarters in New York was the most foreign idea of all. No one liked it, not even Edward who proposed it, but the Company could only take this big step forward in the East. Fur workers, highly specialized craftsmen, were centered in New York and would not consider an untried venture on a Wisconsin farm. The new enterprise must in the beginning be near the markets. Yet for the first time the needs of the Company were in conflict with the desires of the brothers.

"I couldn't leave the ginseng," Walter said.

Henry was even more direct. "And I wouldn't live in New York, even for the Company. There are some things no man should have to do."

John did not bother to state his intentions. So thoroughly had he established his right to a detached existence that he knew no one would expect him to live otherwise.

Edward agreed to see the showrooms and factory into production, but with reservations. "It's only a detour," he said. "Once we are established, we can bring the factory to the farm."

The last step in the circuit from pen to wearer was begun. The introductory eastern auction was held in the fall of 1940 in the new headquarters, a floor leased in a large building on Seventh Avenue, chosen and arranged for manufacture. The factory was opened in January, 1941. Edward commuted between Hamburg and New York. Johnnie Fromm, who had completed college and two years of business administration at Harvard, brought his family east and learned factory methods as, when a boy, he had learned to raise foxes. Fromm pelts and garments could now be purchased in New York. The great fur center regarded the Company as permanent invaders, but the Fromms looked forward to the time when this temporary exile from Wisconsin would end and the Company would again be a close-knit unit. Pen and fur workroom could go hand in hand.

Meanwhile varied problems crowded in. In 1940 war factories robbed the farms. Where husky youths could once be had for ginseng crews, now grandfathers and girls must do the work. Digging root requires muscle and, with additional man power unobtainable, harvesting twenty-two acres before frost was impossible. Mature roots left in the ground until spring might rot and be worthless. Fall approached, and there was still no solution. A machine to serve the purpose had never been built.

The ginseng boss, Herbert Kleinschmidt, shopping in town, saw an obsolete double potato digger in a dealer's warehouse. It had proved unsatisfactory for potatoes, but its width would exactly span a four and one-half foot ginseng bed. The center transmission presented a problem, but Herbert was sure he and Walter could install a central plow to channel roots and soil. He hurried to the farm and told Edward, who bought the digger by telephone, sight unseen. Power would be the greatest problem. The digger must travel slowly through a bed, displacing four and one-half feet of soil, and shaking earth from roots on a vibrating apron.

Walter and Herbert took it to the blacksmith shop. Ten days later they produced a machine that worked. A center plow channeled roots. Side boards held roots within the bed. The vibrating apron spewed roots onto the ground at the rear. One tractor drew the equipment and a second tractor furnished power. The two-tractor plan had been the solving inspiration, and neither man knew to whom belonged the credit for the idea.

"All we cared was that we'd saved the crop," Herbert said. "We had to find a way to do that." Having to find a way, and the sense of satisfaction when the way was found, probably accounts for the great number of homemade tools invented for a special purpose on the Fromm farm. This spirit began at the top, and in the early years. And as workers were added they have shared it, until the attitude of "having to find a way to do it" has sprawled as widely as the farm itself. Demands on ingenuity have always been a part of the adventure of the pioneer, and the Company has never ceased to be that. Nor has it ever become anything but a farm.

"You can't run a farm the way you run a business," Edward said. "Every man on a farm is important."

The greatest achievement of Walter and Herbert was the bed-making machine they devised when weather and the labor shortage of the first year of the war combined against ginseng. Preparing soil and shaping the raised beds had always been done by hand, and a crew of ten men could make the beds on only four acres in two weeks. Continuous rain made early preparations of beds impossible. Putting in a crop of ginseng seed appeared hopeless in the short planting season.

Once again Walter and Herbert went to the blacksmith shop. They had always hoped to dispense with sideboards, which were costly, a source of constant trouble, and lasted only through two crops. Frost heaved out supporting stakes and required spring repairs, and the new digging machine now made it necessary to remove all sideboards before the harvest could begin. The inventors decided their brain child would not only pulverize and prepare the soil, but would pack it so firmly that board support would not be necessary. Devising a piece of equipment to perform these multiple duties provided a lot of fun. One thought of a gadget, and the other came back with an equally inspired idea. The machine, as finally produced, was headed with a heavy metal dragger to level the ground. Following it was a steel pan weighted with rocks to act as a crusher. The shaper was a fixed frame of two heavy hardwood planks, four feet six inches apart and set at an angle to leave a well-shaped bed. Harrowers and eveners were mounted between the planks. A heavy roller came last to smooth the sides and make them harder. The men used odds and ends of metal, anything they could find to serve the purpose.

Finished, the machine looked like the achievement of a pair of demented magpies, but it laid beds with the ease of a hen dropping eggs. Tractor-drawn, it moved across the land. Two men could make four acres of beds in a day. The cost per bed was reduced from ten dollars to four cents.

In one week the Company put in its fall planting on schedule. Ginseng was carried to its final mechanical process, for now only weeding and picking up harvested root need be done by hand.

"We could have thought of that machine years ago," Walter said, "but we didn't have to."

Ingenuity devised many short cuts, as war drained young men from fur and ginseng. Labor, which had once been so plentiful, became increasingly precious. This threatened Henry's reforesting project, begun in the middle thirties. Henry had always planted trees, just as he had always carried tools in his car to repair a culvert or to remove an obstruction on the company roads. The company forest had always held a special significance for Henry. To him, trees, unlike ginseng, were a physical assurance of perpetuity. He was grateful to ginseng for feeding foxes, but trees could always stand on the vast holdings. Reforestation had caught his imagination, and he had plunged into it with all the fervor he had given to silver foxes.

Henry kept a tally. He considered years in which he planted only half a million trees as merely keeping abreast of possibilities, but when a million trees were set in the ground he'd made a big step forward. Sometimes when his planting crew was sorely needed elsewhere, the others spoke of it as "Henry's project," but he never called it anything but "Company trees." And he guarded them with all the zeal he would have given to any other property of the Company. When the first selection, white pine, fell victim to blister, Henry's anger drove crews through the forest to remove wild current, gooseberry, and other shrubs which spread the infection, but at last he admitted he could not make the forest safe for white pine, and accepted spruce and Norway pine. Now, to offset labor shortage, he devised techniques and machinery which would enable the project to continue. A million trees would plant a section, but for the war years he must be contented with half this acreage.

"We'll never live to see those trees mature," he said, "and perhaps our children won't. But their children will have at least twelve thousand acres of forest for selective logging, and that's the way logging will be done in their time."

Young Henry and his sister, Ardene, were still away at college, but Henry never doubted that sometime they would return and that a third generation would live at Hamburg to serve and be served by the Company. In company trees he found expression of this conviction.

After farm auctions ceased and Federal Furs no longer existed, Dr. Young, the marketing specialist, took over farm health problems. Veterinarian and a pioneer in fox ranching, he had a real enthusiasm for the physical welfare of fur bearers, and these problems were at hand. The lull following control of distemper was short. Pen mortalities were increasing, and too many fox death certificates read "gastro-enteritis." Dr. Young set up a laboratory in a corner of the warehouse, made autopsies and then sent for Edward.

"You've lost plenty of foxes with distemper, but do you know how many you've lost from hookworm, lungworm, and just ordinary roundworms?" he demanded. "Know what hookworms do to foxes? Just what they do to people."

The fiery little doctor had become an impassioned crusader. "Look at this lung!" he exclaimed. "Not enough good tissue left for an active fox to breathe with. Start a fox like that running on the range, and of course he's gone! As for roundworms, the chances are your pups get a dose of them with their first milk from an infected mother."

The Company, which had gone through thirteen long years of epidemics, now faced a fresh threat to foxes. Keepers and owners had been aware of some parasites, but hadn't realized they had made so big an invasion. While Dr. Green and the Company had been gunning for the big killer, all the lesser killers had moved in on them. Keepers and John and Henry refused to believe the situation was as serious as Dr. Young insisted. Because all foxes are vulnerable to parasites, from time to time vermifuges had been administered. But ordinary vermifuges do not eradicate the hookworm.

This is a tenacious parasite. It has a cup-shaped mouth with cutting plates, and can fasten to walls of the intestine and live on the blood of its host. The warning symptom is the poor condition of the herd.

Dr. Young continued to weigh foxes, perform autopsies on those that had died of oedema, and showed the evidence of pinhead hemorrhages. Men who had the custody of foxes tried to avoid him, but the doctor was as tenacious as the hookworm itself and at last everyone admitted a wholesale attack on hookworm must begin.

The early method, use of carbon tetrachloride given in hard capsules, was thoroughly in disrepute. Ranchers who had tried it had lost as high as 75 per cent of their herds. The drug caused a slow destruction of the tissue of liver and spleen and if, in administration, the capsule were broken and the fox inhaled the drug he was asphyxiated. Later, carbon tetrachloroethylene in a soft capsule was used. This drug had no bad after-effects and soft capsules were safer, but the treatment still held danger. The capsule must be placed well down the throat and past the larynx.

Tools had been devised for giving medicine to foxes, but Lawrence Schult, boss of the treatment crew, had refused to use the metal speculum to hold the mouth open because it was inserted in front, forced the jaws apart, and was apt to break the teeth. Also its manipulation was almost impossible while holding a fox. The forceps for inserting a capsule was equally unsatisfactory. It was of poor workmanship, did not control the capsule securely, and injured throats. Lawrence used the earliest method, a round notched stick of wood, inserted at the side of the jaw and turned to keep the throat open, with a small rubber hose for insertion in the throat. It was slow, but it did not injure foxes.

This technique, however, held little hope for wholesale pilling. In a ten-hour day the treatment crew could pill only four hundred foxes, and control of hookworm demanded that pelter pups be given five pills at monthly intervals, breeder pups six or more, and adult foxes one pill; two if possible. The men needed tools that could be used with speed and safety; even with the greatest care the loss from asphyxiation was at least one per cent.

When the first fox died in Lawrence's arms he could not understand what had happened. Apparently science had discovered another way to kill foxes. Dr. Young showed by autopsy what had occurred. Lawrence did not grasp the idea at the first autopsy, or in half-a-dozen, but at last light broke. He saw what he had to do to pill with safety.

"And that's how I learned," he said, "and how I come to believe that Doc was right on this pilling business. But we had to find a way to do it."

Lawrence went to the blacksmith shop with a set of fine German surgical instruments and an idea.

He developed a new speculum built on the plier principle. It was inserted in the side of the mouth, and held the jaws open without causing struggle. This could be locked in position, thus leaving the fox's head in complete control of the handler. He designed forceps in three sizes, for young pups, medium pups, and adults for inserting the capsule in the throat. These were curved to conform with the shape of the throat, with capsule grips at the end.

With the new tools and a trained crew, two thousand foxes can be pilled in a ten-hour day. With men not available, the Company employed boys and girls just out of high school, and in so doing achieved a super-assembly line plus a sporting instinct. Youth has pep and none of the caution that causes an adult of more than twenty-five to hesitate momentarily before reaching for a fox. A treatment crew consists of nine or ten boys and four girls. They can catch a kennel of pups, vaccinate for distemper, pill, and return to the kennel in five minutes. The foxes have no time to become nervous, and scarcely know what has happened to them before the crew has moved on to the next group.

Teamwork is of a high order. Each boy selects a pup, runs it down, catches it by the tail, slides a hand down the back, grasps the neck and brings it out of the pen. A girl stands at the door to swab with disinfectant and make sure every pup has been caught, a card on the door recording the number. The "grabbers," each carrying a fox, walk in a procession around a circle from the swabber to a second girl, who administers the injection. Foxes are held out to her almost as fast as she can operate the needle. A third girl "folds" the fox for pilling. This is accomplished by folding the hind legs over the front so that the grabber can hold all four legs and the tail with the same hand. The girl then folds the brush over the legs. A fox is folded in a few seconds, and is then in the grabber's complete control to be offered to the girl who operates the speculum and then, with the neck curved in exactly the correct position, for Lawrence to insert the forceps down the throat and release the capsule.

This system made it possible for the crew in one season to give six pills to each of 35,000 pups and one to 19,600 breeders.

"That's 229,600 pills in one season," Dr. Young said. "We couldn't have done it without those tools Lawrence Schult made in the blacksmith shop."

This extensive pilling project was achieved within a year. It had become a race between the Company and the worm. Dr. Young moved into a real laboratory. The little building which had served as a gatehouse for the auctions was enlarged, and equipped to handle the diseases of fur bearers. The hookworm continued to prove the doctor had been right. In one unit a thousand pups were lost in a crop of 3,200. Pen deaths rose, as did those on the range. And now autopsies showed the lungworm was beginning to present almost as great a hazard. This parasite, however, could not be controlled by pilling.

It is treacherous because it can be widespread before a rancher is aware of it. The life cycle of the lungworm that attacks foxes is still not definitely known, but its eventual destination is the lungs and air passages. No drug to eradicate it has been discovered. The only defense is to remove the fox from infested soil. Spring is the dangerous season, since then heat and moisture become allies of the eggs, and a wet spring is especially dangerous, as eggs hatch in the ground. Pups are vulnerable. At Hamburg the mortality mounted. Lungworm became as serious a menace as encephalitis had been, and if deaths continued to increase at the same rate, in another year the company might lose half the puppy crop.

Despite the wartime lack of wire, lumber, and crew, puppies must be taken off the ground. In the past years of ceaseless construction the Company has purchased more than a million and a half posts, and the wire netting, if rolled out end to end, could have more than reached across the continent. Now it needed more, at a time when it was almost impossible to buy wire netting;

but the future of the herd depended on the purchase. The Fromms made wire-floored kennels a first consideration, and in 1945 had half the puppies off the ground. A year later every silver fox, when old enough to leave its mother, was put on wire.

Mink do not have worms, a fact that endears them to their keepers, but they have other and distinctive troubles. One is stones in bladder and kidney. Why mink should have calculous deposits, no one knows, but it is so common a cause of death that the keepers assume this to be the answer until an autopsy reveals otherwise. When the death rate from calculi climbed to 45 per cent of the deaths from all causes, Dr. Young turned to medical reports of research in this disease among humans. A theory had been advanced that it might be due to an overdose of concentrates, A and D vitamins, with D the chief offender. This was nothing more than a suspicion, but it suggested an avenue for experiment. The cod liver oil that had been used for mink was fortified with D vitamin, and Dr. Young and Edward changed the oil and cut the daily ration in half. Bladder stones continued, but autopsies showed the calculi were now grains of sand instead of stones the size of a man's thumb, and mortalities were lowered to 22 per cent of all fatalities. There was a chance they were on the right path. Medical research among mink might even have value for humans. They cut the oil ration still further and watched the results.

"But the experiment has not been carried far enough to justify any conclusions," Dr. Young said. "We might even be on the wrong track altogether, and we can't consider that we have reached a conclusion until we have the trouble beaten."

There will always be frontiers for exploration. No one knows when a virus may accommodate itself to a new and comfortable haven, make an adaptation, and flare up. Other mink diseases, nephritis and fatty degeneration of the liver tissues, have yet to be conquered. Pneumonia is also a problem. A creature which, in the wilds, customarily fishes in creeks, swims in icy water, and is often chilled by cold winds when drenched, is extremely susceptible to pneumonia in pen life and must be protected from wet and cold. Perhaps pneumonia deaths in the wilderness are greater than have been realized, and this may be true of other diseases. Dr. Green's study of the ten-year cycle of the population of the varying hare proved it to be the result of shock disease. Parasites and viruses attack animals in wild life, and perhaps fur farmers are dealing with natural hazards that account in some measure for the reduction of wild fur.

Left to herself, nature has always achieved a balance, even though she has been forced to drastic measures on occasion. Mink, foxes, beavers, buffaloes, wolves, or bears might have overrun this continent had it not been for diseases, birth rates, and carnivorous foes. The defenseless rabbit survived through fecundity, and buffaloes had enough grass because cows dropped only one calf a year. As late as 1947 crowded marshes were relieved by an epidemic among muskrats. Predatory fur bearers were limited by food supply. Their numbers were kept down by a periodic disease which in great part destroyed the varying hare. Even the Indian fitted into nature's scheme. He only nibbled at the herds of deer, buffalo, caribou, and antelope.

When a white man stepped ashore in America he

began to upset nature's balance. Fur was the land's first product. Fur drove explorers across the continent and north to the Arctic. Fur opened the western United States, and the trade was so devastating that it eliminated itself in two decades. In this century the airplane and outboard motor have carried skillful and aggressive white trappers into the most remote districts of America, and the Russians have adopted similar tactics in Siberia. The last sources of wild fur have been tapped.

Man prepared to meet this depletion. Without knowledge of his project, he began with crude cages in farmyards. He met reverses, but he kept on. New animals were domesticated and made to serve. Today fur breeding has been carried past the experimental stage. Fur farming will always have hazards, like any other branch of animal husbandry, but these hazards are challenging. The industry has proved it can supply a product so necessary in a world that no longer ranks fur as a luxury for the few. The industry has also proved it can supply better fur than is caught in the wilds. Selective breeding, proper housing, correct feeding, scientific care, and a controlled pelting period have improved the natural product.

Mature and established, the fur industry was ready for its most exciting period. Mutations, once only isolated accidents among fur bearers, were now appearing in herds, and it was possible to fix and hold these rare and intangible shades. This opened a new era, and on top of this came the even more startling discovery that these established mutations could be used to produce still more breath-taking beauty. Men who raise fox and mink find themselves in a land which today has no boundaries.

Chapter Twenty-four

THE SILVER FOX WAS A MUTATION AND A RECESSIVE, and fox breeders probably saved it from extinction, since aggressive trapping would have reduced the chances of one silver meeting another of the same strain. But breeders, having rescued this mutation, barred all others. The pearl, platinum, and white-marked foxes were killed in the early days of fur farming.

Mink, too, produced variations. In 1892 Henry Poland, a biologist, in his book *Fur Bearing Animals*, described the varieties existing today. Many trappers caught a silverblu, a pastel, or an albino, and had to sell the pelt for almost nothing because it differed from the accepted standard shade. These wild pelts undoubtedly were not as beautiful as are present mutations improved by selective breeding, but they were the basis of these. In the thirties mink mutations suddenly cropped up in ranchers' herds, and their appearance at this time may be explained by the history of mink farming.

In early days mink farms specialized in one of three

types, pure Yukon, pure eastern, or middle western. This last classification was known in Canada as Lake Superior mink and in the North Central states as Mississippi Valley mink, since it was found along this river and its tributaries. Formerly all three types could be bred with considerable profit, and mink farming went through'an unhealthy period of promotion and speculation much like that of the early days of silver fox ranching. This was ended abruptly by the depression following the First World War, when the pelt of a middle western mink was worth only three dollars. Ranchers who survived this slump in mink values changed to the more valuable types, the eastern and the Yukon. Herds became mixed, and the inevitable cross-mating may have stimulated mutations.

This theory was offered by an old fur man as a possible explanation of why mink ranching, which had provided no excitement for twenty years, should suddenly take on all the thrill and suspense of prospecting. Now a mink herd might at any time produce a mutation which held potential wealth. The time and place of this miraculous appearance of a new color phase was as unpredictable as lightning. It was an incalculable act of nature, a change in germ plasm, but it held golden opportunity for the man in whose herd it occurred. Every rancher prayed for a mutation.

Such a possibility was unknown in 1931, when a female mink of a strange new color was whelped on a ranch in Wisconsin. She was an illusive shade, a bluish platinum, and the rancher, William Whittingham, liked the color. It resulted from the mating of a native Wisconsin female with a male of the Yukon River district, and it was called a freak. Mr. Whittingham saved the mink, hoping to produce others, but in two breeding seasons her kits resembled the standard male parent. Fearing the color phase was not heritable he wrote to Harry Le Due, editor of *American Fur Breeder*, who had printed several stories of the sporadic appearance of freak fur bearers. Mr. La Due did not then suspect how important mutations were to become, but he had carried on a correspondence with W. E. Castle, Harvard geneticist, and often printed Professor Castle's letters. From the breeding history of the mink and her solid coat color Mr. La Due guessed the mutation to be a recessive, and suggested that she be mated to a son to recover the mutant recessive strain.

This was practical genetics. The greatest difficulty in handling a recessive strain is the ease with which it can be lost. While the dominant has the capacity to reproduce itself and thus is recognized, the recessive, mated to a standard, produces hybrids which show no visible characteristic, although they carry the blood line. This initial time lag in recessive breeding caused the defeat of some early breeders. Once the recessive strain is established it will breed true, but to use the hybrids effectively the breeder must have an understanding of the Mendelian law.

Mr. Whittingham mated the mutant female to one of her sons and two platinum blue recessives were produced. While he was still struggling with genetic formulas and was not too encouraged by the results, Guy Ingham became interested in the problem and joined the venture. Eventually they established the strain, and succeeded in producing litters of this shade.

In 1935 the same mutation appeared on the ranch of Charles Whittaker and he, too, began to develop it.

Quite unknown to these Wisconsin pioneers in mutations William R. Fremersdorf, who owned a ranch near Portland, Oregon, was working on the same problem, although the story of his experiment was not known until more than ten years later. In 1931 a wild platinum blue male and female were captured in the wild country of western Oregon by a trapper. Mr. Fremersdorf bought them and, working in secrecy, began to develop the strain.

His was an original piece of research. He proved the trait to be recessive, produced hybrids, and understood their breeding significance in the genetic pattern. Later the value of the offspring of a cross between standard and a recessive, a half blood, was known, but when Mr. Fremersdorf carried this pair to a herd of forty mutations he was working wholly without the aid of geneticists. He spent years bringing this strain of wild mink to a standard that would satisfy him, and it was not until 1938, after seven years of rigorous culling, that he decided the foundational stock was ready to produce in quantity. He had worked alone. No man had seen his mink, no man had shared his dream. He believed they were the only animals of this color in the world, and in 1939 he produced forty platinum kits. In another year he would have enough to send to market. Those mink were never whelped. Food poisoning almost destroyed the herd. He was left with two males and three females. Discouraged, in ill-health, the work of years swept away, he sold the remnants of his platinums to another rancher.

None of these pioneers had any certainty that the new color would prove of value, that the fur trade would buy it or the public like it, but they believed in it and persisted. The practical application of genetics to fur farming was in its infancy. Even to obtain knowledge of the most elementary laws meant study of a science by men whose trade had not been associated with textbooks. Today university professors are fascinated by the proof that fur farms offer of the workings of genetic laws, but in the late thirties and early forties breeders were, except for articles in fur trade magazines and books on fur farming, working wholly on their own. Unfortunately for them the geneticist entered the field after the appearance of mutation mink. Now genetic departments in universities are of inestimable aid.

In this early period, while mutation pioneers endeavored to produce platinum mink in sufficient quantity to be of commercial value, they were faced with the same immutable workings of the Mendelian law of one to three. In a litter of four from mated hybrids, one kit will be a pure recessive of the mutant coat color, while the other three will be normal-colored mink. Two of these three kits, however, carry the recessive blood strain although they have no visible characteristics to distinguish them from the fourth, a pure blood standard. This 25 per cent chance of an error was only one obstacle along the way of the mutation which was first called a platinum and now is known as silverblu. After the recessive coat color was established in even a small number of animals, these had to be brought back to the quality of the original standard herd. Ranchers who had spent years producing mink with deeply furred coats of soft velvety texture could not now sacrifice these qualities, and recessives recovered from hybrids do not always show the quality of the best of the original stock. This had to be replaced. Also the new color must be made clear and sharp. Animals with the faintest tinge had to be culled. This new color phase must have all the beauty of the fine ranched mink with the added appeal of its elusive shading. Nature had dumped a fascinating problem into the laps of these pioneers, and their perseverance pushed back the boundaries of fur farming.

In the meantime another mutation had appeared, a white mink with black markings, and a dominant trait, which eventually became known as the Royal Kohinur. Why American fur farmers should have gone so far afield to find a lush and undescriptive name for a new mink color will undoubtedly baffle purchasers of this mutation for many years to come. The pattern coat has nothing to suggest a diamond, and royalty has long since ceased to be the sole possessor of unusual or rare fur. But this second mutation in five years made breeders mutation-conscious, and they scanned their herds for whims of nature.

Equally exciting events had taken place in the fox world. The white-marked fox, which originated in Canada, was being bred and perfected in the west. The Norwegian platinum fox had been accepted as a new breed, and platinums were reported on northwestern ranches. The pale and silvery fox had caught on in public favor, and in 1940 a platinum pelt was sold in a New York auction for $11,000. Even as a promotion project this sum was staggering. The forecast of Ned Dearborn, a biologist who said in 1922, "No one knows how many incipient breeds of foxes are in existence," was proving true.

Silver fox men were in a quandary. Platinums and white-marked foxes might prove to be only a whim of fashion, too ephemeral to warrant any change in the blood strain of a herd. The silver fox had been esteemed since the first pelt had been shown in Europe, and the Fromms had spent twenty-five years making their silvers brighter. "We can't chase every will-o'-the-wisp," Edward said. "I don't think women will like these gaudy foxes."

Henry reached his decision when he went on a western buying trip in 1940 and was captured by the brilliance of twenty white ring-necked foxes on the Black Forest Fox Farm. The ranch had gone into receivership and Henry was offered the lot.

"Even in the darkness of night they shone like diamonds," he said. "The color picked up light and you could see the outline of the whole fox."

Entranced by their possibilities, Henry bought the twenty on approval, and sent one fox to Hamburg as a sample. This caution was unlike a Fromm, but Henry had misgivings as to the reactions of the others. His apprehensions were justified. John and Edward thought the new fox garish. "Women won't like foxes with white patches," John said. Edward did not care for the white rings around the necks any more than John. To them this was just a silver fox gone wrong.

John recalled this incident two years later, when the breeding value of the white-marked fox was discovered through live fox shows, which now fulfilled the real purpose of any blooded stock exhibition. Breeders exhibited their finest specimens, and others saw what had been achieved and went home to try to do likewise. Perfection of fur was the acknowledged goal, and ribbons were awarded for the pelt of an animal rather than for a long line of illustrious ancestors. Also, standards had widened. Platinums, pearls, and white-marked foxes were now shown in separate classes, but judges had difficulty in choosing the grand champions. When the white-marked winner was compared with the silver that had captured first prize in its class, the white-marked was always brighter than the best full silver. The fur trade, too, commented on this fact.

Ranchers considered this phenomenon, and in experimental breeding discovered that the white-marked fox could be used to brighten a strain of silvers. Previous attempts to brighten silver by platinum crossings had not been successful; the platinum diluted all the pigments. Black became gray, the underfur suffered deterioration in color, and the silver lost its sharpness. But the white-marked fox was a sure, quick, route to brighter silvers. The offspring of a mating of silver and white-marked foxes, if crossed back to the silver, produced pups in which the silver was brighter and the black sharper, while the underfur remained the slate blue of the silver fox. Ranchers who had worked for more than ten years to overcome the handicap of a dark blood line were now able in two breeding seasons to bring their herds to the brighter tone demanded by the fur trade. Owners of the darker silvers could now catch up with fashion, and one crossing with the white-marked mutation added dollars to each pelt. Silver fox farmers bought white-marked foxes, and the Fromms prepared to make their foxes even brighter. A characteristic of the white-marked fox Henry had noticed in 1917, when the Fromms had a female with a white paw, might have served as a shorter path to their goal.

"We could have made those ring-necks into good

foxes, once we got the white patches off them," John said. "I guess we were like those old fellows on Prince Edward Island who were so sold on black they couldn't see the beauty in silvers. We'd been chasing an idea and thinking silvers for so long we weren't open-minded."

But no fur breeder could have remained traditionally minded in the stirring days of the early forties when exciting mink mutations were beckoning ranchers to adventure. No one knew whether these new colors would be popular, but a few of the more daring breeders purchased mutation stock. It was an expensive gamble, and little stock was available. Trios of platinum and, Kohinoor cost at least a thousand dollars, and often more. The Fromms bought some trios of each color, and discussed the advisability of changing their herds over to the mutations.

In the meantime other color phases were cropping up on ranches. Some appeared without warning. Some were the results of experimental breeding. Ranchers recalled that silver-haired mink once had been carefully culled and considered of no value. Now men experimented to breed them, and in Michigan and Saskatchewan a new shade was produced that was later given the name of blufrost. This variation was a two-toned mink with a light bluish underfur and dark guard hairs of black or brown enlivened with silver. It was a dominant, and in 1941 only a few dozen of this color existed. Pastel mink, a recessive, was whelped in southern Wisconsin and on some western ranches. This was a delicate shade of taupe, and varied from light to a soft chocolate brown. It, too, existed in extremely limited quantities. Albino mink, spotted mink, steel blue mink and ebony mink were reported. These variations were similar to those described by Henry Poland when he wrote in 1892: "The usual color is various shades of brown, albinos and nearly black, mottled, and drab-coloured examples are sometimes met with, as well as animals with white hairs sprinkled in the brown fur; there is often a white spot on the throat, somewhat similar to that of the Marten; a white line or spot is also sometimes found underneath, varying much in length; the tail is generally brown or dark brown, of a darker shade toward the tip, and is sometimes tipped with white; the whiskers are usually brown or dark brown; the ears are short; the underfur is usually bluish-brown, and in black animals, dark blue; sometimes the underfur is white. There is a deeper ridge of color on the back. Sometimes skins spotted with white are found.

"The fur, as in most amphibious animals, is short; it is the very best for wear, lasting for many years, and sometimes for a generation or so.

"These skins are usually manufactured into muffs, etc., both in the natural state, and dyed and pulled to imitate seal. They are also used for coat-linings, and the tails are made into capes, etc.

"Some years ago an attempt was made in the United States to breed Minks for the sale of the fur, but this enterprise ended in failure. These breeding establishments were called farms."

So few animals of each new color existed that it would be years before their appeal to the public could be tested, but mink mutation breeders were a small and stalwart band of adventurers. They had to be. The fur trade had definite misgivings about these startling departures from accepted standards. Geneticists had only become aware of the stirring events. Ranchers were yet having to find their own way in unfamiliar genetic patterns. The old fractional measurement of heredity—quarters, halves and eighths—was valueless. Breeders must learn genetic laws, must recognize dominants capable of reproducing themselves in half the litter, and recessives which must be bred together to recover the hidden strain. Each man had to have the courage of a conviction that he was on the path of something rare and very lovely, for only faith could take him through the early, lean years.

In 1942 men who had pioneered the platinum mink met to consider its presentation to the public. Marketing presented inflexible conditions. The new color could not be offered until it was in sufficient quantity. A mink coat requires sixty or more well-matched skins, which are selected from several hundred. One or two garments of this new shade were not enough for ordinary retail channels, for so limited an offering would make the platinum only an oddity in fur to be avoided by the conservative. Fur houses would be fearful of this reaction, and a mutation on which ten years of preparation had been spent would suffer an unfair handicap.

But the way should be paved for the sizable crop of 1943. The pioneers decided to present the only platinum mink coat in the world to the American Theater Wing to be auctioned for the benefit of the Stage Door Canteen. No single rancher had enough pelts, but more than a dozen joined in the venture. The selection of the individual mink to be given was made by Herbert Mezger and was probably the most spectacular feat of grading ever accomplished in the fur industry. Mr. Mezger is one of the three judges at important fur shows of the country and is on the staff of the New York Auction Company. Of necessity, the mink were selected while alive and Mr. Mezger traveled from ranch to ranch, carrying the color in his eye and selecting only animals of the desired tint. Even grading mutation pelts is difficult as the delicate color has many shades, and these shades can be determined only by comparison. Grading on the hoof had never before been attempted, but Mr. Mezger did it, and successfully.

"We need three of your herd," he would say at one ranch and, taking four at the next, ten at another, he kept on until the requisite sixty had been selected. Men parted with precious breeding stock which they would have pelted for no other cause. A photograph, the story of the coat's making, and an announcement of the auction at the Waldorf-Astoria on New Year's Eve, appeared in *Vogue*. The coat was displayed to fashion editors in the New York showroom of Fromm Brothers, where one of the pioneer breeders told the history of the color phase and showed live platinum mink. The press took pictures of the lecturer and the mink, and in its zeal to get a perfect picture called, "Closer! Closer!" until the rancher held the mink so close it bit his nose. This ended mink modeling but made the headlines.

Fashion experts were fascinated by this hasty brush with science, and *Women's Wear Daily* asked Johnnie Fromm to write an article explaining the genetic formula of the mutation. All this interest and excitement in a new color phase in mink led to the confident expectation that the coat would bring at least twenty-five thousand dollars for the Stage Door Canteen. But ap-

Alwina Fromm with Arthur, Edward, Henry,
John, and Walter.

Photograph taken in 1892 of farmhouse which served
family and ginseng crew until 1920.

Country school, 1905. Henry, sitting left; Edward, sitting right; John, standing left; Walter, third from right.

John and Henry with pups caught by Walter in padded trap, May, 1910.

Fromm boys haying.

Litter chopped from hollow log.

John, Henry, and Edward with red fox litter
dug out in 1911.

Picture that won
Funsten $50 prize.

Henry and John bringing home wire fencing
bought with prize money.

First big pelt sale, fifty-seven red foxes.

Edward with ginseng crop, 1910.

Washing root with family car as power plant.

Ginseng arbor.

Washing with power from their first stationary engine.

Fort Moreland.

Mr. Moreland, center, with red and cross pups
from his silver fox.

First block of pens.

Kaiser.

The Fromm double fox house.

Foxes on range in late twenties.

Range feed cart.

Feeding in the forest.

Walter Fromm, Herbert Kleinschmidt and their
washing machine.

Modern method of digging root.

Center of Fromm farm tod

varehouse in background.

Silver fox of the present day.

Selecting foxes for mating.

The tame fox at Thiensville.

Progress in breeding for silver since 1910.

One of the Fromms' first silverblu mink.

A standard.

A Kohinur.

1947 silverblu.

Edward, Walter, Henry and John in a mink unit, 1947.

One of the mink furring ranges.

Present-day fox when he enters furring range
in September.

Three months later when his coat is prime.

Harvesting fox crop.

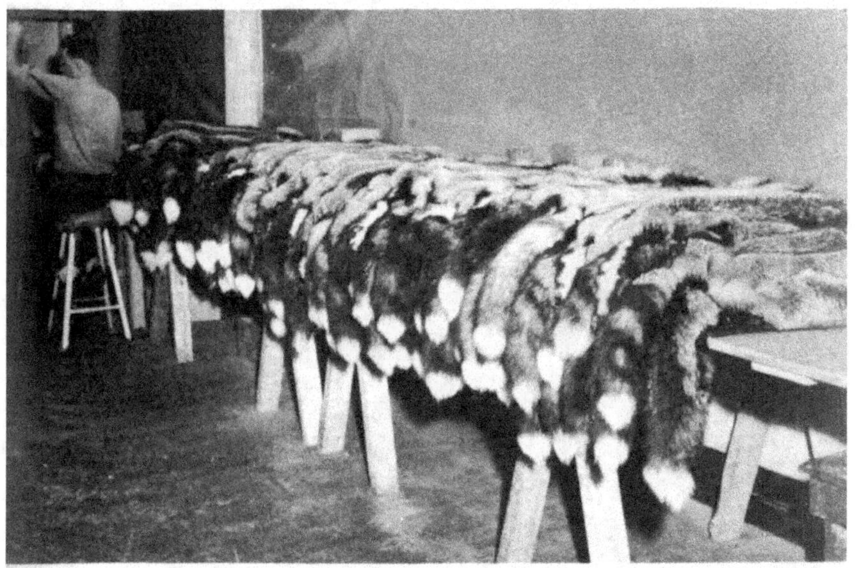

Examining pelts.

Grading pelts.

Edward and callers at the 1939 auction,
which was broken off.

Buyers at a Hamburg auction.

Dressing fox pelts in Merrill factory.

"Nailing" mink garment.

Operators working on fox jackets.

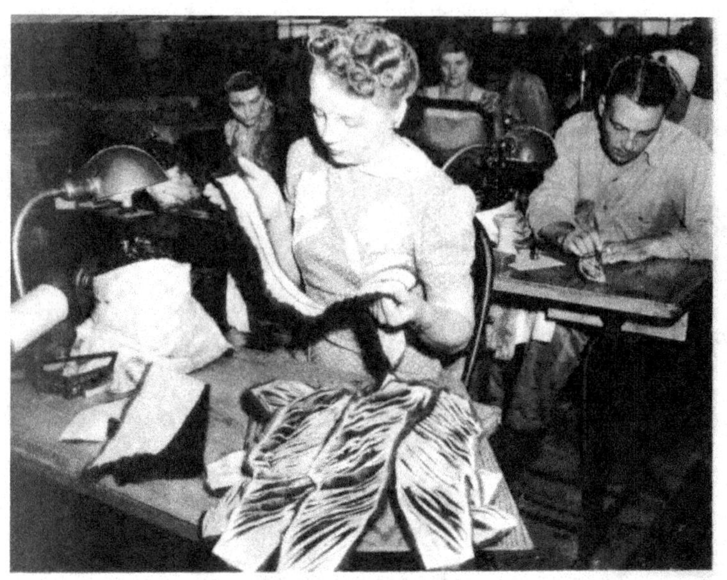

"Letting out" mink.

Johnnie Fromm and the body of first mink coat
made by the Company.

Hamburg farm, office in center.

A few of the thousands of fox pens.

parently the public was not aware that the coat was a donation. Or it might have been that war-mindedness made so spectacular a luxury purchase seem untimely. Myrna Loy bid nine thousand dollars. Other bids topped hers, and then the contest stopped and Edward Fromm, the auctioneer, raised the price by accepting fictitious offers. Finally the American Theater Wing bought back the coat for eighteen thousand dollars. Later it was disposed of for nine thousand.

Men who had donated precious breeding stock were disappointed, but at least America knew mink were now appearing in a new color. The Breeders' Association rechristened the mink "silverblu" and began a campaign of national publicity. The fur trade and the public were already talking of the silverblu before the first crop was offered in January, 1944. A full-page color advertisement appeared in the December issue of *Vogue*, and fur houses had an opportunity to gauge the interest of customers.

From the moment the sound of the auctioneer's hammer marked the purchase of the first lot, it was evident that the new and glamorous mink would be accepted. The "ups" of the callers came so fast that one sounded like the echo of another. The first coat bundle was sold for $185 a pelt and later bids went higher. One bundle of sixty-five pelts soared to $265 and the prices averaged $147.25. The faith of men in a new-found beauty had been justified.

Almost two years earlier, Herman Bock of the Bock and Mohr mink ranch in Wisconsin, had written an article on mutation breeding which appeared in the June, 1942, issue of *American Fur Breeder*. He gave the genetic facts of the new mutation to his fellow ranchers.

Genes in the germ plasm, he said, not the proportion of the blood ancestry, determined the color of the new mink. The various matings were illustrated by diagrams in which the rancher might see the exact result of mating pure platinums, half bloods with dark mink, and half bloods with platinum.

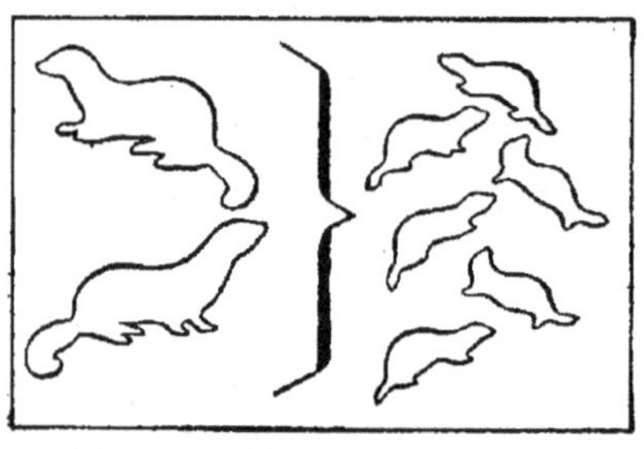

MATING PLATINUM WITH
PLATINUM

MATING PURE DARK WITH
PLATINUM

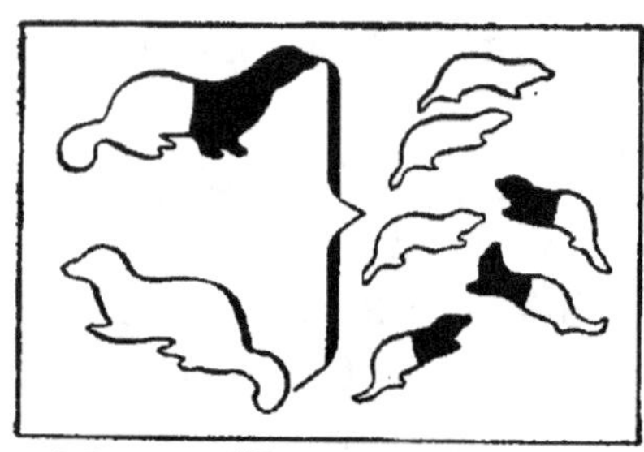

MATING HALF BLOOD WITH
PLATINUM

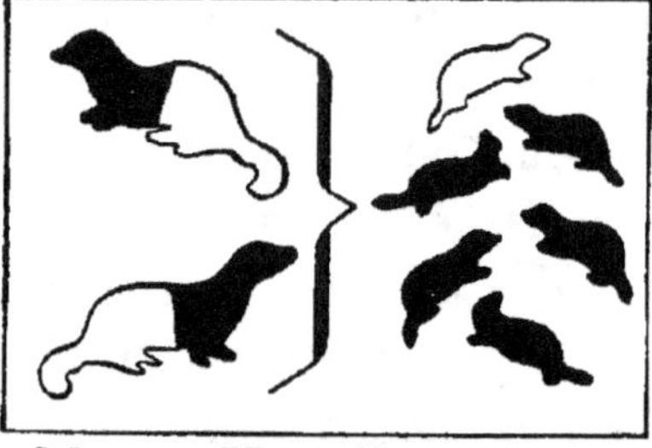

MATING HALF BLOOD WITH
HALF BLOOD

Thus, he pointed out, a rancher might breed to produce all platinums, pursue a slower course by mating half blood with a platinum to produce a split litter, or an even slower course of mating half bloods with half bloods. It was an exceedingly clear and comprehensive article. However, among mink ranchers in the excitment of mutation breeding, the emphasis centered on trios of pure platinum. The price of this breeding stock was fixed by the Association with every member pledged to observe them. Pure bloods were costly, although the half blood of dark color had no price rating. Even as pelts they were considered undesirable since they were somewhat lighter than the standard parent and darker mink were in fashion favor. But Johnnie Fromm, in preparing his article for the *Women's Wear Daily*, became increasingly aware of the value of these half bloods.

"If we could pick up some half blood females and buy enough pure blood males to cover them, we'd get half litters of silverblu," he said to Edward.

"What makes you so sure?" Edward asked.

"That's the way it works genetically," Johnnie said.

"And how do we know the public is going to like them?"

"We can't until the mutation is on the market," Johnnie said. "But after the new color catches on we'll have to pay real money for the half bloods."

Edward and Johnnie went shopping. The company bought 106 half blood females for forty dollars each, and a dozen pure blood males to cover.

"Johnnie wants to try an experiment," Edward said to the rancher. "He's wondering if he can do something with those half bloods."

In the following breeding season the half blood females produced four hundred kits. Half of these were silverblus, and in a year when trios of this color were selling for twelve hundred dollars. The remainder of the litters were half bloods, and now their breeding value had been established. Thus the Fromm silverblu herd, one of the country's largest, was begun.

But even more exciting events were taking place in mink mutations, events which were bewildering and yet held dazzling possibilities. It was found that mutants could be crossed to produce even newer and more elusive shades. Some of these combinations were discovered by accident, when half bloods of recessives were unintentionally bred to dominants. In other instances there was a definite attempt to superimpose a different shading. When pastels first appeared, and only a few pairs existed, ranchers feared this mutation resembled the wild mink too closely to have a real value. A mutation must be discernibly different to justify the difficulties of mutant breeding. It was suggested that the Kohinur or the blufrost, pattern mutants, might add an interesting differential. This was tried by a few men and the golden cross resulted.

Another double mutation on the Fromm farm was wholly an accident. Supposedly pure blood Kohinurs, unknown to them or to the rancher who had bred them, were half blood silverblus, and these quite unintentionally were bred to half blood silverblus in the Fromm herd. Even breeding cards were not always a protection in the confusion of new strains. The kits of these litters were a soft pearl shade with the black cross markings of the Kohinur, and were so interesting and attractive the breeding program of the following year was planned to produce more of this new pearl mink. In 1945 when the mink breeders held a show and each rancher gave a prize animal to be auctioned for the benefit of the Association, the Company sent a male pearl mink, intending to buy it back, since it was a valuable breeder. Apparently other ranchers agreed with the Fromms, for Edward had to bid $2,300 to make the purchase. Then, so unpredictable is the behavior of male fur bearers — or perhaps the excitement of becoming a traveled and admired mink altered his point of view — that this male, formerly a dependable breeder, sired only one more litter and retired to a life of leisure. Now keepers exhibit him to visitors, quote his purchase price and add, "but it's no use trying to make him work."

These double mutations proved there need be no end to the possibilities of lovely shades of fur, but the fascinating combinations must wait on immutable conditions. Mink produce young only once a year, and at the end of two years, working with a dominant and a recessive, the best result to be hoped for is that a quarter of the litter will be the shade desired. Crossing two recessives is still less productive. Dr. Seth S. Osborn described this procedure in a paper read before the mink breeders' association.

"In the crossing of two different types of recessive mutation mink," he said, "we should be able to develop a new type of mink by the following procedure; for example, let us take the pastel and the platinum; the first cross of these animals should produce an entire litter of brown half blood platinums, that are also half blood pastels.

"Now what most of us have been doing for several years, is crossing this half blood back either way to the original mutation. This method is wrong. These brown half bloods should be bred together; from sixteen kits we should obtain nine darks, three platinums, three pastels, and one blend of the two colors. This is the animal we are looking for. This one-in-sixteen animal can be used to breed back to any animal that carries both factors."

The possibilities of shades not yet glimpsed sent ranchers to textbooks. They spent their evenings working out genetic tables and struggling with unfamiliar science. Terms which had been mere words to them five years before — genes, chromosomes, alleles, homozygous, heterozygous — now had meaning. Men began to talk of the time when not only two but three mutations were superimposed. In this triple crossing the breeder must seek the one-in-sixty-four animal from hybrid parents. It can be found, however, by a genetic short cut. Under the most ideal conditions three breeding seasons, 34 matings, and 160 animals are the least which must be involved in the entire experiment.

"That's the 'hope-to-be-beautiful' mink," said Johnnie Fromm. "And it will be a long time before we see it."

But sometime this boiled-down essence of three mutations undoubtedly will be shown to the world, for mink mutation men are a young and eager crew. There was no need to emphasize that one of the purposes of the breeders' association is the exchange of knowledge. Mutant breeding is as insidious as bridge. Two members could not meet and fail to talk about it. A tantalizing gamble, an intellectual excitement, and a new zest had been imparted to fur farming.

One of the early acts of the Association was to end the confusion of a new and startling nomenclature. This included names of originators, colors, trees, regions, mountains, glaciers, and even poetic phrases. Breeders themselves were confused, geneticists baffled, and the fur trade more so, and future purchasers undoubtedly would lose any enthusiasm in their bewilderment. Now silverblu includes any combined mutations in this shade; the patterned white and black mink is

Royal Kohinur; blufrost describes the silvered sable-toned mink; royal pastel covers the various blends in blonde, golden and brown; the spotted mink is called choker; and blue, white and ebony are other classifications. New names are to be used only to describe an entirely new mutation. At last breeders, geneticists, the fur trade, and purchaser can use a common language.

Under these names the mutations were introduced to the public. Kohinur and blufrost reached the market in 1945. Royal pastel was first sold in February, 1946, in a Seattle auction. The entire offering of 1,850 skins brought an average price of $115, the top bundle $172, and it was evident another mutation favorite had arrived. In the same year 18,656 silverblu skins were sold in New York at an average price of $91.83 with the top bundle of sixty pelts bringing $190 a skin. In 1946 more than fifty thousand mutation mink skins were auctioned in the United States.

Various combinations of mutations have been presented. In 1947 a new shade known as Breath of Spring, a combination of silverblu and blufrost, was offered, as was also Golden Cross, a new green-eyed pastel. Already the trade is talking of an Aleutian blue of which at present there is only a handful. Its beauty makes hardened mink men speak like poets.

Each year more mink and fox ranchers catch the contagion of mutation breeding. Whole herds have been changed over. On the Fromm farm 90 per cent of the mink and one third of the fox population are mutations. In the years when mink were suddenly appearing in new colors, foxes have not confounded their owners with transformations, although in at least two instances a brown fox, a recessive, has appeared in the United

States. One is being developed on the Fromms' Thiensville farm; the other, a quite different shade of brown, was whelped on an Ontario ranch and is now the forbear of a number.

But at any moment new mutations may crop up, and fur ranchers can still dream and hope. Perhaps the blue fox will be the next to startle owners. It has threatened to do so, having produced examples of a fox of lovely bluish gray and white, with no suggestion of brown in the coat. Some disappointed breeders have declared this fox to be a freak because the color phase apparently would not reproduce itself. One breeder struggled with the problem for five years before he admitted defeat. The same color has cropped up on other ranches and always, despite its history, owners dared to believe that nature might have sent them a Christmas present. Two of these foxes appeared in one litter on the Fromm farm, both females. Neither produced young the first year, but the same color popped up in another pen. This was tantalizing, and then one of the females produced nine pups of this new shade. Five of the precious litter died and the other four of this rare phase may not survive.

Even without new types the fox mutation picture has become different in the last ten years. Incredibly beautiful foxes are being produced with the present mutations. Platinum now includes a wide range from blue to almost white, and the platinum fox of Utah is a gorgeous creature. The radium fox, which has a dark underfur and so great a profusion of wild white hair that the poorest specimens resemble porcupines, has been improved. Now at its loveliest it approaches a pure bred platinum and yet retains the two-tone effect. Its greatest possibilities may lie in combinations with other mutations, for it promises to have the same usefulness in breeding as the white-face. Fox mutations have also been combined in new tones. The white-face and the pearl have produced a color known as pearlatina, and the platinum and the pearl combination have produced the glacier blue. The various colors of foxes are as bewildering as those of mink.

The genetic facts established are even more bewildering than the colors. Pearl platinum foxes come in two entirely different mutations. Since their genetic origin is different even though their appearance is similar, the behavior pattern follows the rule of different mutations and, when bred, offspring return to standard strain. This is true also of the silverblu mink. The silverblu strain from the wild platinum mink in Oregon is a wholly different mutation from the silverblu which appeared in Wisconsin. Kits from a cross-mating are standard, normal-colored minks. Gradually the geneticists, with the aid of fur farms as laboratories, are documenting these biological facts. The discovery of a lethal factor in platinum and in certain strains of white-marked foxes cleared up the mystery of their smaller litters. Its existence in platinum foxes was discovered in Norway, but it was proved to be true also of white-marked foxes in a study made by Dr. Leon Cole and Dr. Max Shackleford of the genetics department of the University of Wisconsin. This is a duplication of the famous case of the yellow mouse used in genetic textbooks as an example of the behavior of the lethal factor. In these fox strains a pure blood pup cannot be born, as the lethal element causes the pure blood animal to die early in development. Ranchers had believed the pure blood platinum would be paler than the half blood, and actually a few very pale platinum pups have been born, but were too weak to be kept alive. This lethal factor, which decreases litters of purebred platinums or white-faces by 25 per cent, has resulted in these strains usually being mated with silvers.

The fur farm has been a fruitful territory in which to prove genetic laws, and a geneticist working in the field has been invaluable to the fur farmer. As new facts are discovered, combinations of mutations developed, and even more elaborate combinations contemplated, the farmer needs the scientist even more than he did in the early yers. He is now swimming in deeper water.

Often the geneticist is in equally untried currents. Ben La Stofka, a straw boss on the Fromm mink farm, showed Dr. Shackleford a litter that had resulted from a crossing of two mutations. Ben hoped to overlay this effect by a mating with half bloods of a third mutation. Dr. Shackleford tore a blank sheet from his notebook and drew the squares of a genetic chart of inheritance.

Sunshine filtered through the maple leaves overhead. The community mink nursery was quiet. The litters of kits which mothers had dragged outside for an afternoon nap were sleeping peacefully. Nearby mink matrons watched the two men curiously, to see what might be going on at a neighbor's pen. The kits in question, possible forebears of still more beautiful mink, yawned and curled up in a compact heap. At the end of the computation Dr. Shackleford pointed at the little square which held the combined letters of the strains.

"That's the one you're looking for," he said.

"But what will it be like?" Ben asked.

Dr. Shackleford shook his head. "I don't know," he

said. "But I do know it will be worth seeing."

That is where mutation breeding stands today. It is concerned with the future. The public will decide which mutations it prefers and standardization will come through this preference, but this is not the whole answer. All the materials that have been gathered will be the tools of the breeder. Even the color phases that have failed to win favor are important in his palette. He knows which will be useful to purify and enliven present colors, which can be blended to produce elusive hues. No color phase has been wasted effort, and it would be a pity if so early in the experiment, mutation breeding lost its flexibility. Even mistakes hold a challenge; they may be the first steps toward a triumph. White markings, areas that must be wasted in manufacture, and unfortunate combinations in contrasts between underfur and guard hairs can be bred away. Nothing is impossible in the mutation field, and therein lies its greatest promise.

Some day a woman can select the elusive shade that will be the most attractive frame for her hair, eyes, and skin, and best accompany the colors she wears. Instead of a few varieties of mink and foxes there will be scores. This will be an exciting experience for women.

It holds an even more exciting adventure for the breeders. Probably no field of animal husbandry has a greater opportunity or a larger group of alert and well informed fur farmers. Comparatively small ranchers have produced entrancing colors, and are now engaged in making those colors more clear and more consistent, in giving pelts character, fine texture, thick pile, sheen, attractive contrasts, and leather that is soft and pliable for the draping of luxurious garments.

The first era of mutation breeding is past. Everywhere fur ranchers have turned to science and to textbooks. Now, galvanized by the excitement of intellectual discoveries, they are ready for the future. Fur production is coming into its maturity. Its leaders must be a strange combination — students, fanatics, practical business executives, madmen, and creators who are driven to produce something more beautiful than has as yet existed.

Somewhere such a man is working today.

Chapter Twenty-five

ALMOST FROM THE FIRST THE FROMMS' NEW YORK
factory was the nation's largest maker of silver fox garments and well up in the middle group of mink manufacturers, but it was managed largely by remote control. This was not the Fromm way of doing things, but
the Fromms did not like cities. Walter, John, and Henry
would not consider a metropolitan existence. Seventh
Avenue was an alien world and they would have none
of it. They insisted that they were farmers, and when
the Company tried to interest Arthur in assuming eastern management he, too, did not care for cities, and was
absorbed in a research project in ginseng spray and
humus. He had taken postgraduate work in the University of Wisconsin and, fired by new discoveries in
horticulture, was eager to complete a series of experiments. He succeeded, but only just before his death in
the fall of 1945. Some of the formulas had not been
recorded, and no other Fromm was equipped to carry
on this scientific research.

When Arthur refused to become interested in making

fur garments, his son Johnnie prepared to stand by in the east. Johnnie, too, did not care for cities, and he began to look forward even more eagerly than his uncles to the time when garments could be made at home. The Fromms were convinced that this would be possible, but the plan to do so was strangely un-Fromm-like in its leisurely approach. They talked often of a small factory in Wisconsin to supplement the New York venture, but always as something in the vague future. In the early years they would have laughed at such postponement, but the brothers were growing older. Even Edward went less often to New York and depended more on the long-distance telephone.

Johnnie remained in New York through the beginning of the 1945 summer, a victim of heat, humidity, and a yearning for the fishing streams of Wisconsin. When Seventh Avenue pavements sizzled, postponement of a home factory seemed a needless waste of years and energy.

Every precept of the fur trade warned him that conversion of raw pelts into garments was a highly specialized craft. Workmen were supposed to be born to it, and were centered almost exclusively in New York. In a few previous attempts of other maufacturers to establish factories outside of New York, the International Fur and Leather Workers' Union, C. I. O., had quickly won its argument for a centralized industry. Nevertheless Johnnie believed fur skill could be acquired. He had watched the making of garments and it had not appeared too difficult for an intelligent worker.

Soon afterwards several mysterious losses occurred. A fur sewing machine disappeared, as did a jacket bundle of matched silver fox pelts, and a pattern. The shop foreman and workers wondered about this. Johnnie went home for a vacation. Later other sewing machines, sent out for servicing, failed to return. Partly finished garments were taken from the shop to be photographed and never seen again. Bundles of matched pelts and patterns were mislaid. Rumors spread through the union. The Company heard of these disturbing events but Johnnie, vacationing in Thiensville, said nothing. At the end of two weeks he appeared in Hamburg with a finished silver fox jacket.

It was a professional job. Johnnie, a good sportsman, had chosen the most difficult model, with a collar and reset sleeves. The sleeves, made of a single skin, required that a pelt be split and converted into a pair of matching pieces. He did not have a form to work on but his wife, Barbara, served as a model. To lay out, cut, and sew such a jacket in a first venture as a fur worker, and complete it in two weeks, was an astonishing record. Johnnie contended this proved ability in fur work was not necessarily inherited.

"It certainly does," said Edward, suddenly alert as the final piece of the farm unit pattern fell into place. He examined the workmanship. "That's a good jacket. What did Barbara think of it?"

"She thought it was all right," Johnnie said, "and I don't believe it was because her husband made it."

Edward handed the jacket across his desk.

"Tell her the Company wants her to have the first silver fox jacket made in our home factory," he said.

Within a week the missing sewing machines appeared in Hamburg, as did the matched jacket bundles and patterns, as well as a fur worker from the New York shop who could design and cut and, even more important, who preferred small towns to cities. Factory quarters were found in Merrill, eighteen miles from the farm. A fur workers' union in the A. F. of L. was established. Local workers were enrolled, and before suspicions of the New York union were aroused the new shop was started. Never did a factory get under way with less fanfare.

The Company did not expect large production. Workers were inexperienced and could not be trained to produce fur garments in less than six months or a year, but a factory on home ground had emotional value, and many on the pay roll were from families of employees who had worked for the Company twenty years. As long ago, when neighbors had come to dig ginseng and harvest and feed foxes, now their sons and daughters were at work getting the fur crop to market. In time this factory might become an important avenue in the scheme of pen to wearer.

Suddenly it became the only avenue. Officials of the fur workers' union discovered that a shop had been moved out from under them and called a strike on the New York factory. The Company offered a contract in the Merrill factory and assurance that it would not become more important in point of wages or total employees than the New York shop, but this carried a provision that a certain number of employees should be beginners and the wage scale adjusted for apprentices. The union balked. To countenance a Wisconsin factory would open the door for others and weaken the union's insistence on centralization. The Company, however, maintained it was a Wisconsin corporation and entitled to be considered an exception.

The Fromms knew they were in an extremely vulnerable position. The union had won previous arguments with other manufacturers, and was sure it could do so again. It had the weapons. A fur factory could not hope to operate with inexperienced labor, and union pressure could not only keep skilled workers out of the Merrill factory, but could affect allied industries and close the door to the sale of raw fur.

"Garments were our only outlet," Edward said, "and we had an inventory of thirty thousand fox pelts and between twelve and fifteen thousand mink skins. The union knew this, and knew that even if we had a thousand willing green hands on our Merrill pay roll we were helpless in manufacture. We needed key men to train the beginners and we didn't pretend we could operate without them. But we didn't intend to close the Merrill factory."

The Company still hoped an exception would be made, but two weeks later it received the union's decision. The Merrill factory must be closed. The union was in an unassailable position and did not have to make terms.

But it overlooked one factor. The New York strike was called in summer, in the dullest season. The Fromm factory had always operated throughout the year, and its employes had no quarrel with wages or conditions. They had been called out on strike without being given an opportunity to vote, and now a dozen of the older workers offered to move to Merrill and go to work.

"With this nucleus and our local employees, we began to manufacture," Edward said. "It was not what we had planned. The local factory was premature, but now we *had* to produce garments in Wisconsin. There was no other way out."

Having to do a thing was an old and familiar pattern. The venture started slowly. Only a few garments were finished at the end of several weeks. Production improved, but through the winter the eastern workers found a small town monotonous and gradually drifted back to the city until only three remained. Meanwhile local men and women were proving that the fur craft could be learned. In the New York factory three dozen garments had been produced each day. In Merrill, after a year's operation, the 130 employees, all except three of whom had no previous training in fur work, were producing thirty. A few men who had begun as machine operators were able to cut garments under supervision. The factory was shaking down.

The fur workers' union in New York and the Fromms were still in deadlock. All attempts at mediation failed. The real issue had come into the open. Until the Merrill factory was closed, the New York workshop would be strike-bound. The union was adamant on this.

"They offered to buy the Merrill factory and close it for us," Edward said. "But we wanted to go on manufacturing here at home."

The Fromms maintained that if a man wished to make anything anywhere in the United States he had the right to do it, and with this contention they suddenly found themselves exponents of a theory that was attracting national attention. In seeking to convert raw skins into garments at the source of the fur supply, they had become a part of the battle over the decentralization of industry. But success in the home factory did not mean total victory. Union pressure closed avenues for the sale of raw pelts and shut off many eastern retail outlets for the Company's garments.

The Company, however, had proved fur could be manufactured outside the national center. At the end of the first year, when only three eastern workers remained in Merrill, the Company appraised the venture. The expected spoilage had been astonishingly low. Only twenty-five garments showed imperfections, and these were slight. The general average of the Merrill product was better than that in the New York factory. The Company now had a much clearer idea of the costs of production, which in the east had been shrouded in some mystery, and this, with a lowered overhead, had enabled it to use more fur and make a better jacket for the same price.

Co-operation between management and labor was gratifying. Employees, starting at scratch and knowing their limitations, were eager to learn a new trade, and this spirit made the shop a close-knit unit, and a friendly one. Workers were interested in the product and developed a craftsman's pride. The factory now seemed a part of the farm unit, as close as the fox and mink pens and ginseng gardens. For the first time fur coats and jackets hung in the Company's office, and the brothers proudly carried them home to show to their families.

Second-generation Fromms now took an active part in manufacture. Johnnie, who had been instrumental in starting the factory, was brought from Thiensville to be Edward's assistant, and the Company built a home for him in Hamburg. Mark Koenig, who had married Henry's daughter Arlene, entered the Merrill office after his discharge from the army, and a year later headed the factory. The Company enlarged Henry's house to make room for the young family, which already had a small daughter. Young Henry came home from the army with a wife and son, and learned fur farming by working in the pens until he was made assistant to his Uncle John. Another Fromm had become a fur farmer, and the company built a house for him on the home acres. This construction for the young families seemed only a logical extension of the brothers' own home building period in the late twenties. Henry's vision of a third generation to serve the Company was coming true. The Company needed its youth.

Merrill liked the factory. The plant paid the highest wages in town and had a waiting list. Many were returned soldiers unwilling to go back to old jobs and looking for a new craft. "I was a school teacher," one said, "but after three years in the army I'd have had to take a refresher course, and anyhow I didn't want to teach. I tried the sash and door factory and got tired of working on one kind of window frame. This job keeps you on your toes. Gives you a chance to use your head." In a year he had advanced from operator to cutter of silver fox jackets. "Look at this! I've got to make a jacket out of four skins. See how I fitted in this piece from the neck? The fur swirls around as though it had grown there."

A successful cutter of silver fox must have a dash of creative spirit, a good eye for color, and an understanding of the anatomy of the animal to fit the pelt into a garment. Markings, texture, and even length, of fur vary, and since each pelt is slightly different from all others and a jacket bundle has been matched as closely as possible, the jacket must be contrived from this material. Odd bits from other pelts cannot be used for piecing. This is a challenge to ingenuity.

Mink cutting is even more specialized. A cutter must have a keen eye for the most minute gradations in color and texture, and a good head for arithmetic. Making a mink coat has become an elaborate process since the invention of the fur sewing machine in 1895, which made it possible to sew very narrow strips together with great speed. A mink coat has about five thousand seams yet must look like a single piece of fur, and the short furred mink does not supply camouflage for errors. A skin is first split into two pieces down the back and then, with the central character stripe, or "grotzen," as a guide, is cut diagonally into many long thin strips, and these pieces are replaced at such an angle that they make a matched fur two or three times the length of the original pelt. This process is called "dropping."

Sewing machines are run by both men and women, and each cutter, either in fox or mink, has five operators. This group carries on the making of a garment as a unit, and it is the cutter's responsibility to see it is well done. He plans, cuts, distributes the pieces, and eventually fits them into a final product. Operators watch the garment grow and can share the cutter's problems.

"Even stitching fur is different from running a sewing machine in other factories," a Merrill girl said. "When I sewed shoes I saw only one part. Here I make a sleeve or a back or a front, and when we get a jacket together all of us can see what we have accomplished."

The finishing department, where linings are sewn in, was easily staffed in a community where any number of older women were skillful with a needle. Linings might become monotonous, but a group sewing together found it much like taking one's work and dropping in for a visit with a neighbor, and it was far less lonely than home dressmaking.

The Company had counted on the native intelligence of the small town worker who has turned his hand to many jobs; after these people had learned the feel of fur they were able to cut, match, nail, and sew garments. The labor turnover was less than 5 per cent, and this occurred mostly in the first weeks when the employees tried a new job to learn whether they liked it.

The Company had not planned to dress its own pelts. This is a secret process; no books have been written on the subject, and even the ingredients used are known only to the craft. But this was another trade which had to be mastered, as Edward reported in a fur trade journal:

"In opposition to our Wisconsin operations, the New York fur workers' union induced the dressers' union not to work on our pelts. Hence it became necessary for us to do our own dressing. Fur dressing is a technique dating back to the dark ages and kept dark right up to the present. It is simple in principle, but complicated in practice. After many trials and a few costly errors, the pelts began coming through as beautiful as New York's finest. The New York union has done us a favor."

Dressing furs, like good cooking, is done partly by rules and partly "by ear." A man must learn how a pelt should feel and look. The skin is softened, fleshed, then put into the "bite," or pickle, dried, drummed in hard maple sawdust, and oiled. The last process depends more on the "ear" than any other, and only through practice can a worker learn how little or how much oil each skin should have. The skin is then put into the "kicker," which works the oiled pelts, and this, too, must be done with caution. More drumming and stretching follow, and between drummings the pelts are spun in a revolving wire cage to "cage out" the sawdust.

Working pelts is done either by electrically driven or bench fleshing knives. Fleshing mink pelts, a delicate process, could be done only with bench tools, and extra leather must be shaved off so skillfully that the pelt is soft and light as chamois and yet undamaged. This, too, can be learned only by practice. At the end of the year the Company was dressing even the delicately shaded mutation skins.

The Company, confident of the ingenuity of the small town worker, prepared to produce 175 garments weekly, engaged more employees, and raised wages. Even after this advance, the scale was less than in New York, but the Merrill factory operated at capacity all the year, and in the east the season was from six to nine months. Workers took this into consideration, as well as the lowered living costs of a small town.

"We know we aren't getting New York wages," one man said, "but neither is this New York. I've worked for higher wages in the east and felt a lot poorer. Here we live in better houses, can enjoy a visit with our neighbors, and send our kids to school with their friends. Most of us own cars. Wages stretch twice as far. Food costs are about the same all over, but we can have fun here without spending a lot of money. In New York it cost me as much to get to the country as taking the wife and kids to the movies and buying a dinner. Here all we have to do is step into the car. And this is a union shop and I'm getting union wages."

He was referring to the wage scale controversy. Men in Merrill knew the eastern union spoke of them as scabs, and they didn't like it.

"I had a chance to learn a new trade and I took it,"

one said. "I'd have been crazy not to. In New York they'd never have given me a chance to learn to be a cutter. Now I am one. This is America and a fellow has a right to any job he can hold down. What do those men in the east mean when they tell us we can't do fur work in Wisconsin?"

Clearly the Fromms were not the only ones who intended to be stubborn about the right to make fur garments where they pleased.

In the fall of 1946, when the price of silver fox declined, stubbornness again served the Company. The unpredictability of the silver fox is not wholly in the nature of the animal. Its price has always varied according to fashion's rulings, and now short-haired furs were popular. Makers of fox garments turned to furs in more certain demand, and this sent fox prices even lower.

Then the single farm unit, pen-to-wearer idea proved its worth. While other breeders were victims of the trade's reluctance to build up inventories in silver fox pelts, the Fromms were able to sell their pelts as jackets. Overhead and production costs in Merrill were less than in the east, and the finished garment need carry but one profit. This was small, but enough to maintain the herds until silver fox returned to favor.

That it would do so the Company never doubted. With the fanatical zeal it had once thrown into the battle for bright silvers, it now prepared to keep the public aware of them. Not only did it manufacture jackets but, to insure these garments being shown in the shops, it backed its faith by selling on consignment. Retailers thus continued to offer silver foxes.

Two circumstances made this vigorous campaign possible. The vast herd subsidized the manufacturer, and again ginseng come to the rescue. For more than forty years the two threads had interwoven, and in 1946 root stored so long in the warehouse could be shipped to China and sold at prices that justified the thirteen-year gamble. Once more ginseng could feed silver foxes. Even Henry, who had never cared for it, became grateful, although for him the vast gardens would never hold the emotional satisfaction of the Company's forests. For some years the annual seed planting had been restricted to ten acres, a mere trifle to Walter and Herbert Kleinschmidt, who had longed for the time when their bed-making machine could really demonstrate its prowess. With a reopened Chinese market, the Company determined on a twenty-five acre planting, and in a week the machine left twelve hundred beds behind it. Five years must pass before these seeds can be harvested, but to a company that has grown ginseng and silver foxes, five years is only tomorrow.

Through the fall and early winter of 1946 the Company continued to manufacture and promote silver fox. Having proved the success of the farm unit plant it was in a position to discuss the matter with the union, and offered to reopen in New York on condition that the Merrill factory was to be continued. The union refused and negotiations were broken off. Compared with other controversies that commanded national attention, the determination of the Company to manufacture in Wisconsin was a mere skirmish on the labor front, but to the Company it was tremendously important. It was more than a business obstacle, even more than a weapon in the promotion of silver fox. It was part and parcel of the company idea, as vital to it as was centralization to the union. To the Fromms the question was no longer a matter of the rights of an individual or even of a group of individuals. It had become a company right. The battle might have had somewhat the appearance of a slingshot attack on a giant, but with the Fromms it had taken on a terrible earnestness. To a company which had spent almost forty years in building a herd of foxes a CIO union was no more powerful an adversary than others which had attacked it in the past.

Then in December, 1946, the picture changed for each opponent. Raw fur prices suffered the most spectacular decline in history. Silver fox went lower than anyone had believed possible. In a year when they had never been lovelier, when breeding had carried them to a new perfection, the skins were selling for less than the cost of production. The manufacture of silver fox garments almost ceased in New York.

Chapter Twenty-six

THE INDUSTRY WAS IN DISTRESS. FOX HERDS BUILT UP
through years of selective breeding were imperiled. But
for the first time in its career the Company was prepared to meet a threat. Always before it had been
necessary to erect defenses when disaster was already
upon it. This time the Company was fortified because
it was "dug in" at Merrill. Manufacture eliminated
losses, unavoidable for other ranchers, and made
it possible to sell pelts at least at cost. Ginseng was
again a revenue producer, and while mink prices had
tumbled, they still permitted profitable farming. Now
the Fromms answered the emergency by enlarging the
factory, raising wages, and becoming the only firm in
the country to manufacture silver fox jackets in any
quantity.

In the meantime the fur farmers' organizations appealed to Congress to save the industry by softening
the excise tax on fur-trimmed garments to permit a
much wider use of fur. Approximately eight thousand
fur farms represented an investment of one hundred

and thirty million dollars, about equally divided between fox and mink. The pelt value of the two hundred thousand silver foxes, even at the low price of twenty dollars, was four million dollars. Of these the Fromms produced almost one-fifth. The pelt value of the seven hundred thousand mink at twenty dollars was fourteen million dollars. Forty years of pioneering had made this industry possible. Congress evidently recognized its value and, in February, 1947, granted the asked relief.

This put a new aspect on the battle between the Company and the union. The factory employing two hundred workers was the largest in the country, for Merrill was running full time while New York workers were idle. Also, the Company needed New York outlets. Fur trimming necessitated a return to Seventh Avenue and its complicated network of allied fur industries.

Both contestants wanted peace. In March negotiations were reopened. The Company renewed its previous offer and it was accepted. The fur workers union gained an eastern factory, work for members, and a Merrill workshop under a C. I. O. charter, but it conceded an apprentice rating for inexperienced employees in Merrill. A labor organization which had fought for centralization found itself with two hundred new members, either as qualified mechanics or beginners, in a factory over a thousand miles from Seventh Avenue.

The outcome of the two-year battle startled observers, but did not astonish the Fromms. They had always known the Company would continue as a farm unit. Nothing else was possible. For more than forty years the Company had been shaping for this goal. The structure that had formed so slowly and yet so inevitably presented physical proof of its right to survival. Vast holdings — fields and forests, pens and ginseng gardens, roads, homes, and buildings — all were a symbol of permanence.

The 160-acre homestead, mortgaged to buy three silver foxes, had grown to 17,000 acres. Those three silvers and their progeny produced a yearly crop of over thirty thousand pelts. The first small ginseng garden, five by sixteen feet, had culminated in the planting of 469 acres which produced 8,183,000 pounds of root. The few mink trios were the forerunners of a herd which annually yielded 24,000 pelts. Each year ninety thousand fur-bearing animals were housed and fed. The rows of their pens marched over the rolling landscape, and five hundred miles of roads had been built to serve them.

Each fox has three homes in his short lifetime. He is whelped in his parents' pen, of which there are 10,520. When weaned he is placed with seven other pups in one of the 4,500 raised wire kennels. In the late summer he is turned into one of the twenty furring ranges, fenced enclosures in the forest of forty to eighty acres. The mink are more exclusive. Each parent lives separately, and each kit when weaned has its own home. The pelters alone required twenty-four thousand furring pens.

As this animal housing project had used enough wire netting to cross the continent, the task of fastening those strips together and in place was equally startling. Hog rings, made originally to be worn in pigs' noses to prevent rooting, were ideal as fasteners. The Company has used thirty million hog rings, and each one of these millions of rings has been slipped around two strands of wire and clamped shut.

The individual daily attention given each of these ninety thousand animals requires a crew of more than four hundred people. Foxes are fed once a day, mink twice, and although the fox weighs from twelve to fifteen pounds and a mink two to five, mink eat two-thirds of a pound daily and a fox a pound. Thirty thousand horses provided fifteen million pounds of meat a year, in addition to three million pounds of liver and tripe and four million pounds of cereal. Feed pans, water pans, stretching boards, drying-racks, history cards, and pen indicators of vaccine and pilling treatments — all reach fantastic numbers.

This was the project grown from the dream of four farm boys. To them it had been a Company before it owned a fox or a ginseng plant, and it was still the Company. In the forty years of its building, it had become a separate entity, a fusion of them all, and yet not the reflection of any one. The Fromms did not own it; it owned them. Its rights were greater than those of its builders, and they knew there would always be a Company, just as there would always be silver foxes.

It made a significant contribution to the pioneering of a natural resource. It challenged traditional concepts of beauty in fur, and changed a world's opinion. It developed new methods and opened new avenues in the successful management of tremendous herds. It ended two great fur farming hazards through medical research. It brought what once was a rare and precious fur within the reach of every woman.

The Company believed silver fox would always be

desirable. This belief born so many years before, when as boys the partners had talked of silver foxes while they did farm chores, looked after trap lines, or sat around a campfire, never faltered. Bright silver beauty lit a pathway for brave dreams. That way has held adventure and success too, if success means achievement. Except for silver foxes, the great sprawling Company would never have existed. The farm might raise other fur and grow ginseng, but as a protagonist for the bright silver it reached its real greatness.

And now the Company backed this faith. In 1947, when the future of silver foxes looked darker than at any time in its history, the Company did not talk of liquidation or retrenchment. It determined to keep the large herd at Hamburg as a blood strain of pure silver, free even of mutations. Thus when the silver fox returns to favor, when other breeders may have liquidated and the supply is depleted, the Company could still offer bright silver foxes to the world.